A
DANGEROUS
PASSION

A
DANGEROUS
PASSION

LEADERSHIP AND
THE QUESTION OF HONOR

HAIG PATAPAN

SUNY
PRESS

Published by State University of New York Press, Albany

For information, contact State University of New York Press, Albany, NY
www.sunypress.edu

Library of Congress Cataloging-in-Publication Data

Names: Patapan, Haig, 1959– author.
Title: A dangerous passion : leadership and the question of honor / Haig Patapan.
Description: Albany : State University of New York Press, [2021] | Includes
    bibliographical references and index.
Identifiers: LCCN 2020024807 | ISBN 9781438482798 (hardcover : alk. paper) |
    ISBN 9781438482811 (ebook) | ISBN 9781438482804 (pbk. : alk. paper)
Subjects: LCSH: Political leadership. | Honor. | Personality and politics.
Classification: LCC JC330.3 . P39 2021 | DDC 303.3/4—dc23
LC record available at https://lccn.loc.gov/2020024807

To Peter H. Russell, Thomas L. Pangle, Richard W. Staveley

CONTENTS

PREFACE

Honor is a dangerous passion that fuels the ambitions of glory seekers to pursue immortality through preeminence, tyranny, and empire. It is also the source of good leadership that is founded on noble ambition and sacrifice for the common good. These two faces of honor show how leadership and honor are mutually constitutive and that their interrelational dynamic fundamentally shapes the character of political practice. Our contemporary blindness to this leadership-honor dynamic and neglect of the significance of honor and shame in modern politics has caused us to fundamentally misunderstand the nature of leadership. In this book I examine three influential yet divergent and contending accounts of the leadership-honor dynamic to better understand modern leadership and to show how insights from these debates can illuminate a series of pressing contemporary political challenges.

Few, if any, of us are indifferent to the opinion of others. On the contrary, it seems almost impossible not to think of others in all aspects of our lives. Though interested in what others may think in general, we are especially concerned with their good opinion of us. The desire that people should think well of us often animates what we think and do. Frequently it is linked with our hopes and expectations of some discernable advantages, though it would seem that our desires are not always defined by such simple instrumental calculations. Consequently, those who are vain long to be seen and acknowledged as beautiful, the virtuous want to be known as good and noble, and the proud as preeminent and superior. Though some need and seek the good opinion of everyone, and therefore the love of the whole world, most of us will respect and therefore value the views of some select few more than others. We are most sensitive to the opinions of those we admire when in their company, though their absence does not attenuate their influence; they are often in our thoughts, praising, censuring, and passing judgment. Our longing to be loved and admired by those we respect—the passion of honor—is therefore essentially a social passion because it can only exist and be satisfied with and through others. It is also political because each political community defines and therefore determines what is honorable by bestowing the dignity of citizenship, and equally importantly, defining in subtle detail, through laws, conventions, and customs, what is honorable and shameful.

Honor and shame therefore permeate and animate all aspects of political life. They are especially important, however, for leaders, particularly those who are responsible for discharging the authority of foremost political offices. Honor presents two distinct yet interrelated challenges to leaders. Honor of each individual, born or derived from citizenship, or in its modern source and articulation, the dignity of a free and autonomous human being, requires acknowledgement, recognition, and respect from each other and especially from leaders. Though the precise demands of such esteem and deference will obviously vary according to the specific orders of honor and exigencies of circumstances, the unavoidable truth is that all leadership demands acute sensitivity in giving proper honor or respect to followers, not only because they deserve it, but also in order to achieve any success or advantage in leading. Above all, leaders must not dishonor followers by shaming them or slighting all those things that they value, especially family, friends, homeland. The importance of honor therefore explains why leaders cannot simply rule the way a shepherd may care for a flock, or a farmer grow crops, ordering, arranging, and distributing as they see fit, irrespective of the opinions, wishes, and hopes of their followers.

This specific demand for honor is compounded and complicated by the allure of honor for leaders. Those who long for honor above all, because it cannot be bought and therefore seems superior to mere gain, and because it seems impervious to time, leaving a legacy beyond their lives, are naturally drawn to political office. Politics most comprehensively satisfies the desire for honor because the office itself bestows honor, and because leadership and exercise of authority allow the greatest display of virtue, which is admirable and praiseworthy, for now and into the future. In seeking office and discharging its duties, leaders are always thinking of their honor, present and future—what their followers think of them and how they will be remembered. This powerful longing for honor has far-reaching consequences for good leadership.

Leaders who seek office, to the extent that they also seek honor, will be defenders of what is honorable. They will be guardians of those laws and conventions that define the noble and the good, the just and the unjust, and therefore the codes of honor and shame that define and shape the lives and practices of all communities. In defending, and in crucial respects sacrificing, to defend these principles we see the noble and beautiful face of honor. It is the honor of the patriot who gives all for his country. This admirable face of honor can also have its darker aspect. A "my country right or wrong" disposition can sometimes be deaf to reasonable persuasion and intransigently resistant to change, while those leaders who want to gain the love or admiration of their followers may be tempted to pander to their wishes, appearing contemptible in their attempts to please, or, more seriously, neglecting their office by not pursuing unpopular but necessary actions.

This noble face of honor should be distinguished from its other aspect, which we call glory. The desire for honor will in some manifest itself in a longing for excellence in virtue. In these cases, the love of honor points to glory as recognition of superiority in excellence. Consequently, glory or preeminence in virtue introduces and justifies love of victory. Such a love for distinction, the honor of being first or the winner, is the source of the noble ambition that manifests itself in magnanimous actions for the public good and is the source of grand enterprises and major innovations. Yet the desire for preeminence is so powerful in some that when frustrated they may be tempted to question and even overturn what is honorable. Honor as glory is therefore also the most dangerous passion. Glory seekers who are the great political founders and innovators are also potentially shameless tyrants, hubristically disregarding what is proper and honorable to satisfy their indefatigable passion for preeminence.

It would seem, therefore, that honor and leadership are inextricably bound up, that the question of honor cannot be adequately posed or interrogated without understanding the nature of leadership; and that in turn, leadership cannot be understood without reflecting on the importance of respecting the dignity of followers and the contending notions of glory and honor that move leaders. An overview of the foremost works of political philosophy, not to mention historical and poetic accounts, confirms this judgment. This makes the relative neglect of the passion of honor in contemporary leadership studies seem even more puzzling. Given its obvious practical importance, and the long history of philosophical and literary reflection on the theme, why have contemporary students of leadership paid little attention to the question of honor?

This perplexing question proves to be a stimulating and valuable provocation, compelling us to return to and recover those rich and profound meditations on the nexus between honor and leadership. To understand how leadership and honor are mutually constitutive—the leadership and honor dynamic—and how they continue to influence our contemporary views of both, this book selects those crucial junctures that best articulated this dynamic and revealed their insights in the clearest terms. In this book, I focus on three distinct, prominent, and competing views on the leadership-honor dynamic, articulated in the thought of Plato, Machiavelli, and Hobbes. In Plato we find the first comprehensive account of the crucial importance of honor in politics and its decisive role in understanding leadership in all its subtle and striking aspects, from noble aspirations and public-spirited sacrifice to the dangerous impulse toward tyranny and empire. Machiavelli seeks to rehabilitate honor from its pious ignominy, but in so doing liberates it from virtue traditionally understood. Educated but untrammeled *gloria* becomes for Machiavelli the only passion that, in its self-regard, necessarily looks to others, binding the few and the many in a republican community of free citizens. Hobbes endorses Machiavelli's insights yet rejects its core reliance on honor. His ambition is to rid politics of the pathology of pride, repudiating the madness of glory for the safety and comfort of the innovative, contractual state founded by calculating rights-bearing citizens.

Each of these approaches, whether it is classical magnanimity, Machiavellian *gloria*, or Hobbesian dispersed leadership, seeks to understand and address the relationship between leadership and honor. In doing so, each envisages a comprehensive settlement that defines and institutes a new political vision. The most influential in contemporary thought, I suggest, is the Hobbesian, which has left a legacy endorsing dispersed leadership while reinterpreting honor as the dignity of individual recognition. This dominance has not, however, simply silenced the alternative views; classical magnanimity and Machiavellian glory continue to assert their voices and perspectives in the debate. To gauge the relative influence of these contending views and test the merits of the insights recovered from our engagement with these thinkers, it is instructive to turn to contemporary debates on significant aspects of leadership and honor. We do so to see if our new perspective yields greater clarity about the leadership-honor dynamic, as well as providing new means for addressing and resolving contemporary political challenges.

This book is in four parts. Part 1 explores the extent to which the contemporary leadership scholarship neglects the importance of honor for understanding leadership ambition. Part 2 examines the nature of the leadership-honor dynamic and therefore is of interest to those who want to investigate the theoretical origins of the different ways leadership and honor are mutually constitutive. Each of the three chapters in this part articulates divergent yet influential accounts of the leadership-honor dynamic—classical magnanimity, Machiavellian glory, and Hobbesian dispersed leadership. The insights we gain from these different conceptions of leadership and honor provide the theoretical foundations for part 3 on the politics of the leadership-honor dynamic that examines the challenges confronting contemporary leaders and therefore is of particular interest to students of leadership studies. "Rethinking Transformative and Transactional Leadership" evaluates MacGregor Burns's influential distinction to reveal its theoretical provenance not only in modern psychology but also in the classical conception of magnanimity. "Idealistic Leadership of Lee Kuan Yew" examines the life and ambitions of Singapore's founder for new insights into the nature of political founders. "Flattery of Advisors" focuses on the neglected danger of flattery for leaders and the extent to which *parrhesia* or honesty can overcome it. "Anti-politics of Fame and Identity" examines how the politics of honor is manifest in two opposed trajectories in modern politics. Fame as honor uncoupled from virtue issues in celebrities as new aspirants and contenders to leadership, while attempts to recover individual dignity result in identity politics, confronting leaders with new challenges to their legitimacy and authority. Finally, "Patriotism and National Pride" shows how love of one's country is a potent and volatile passion that moves citizens, posing a distinct and subtle demand on leaders who need to acknowledge such love while moderating its dangerous excesses. In part 4, the concluding chapter, we note how the leadership-honor dynamic can usefully be deployed for future research to illuminate a broad range of pressing contemporary challenges, which include the tension between innovation and conservativism, the nature of moral leadership, in particular a deeper and more nuanced understanding of tyrants and modern authoritarianism, and finally the need for modern democracies to acknowledge and celebrate the noble ambition and sacrifice of their leaders and followers.

There is much truth in the view that the importance of honor for leadership, in all its variety of color, depth, and vigor, can only be adequately captured by the works of muses, in poem, plays, paintings, and sculpture. These, at any rate, were the means leaders traditionally favored to celebrate and commemorate their legacy. Yet it is the very charm of these works, beguiling us with the nobility, grandeur, and indeed the promise of immortality of honor, that must give us pause and compel us to consider why honor may be both the most noble and most dangerous of passions and why it is an important question for understanding leadership.

PART 1

INTRODUCTION

CHAPTER 1

LEADERSHIP AND
THE QUESTION OF HONOR

Leaders on assuming office will say they are humbled by their elevation. They will thank their supporters, vowing to lead for all, while affirming that it is an honor to hold the office whose responsibilities they will discharge with care and diligence. They will declare their pride in their nation and pledge to protect and enrich it. These declarations are often dismissed as mere rhetoric, empty words ritually recited by all leaders. Yet even when not heartfelt, the expectation to display humility in victory, while acknowledging the dignity of office and pride in one's country, suggests that honor and shame are an important part of political life. Once in office, all leaders are naturally solicitous of the dignity of their followers and ever vigilant not to offend them. In democracies especially they will praise the goodness and wisdom of the people and in all places defend the noble achievements, proud history, and great name of their country.[1] All the while they will have an eye to the future and their own legacy, being especially concerned with "making a difference," standing out, or being remembered for their "signature" achievements. And once out of office they will fiercely defend their name and reputation, cooperating with historians and academics who wish to memorialize their achievements. In some cases, they will write an autobiography to "set the record straight," correcting unflattering interpretations of crucial events and major initiatives. Honor and shame thus suffuse all aspects of the lives of leaders, determining their original decision to seek office, the actions they pursue while they have authority, and their subsequent attempts at preserving their good name and reputation on leaving political life.

Of course, few of us are immune from the charms of honor and the power of praise and blame. In the *Essay Concerning Human Understanding*, John Locke (1979, Ch. XXVIII, 12, p. 357), one of the theoretical founders of liberalism, explains the potent and inescapable reach of what he calls "The Law of Fashion or Private Censure":

> And as to the Punishments, due from the Laws of the Common-wealth, they frequently flatter themselves with hopes of Impunity. But no Man scapes the Punishment of their censure and Dislike, who offends against the Fashion and Opinion of the Company he keeps, and would recommend himself to. Nor is there one of ten thousand, who is stiff and insensible enough, to bear up under the constant Dislike, and Condemnation of his own Club. He must be of strange, and unusual Constitution, who can content himself, to live in constant Disgrace and Disrepute with his own particular Society. Solitude many Men have sought, and been reconciled to: But no Body, that has the least Thought, or Sense of Man bout him, can live in Society, under the constant Dislike, and ill Opinion of his Familiars, and those he converses with. This is a Burthen too heavy for humane Sufferance: And he must be made up of irreconcilable Contradictions, who can take Pleasure in Company, and yet be insensible of Contempt and Disgrace from his Companions.

As Locke observes, few if any of us are indifferent to the opinion of others, especially those we respect or admire. On the contrary, it seems almost impossible not to think of others in all aspects of our lives, being especially concerned with avoiding censure. While most of us want to avoid the shame of not doing the right thing, a smaller number desire not just the avoidance of shame, but the active recognition of virtue, an acknowledgment of excellence. Some will therefore seek respect for their accomplishments in the fields of business, commerce, and industry, others as jurists, judges, or lawmakers. Still others will seek recognition as artists—poets, sculptors, painters, or musicians. But the most admirable, because it superintends and directs all of these and more, is the political. It is therefore not surprising that those most hungry for distinction will seek the highest political offices. Most if not all political leaders will therefore be distinguished by an abiding and powerful longing for honor.

This intimate connection between leadership and honor, each mutually constituting the other and thus defining the nature of politics more generally, was acknowledged at the very origins of Western tradition in Homer's famous and compelling account of Achilles. At a crucial juncture in the *Iliad*, the Achaian delegation led by Odysseus visits Achilles to persuade him to return to the war against the Trojans. They find him with his close friend Patroclus, playing a lyre and "singing of men's fame" (*Iliad*, Book 9, 189). Achilles, after hosting his guests and listening to their imprecations, rejects their offers, confiding to Odysseus a most intimate and profound choice his goddess mother, Thetis, has revealed to him:

> I carry two sorts of destiny toward the day of my death. Either, if I stay here and fight beside the city of the Trojans, my return home is gone, but my glory shall be everlasting; but if I return home to the beloved land of my fathers, the excellence of my glory is gone, but there will be a long life left for me, and my end in death will not come to me quickly (*Iliad*, Book 9, 411–16).

Achilles is a healer, singer, and also the youngest, strongest, and most handsome warrior, *aristos Achaion* or "best of the Achaians," and arguably the best human simply. Homer therefore suggests that all of us, but above all those who want to be outstanding, the exceptional and talented individuals who aspire to lead, will inevitably confront this profound dilemma and choice concerning honor. Glory or preeminence seems to far exceed, if not be incommensurate with, the benefits of gain and property. We see this when Achilles rejects Agamemnon's exceptionally generous gift, which includes not only returning his slave girl Briseis, the initial cause of dishonor, but tripods, cauldrons, gold, horses, slaves, citadels, and his daughter's hand in marriage. Yet despite Achilles's initial indignation, we see glory is also unavoidably entangled with material gain, property seemingly a measure or symbol of his worth. Glory also appears dismissive or even disdainful of death, yet in longing for immortality, it seems moved by a pride in surmounting death's sting. Finally, though glory is the shining goal, avoidance of shame seems to be the most powerful motivating force in practice. This complex of contradictory longings and desires therefore makes it difficult at any one time to discern what moves Achilles's soul.

These reflections on honor, and how they will determine the choices Achilles will make, are clearly crucial for Achilles himself, but as we subsequently see in the drama of the *Iliad*, his decisions have profound implications not only for his close friends and fellow Achaians but also for the outcome of the war itself, the larger canvas on which Homer depicts the political consequences of Achilles's longing for glory. The overall and dominant impression is of the dangerousness of glory. We see this at the very beginning of the *Iliad* where Achilles declares that, being shamed by Agamemnon, he will leave the war and return home. His desire to recover honor is so powerful that he even perversely prays for Trojan success. Achilles's withdrawal deprives the Achaians of their best fighter, leading to their near defeat, prompting Achilles's beloved Patroclus to enter the war in Achilles's armor only to die in combat. Enraged, Achilles returns to the war, creating carnage among the Trojans, killing Hector and desecrating his body by dragging it behind his chariot. As foretold but not shown in the *Iliad*, Achilles dies from Paris's poisoned arrow to his heel. Yet if the *Iliad* reveals the dangerous aspect of the passion for glory, it also shows it as sustaining nobility and sacrifice. We see this in Achilles's decision to join the expedition to Troy, his valor in war, and above all his decision to return to the conflict, knowing that he will never return to his family and homeland. But Homer's final thoughts on the passion that moves the most promising human beings is found elsewhere, in the epic that celebrates his other great hero, Odysseus. In the *Odyssey*, Odysseus meets Achilles in the underworld, where Achilles laments his choice, preferring slavery to death:

> O shining Odysseus, never try to console me for dying. I would rather follow the plow as thrall to another man, one with no land allotted him and not much to live on, than be a king over all the perished dead. (*Odyssey*, Bk IX, 487–91; p. 180)

In Homer's epics we find one of the earliest and most profound reflections on the importance of honor for leaders. Through his poetry, Homer makes Achilles the preeminent and influential model not only for Greek playwrights such as Euripides and Sophocles, but also for subsequent Roman, Medieval, and Renaissance measures of leadership excellence. It is fitting that it is generally in the works of poetry, paintings, and sculptures that celebrate and commemorate exceptional leaders that we find these seminal and influential meditations on the dangers and promise of honor for leadership ambition. The power of the Muses lies in animating the complex drama, revealing the hidden truth of how leaders respond to honor, how it drives single-minded and dangerous ambition as well as engenders noble sacrifice. In attempting to understand why honor fascinates and enthralls us, we are thus inevitably drawn to the works of great artists. Thus we cannot help but reflect on the dangers and promise of glory when confronting great architecture like the Pyramids of Giza or Versailles Palace or celebrated works such as Michelangelo's *David*, Shakespeare's *Macbeth*, Beethoven's *Eroica*, and Picasso's *Guernica*.

Yet the Homeric approach would, even in classical times, confront a new way of understanding leadership that questioned its premises and challenged its strictures. Socrates's discovery of political philosophy initiated a radically new inquiry concerning human and political things. Socrates, especially in the Platonic dialogues, pursued the most comprehensive dialectical examination of the importance of honor for leaders, how it shapes their actions, and how leaders in turn educate their followers and in doing so shape political institutions and regimes. Socrates, in short, presented himself as the new model of human excellence to replace Achilles. The Socratic insights into the dangers of glory and also its potential for noble ambition, good leadership, and philosophic liberation became influential themes for subsequent philosophers. For Aristotle, the *megalópsychos* or "great-souled" person longed for honor because it is the greatest of the external goods, one usually bestowed on the gods (*Nicomachean Ethics*, 1123b, 13–27; 1123a 35–125b 25). Cicero took up these ideas in the Roman context of the *cursus honorum*, the leadership career path that culminated in the consulship. In his *De Officiis* (2.31), Cicero distinguished *honestas*—honor derived from wisdom, justice, temperance, and magnanimity—from *utile* or the useful. These themes would later be taken up by Plutarch, whose famous *Lives of Noble Greeks and Romans* compares the preeminent Greeks and Romans to understand the character of each and instruct future generations on how to be a good leader. It was an education that would be endorsed by subsequent Medieval, Renaissance, and Scholastic traditions and continues to profoundly shape and define the way we understand the crucial link between leadership and honor.

Yet this influential view was opposed by a radically different way of understanding the nexus between leadership and honor. The intrusion of Abrahamic piety into politics implied a complete transformation of the classical conception. Honor was now an even more pressing question for leaders, but only because it was now altogether questionable, a dangerous temptation rather than a potential spur to nobility and excellence. As all glory belonged to God, leaders moved by the desire for distinction were now committing the grave sin of pride. Because humanity was from *humus* or dust, humility rather than glory and pride marked the new answer to the question of honor. Christ, the Son of God, was born in a humble barn to poor parents. He was the Lamb of God, that most gentle, innocent, and vulnerable of God's creatures. And as Jesus reveals in his Beatitudes, the great virtues were now meekness and humility: "Blessed are the poor in spirit, for theirs is the kingdom of heaven" and "Blessed are the meek: for they shall inherit the earth" (Matt 5: 3–10). To be sure, great undertakings were not only permitted but mandated; but such endeavors were never for personal distinction but always to glorify God: "Let your light so shine before men, that they may see your good works, and glorify your Father which is in heaven" (Matt 5: 19). As the Pope upon his investiture was reminded three times, *Pater Sancti, sic transit Gloria mundi*—earthly glory is ephemeral. The proper disposition was to emulate J. S. Bach, who signed all his compositions S.D.G.—*Soli Dio Gloria* or to God Alone Glory.[2]

It was in the context of this great divergence between classical and pious responses on the proper disposition of leaders toward honor that modern political thought, broadly understood, intervened and responded. Modernity too thought honor was a profound question for leadership, and indeed a variety of answers were proposed to this question. But, in general terms, the modern response took two divergent trajectories. The distinctive aspects of the first can be discerned most clearly in Machiavelli's attempt to recover classical honor but on wholly new terms. Machiavelli thought it was necessary to reintroduce glory into politics to assure good leadership, but he was also acutely aware of the danger of tyranny. His proposal to contrive the dispositions or humors of those who want to command and those who want to be left alone within a republican architecture to secure liberty became the model for subsequent thinkers such as Montesquieu, who sought to marshal leadership ambition and desire for honor as the engine for a new, finely wrought constitutionalism that protected individual liberty. This general approach could be discerned in the American founding, the first modern republican constitution. According to its architects, the American Constitution was founded on the proper use of the passion for honor and distinction precisely because "the love of fame" for the authors of *The Federalist Papers* (No. 72) was "the ruling passion of the noblest minds, which would prompt a man to plan and undertake extensive and arduous enterprises for the public benefit."

The other major modern trajectory was in some respects even more radical, questioning the goodness of honor altogether. It can be found in Cervantes's *Don Quixote*, a coruscating attack on the madness of knights-errant and their chivalrous missions; in Shakespeare's unforgettable Falstaff, nicely poised between Hotspur and Hal, declaiming that honor is "A word," "Air" or "a mere scutcheon" (Henry IV, Part I: V.1); in Montaigne's essay "Of Glory" and Bacon's "Of Vain-Glory" and "Of Honour and Reputation." Yet perhaps no one has been as successful and influential in debunking honor as Thomas Hobbes, who in his most famous book, *Leviathan*, ambitiously claims that the modern artifice of the Leviathan state will now fulfil Job's (41, 1–40) hope of a leviathan that is "king over all the children of pride." Hobbes diagnosed glorying as a form of madness and defined honor as a measure of the morally neutral concept of power. In doing so, he provided a new basis for understanding the relationship between leadership and honor and the new politics it would inaugurate. Hobbes's influential approach is evident in Locke's attack on "dominion," and even in that great critic of the liberal tradition Rousseau, who nevertheless saw in *amour propre* the origin of all human domination and therefore corruption. Subsequent thinkers endorsed this view while attempting to moderate and thereby rectify Hobbes's parsimonious conception of the power-seeking individual. Kant, for example, attempts to retrieve dignity as essential for republican rule, while Hegel argues for mutual recognition as the dialectical overcoming of relationships of dominance. The modern reliance on the concept of honor as "prestige" and the increasing references to dignity, esteem, and self-respect show the persistence of this modern trajectory in recasting the question of honor for leadership.

MODERN NEGLECT OF THE QUESTION OF HONOR

This necessarily brief synopsis and overview suggest that leadership and the question of honor have been a significant and enduring subject of poetic, philosophical, and pious reflection, deliberation, and debate. Honor is important for understanding and explaining what moves leaders as well as how they regard and engage with their followers. Equally, leaders inevitably are arbiters and defenders of all that is honored and, in special circumstances, innovators of what is honorable and shameful. There is therefore a dynamic relationship between leadership and honor where each can be said to constitute the other and, in so doing, define the contours and character of political life. That honor matters for leaders and followers would appear to be an uncontentious, even commonplace observation, were it not for its puzzling neglect in contemporary leadership studies.

Leaders and leadership are explored in disciplines as wide ranging as anthropology, psychology, sociology, and education, although the contemporary scholarship is largely dominated by business and management. It is therefore not surprising that the question of leadership is posed and examined from a range of theoretical perspectives. This diversity also accounts for the different approaches to understanding leadership that have been influential in the scholarship, such as great man, trait theories, behavior movement, contingency theories, and more recent relational, constructivist and critical approaches.[3] Ironically, the study of political leaders, arguably the origin of all leadership studies, now occupies a small part of this scholarship. This is due in part to a confluence of disparate insights that depreciated the role of individuals in politics, including the recognition of material and economic mechanisms, a new conception of "History," and the discovery of the subconscious, subordinating individual judgment and discretion to comprehensive, unseen, and often indiscernible forces. There was in addition the Comtean impulse, evident above all in economics, which favored large "N" studies to develop parsimonious causal explanations for political behavior, implicitly depreciating the role of sui generis individuals.[4] We should also acknowledge the increasing authority of democratic egalitarianism that rejected "great men" and "heroic" individuals as a form of aristocratic atavism, preferring the dispersed leadership of Everyman.[5]

But what is most puzzling is the neglect of the question of honor by contemporary students of political leadership.[6] Perhaps the question of honor has eluded dominant approaches to the study of leadership because of its very complexity. The influence of honor can be discerned in an individual's character and "personality," yet it is also unavoidably constituted by institutional structures, historical legacies, and cultural and religious codes. It is a matter of individual ambition, yet it is mutually defined by the interests, hopes, and desires of followers. Honor, as both a radically transformative and trenchantly conservative passion, reveals the potential for statesmanship and tyrannical hubris, making it inherently a question of both politics and morality. The multifaceted nature of honor means it is too complex to be captured by any one approach, so that it effectively transcended and escaped them all. The theoretical and methodological diversity in the contemporary scholarship reflects a fragmentation and fracturing of the central question, denying a comprehensive account in favor of occasional glimpses, such as the concept of prestige of institutional office, or the importance of individual ambition, or even personality types.[7]

The shift in focus from the characteristics, actions, and behavior of leaders as individuals to leadership as a relational and interactive process promised a more nuanced understanding of the complexity of leadership.[8] Thus the increased emphasis on followership,[9] "post-heroic" leadership,[10] and critical leadership studies[11] showed the dialogic or "post-industrial" nature of these relationships.[12] Yet the question of honor seemed to be missing from these relational approaches. A recent work by Haslam et al. (2010), *The New Psychology of Leadership: Identity, Influence and Power*, is indicative of the promise and limitation of this scholarship. Haslam et al. (2010, 1–19) start with a comprehensive and critical evaluation of the contemporary scholarship on leadership, rejecting "heroic" approaches as "disempowering falsehoods" because they lack clarity and tend to be individualistic, conservative, and undemocratic.[13] They argue that leaders' effectiveness is tied to social identity so that the leaders need to be seen as the "in-group" prototype. Their actions must advance or "champion" the interests of the in-group, they must be "entrepreneurs of identity" (telling the group who they are and what they want to be), actively shaping a unique identity for the group, and they must "embed" the identity, striving toward the practical realization of the group's goals. As the authors put it, "Leadership is essentially a process of social identity management—and hence that effective leadership is *identity leadership*" (2010, 197). Leaders build social identity by reflecting, representing, and realizing such in-group identity (2010, 205–6). That leaders and followers define themselves and engage with each other to produce a "shared social identity," with leaders as "identity entrepreneurs," is a valuable acknowledgment of the subtle and complex nature of the relationship between leaders and followers.[14] Yet, in attempting to understand the meaning of identity and how it is constituted, the authors focus on aesthetics, theatricality, and the use of persuasive speech rather than the way political conversations are informed by the dignity, pride, glory, shame, and humility that animate and constitute all political communities.

Perhaps the most promising attempt to reintroduce the question of honor to contemporary political leadership studies is James MacGregor Burns's *Leadership* (1979), which initiated much of the recent interest in political leadership. Burns's ambition to "fashion a general theory of leadership" resulted in his influential distinction between "transactional" leaders, those who take the initiative in making contact with others for the purpose of an exchange of valued things, and "transforming" leaders who "engage with others in such a way that leaders and followers raise one another to higher levels of motivation and morality" (1979, 19, 20). An important aspect of this understanding of leadership is what Burns variously calls esteem, prestige, reputation, and admiration. According to Burns,

> One generalization seems safe on the basis of both systemic and casual observation: *the most potent sources of political motivation— the key elements of political ambition—are unfulfilled esteem needs* (both self-esteem and esteem by others). (1979, 113; emphasis in original)

Indeed, as we will see, esteem, status, and recognition form an important yet implicit theme of the entire work. Yet, unlike his transformational and transactional leadership, the leader-follower concept, and emphasis on moral leadership, Burns's insight into the significance of "esteem," recognition, and honor has not received the attention it warrants.

Though the question of honor has not been a major theme for contemporary leadership scholarship, recent studies that have focused on honor itself have implicitly confronted its implications for leadership. These studies have explored two different but related questions. The first is the question of "what is honorable," that is, the substance of "codes of honor," and the second is "what is honor," which examines the passion of honor. The question "what is honorable?" has been especially salient in sociological and anthropological studies that show how distinct historical, religious, and cultural legacies uniquely color and inflect what is considered honorable and shameful.[15] It has also been addressed politically, distinguishing between monarchies and aristocracies that recognize, elevate, and encourage the demands of honor; and democracies, where its prescriptions are less numerous and clear.[16] These examinations of what is honorable presume an understanding of what honor is, a complex and difficult question. A number of works have attempted to answer the question of what honor is by exploring the historical evolution of honor, noting in particular its modern decline.[17] Others have sought to examine honor in terms of moral and political philosophy, phenomenologically, or through works of literature.[18] Especially instructive for our purposes have been those works that have sought to examine the meaning of honor through the ambitions and actions of leaders.

The centrality of the founders in American constitutionalism led the American historian Douglass Adair to initiate an important contemporary attempt to understand the role of honor for leaders. In his essay "Fame and the Founding Fathers," Adair (1974) takes his cue from Alexander Hamilton's observation that love of fame is the ruling passion of the noblest minds to challenge Charles Beard and Forrest McDonald, who claimed that the founders were moved solely by self-interest, greed, and desire for power.[19] Adair (1974, 24) argues that though the founders were indeed "passionately selfish and self-interested men," they achieved greatness because the Revolution had led them to "redefine their notions of interest and had given them, through the concept of fame, a personal stake in creating a national system dedicated to liberty, to justice, and to the general welfare." Or, as he puts it, "The 'love of fame the ruling passion of the noblest minds' thus transmuted the leaden desire for self-aggrandizement and personal reward into a gold concern for public service and the promotion of the commonwealth as the means to gain glory" (1974, 24).[20] Adair's influence is evident in Peter McNamara's edited collection *The Noblest Minds: Fame, Honor and the American Founding* (1999), which examines the importance of love of fame for preeminent founders such as Franklin, Washington, Adams, Jefferson, Hamilton, as well as jurists such as Marshall. Two other significant and thoughtful works take up the question of honor and leadership, though each approaches it from a fundamentally different starting point. Sharon Krause's *Liberalism with Honor* (2002, xi) is a subtle and persuasive "excavation" of honor in the American context and is especially concerned with the role of honor in strengthening individual agency in risky and difficult actions in defense of individual liberty. It examines the various conceptions of American honor, ranging from honor in the Old Regime to democratic honor to the love of fame of the Southern Gentleman, and in doing so pays close attention to the way honor informed the leadership of Abraham Lincoln, Frederick Douglass, Elizabeth Cady Stanton and Susan B. Anthony. Finding contemporary alternatives to honor, such as dignity, self-esteem, and recognition, insufficiently spirited and lacking high ambition, Krause's argument is that "a strong sense of agency is crucial to liberal government, and as long as political power is of an encroaching nature liberalism will have need of honor" (2002, 190). If Krause is concerned to show that honor strengthens each liberal citizen's sense of duty, Robert Faulkner's *The Case for Greatness* (2002) seeks to understand truly great political ambition as evidenced in the actions of Washington, Lincoln, and Mandela "to shed indispensable light also upon the lesser kinds, including the ambition of decent but more ordinary leaders, and not excluding that of the tyrant and the time-server" (2002, 4). Faulkner returns to classical political philosophy, specifically an examination of Aristotle's conception of the "great-souled" or magnanimous leader whose noble ambition is subordinated to the good of the country. He contrasts this with the dangers of ambition as evidenced in Thucydides's and Plato's account of the talented Alcibiades and Xenophon's *Education of Cyrus,* providing a detailed examination of the hollowness of imperial ambition. In his "attempt to refresh a reasonable understanding of human excellence," Faulkner (2002, 7) also critically evaluates the limitations of contemporary understandings of honor. He thus counters Adair's view of fame, based on Plutarch and Bacon, with Cicero's account of the priority of duty, critically evaluating Rawls's and Arendt's conceptions of ambition and finally retracing the genealogy of honor with the Nietzschean and Kantian repudiation of Machiavellian and Hobbesian conceptions.[21] Faulkner's approach can also be discerned in more recent works that recognize the nexus between honor and leadership and in the process attempt to recover a role for statesmanship.[22]

These writings reveal a number of important insights into the nature of honor and how it influences leaders. Foremost is the importance of honor understood variously as glory, fame, esteem, or recognition, the diversity in these designations constituting a testament to the complexity of the passion. Though honor seems to be like other passions, in one respect it is fundamentally different—it is above all a social and political passion that can only be satisfied through others. It is the passion that moves ambitious individuals who seek to fulfil their longings through public service and the authority and recognition that public offices confer. Though powerful and ever present, honor's political influence is nevertheless complex and morally ambiguous. Leaders moved by honor may do the "right thing," selflessly defending valued principles and institutions, but their longing for preeminence may tempt them to go beyond the noble ambitions of public office to pursue fame and glory at any price. The various attempts to capture this moral ambiguity in the form of charismatic, leonine, transformative leadership confirm the duplex nature of honor and its profound implications for good political leadership. The honor scholarship therefore underlines the importance—and difficulty—of understanding leadership and honor as mutually constitutive. But to properly understand this dynamic, we need to recover from history a series of profound theoretical debates that explore the nature of this relationship and its implications for political practice.

At the heart of this book is the claim that leadership and honor are mutually constitutive, so that to understand the nature of leadership one needs an overarching conception of honor, and, equally, any conception of honor will inevitably be informed by what we think is good leadership. The claim that leadership and honor are mutually constitutive, or what I call the leadership-honor dynamic, in turn gives rise to the question of what exactly is the nature of this dynamic? Though the reflections on this question have a long and complex lineage, the diversity of the responses can be gathered and comprehended under three major approaches that have informed and continue to animate political and philosophical debates on the subject. I argue that the three thinkers who have been especially influential in shaping these approaches are Plato, Machiavelli, and Hobbes.

In part 2 of this book, "Leadership-honor dynamic," I attempt to bring to life these various approaches and show how they have engaged in a mutual dialogue while issuing in radically different and therefore contending formulations of the leadership-honor dynamic. Part 2 therefore is of partic- ular interest to political and moral philosophers and theorists of leadership who want to understand the philosophical provenance of contemporary approaches to the study of leadership. In trying to understand and articulate their various formulations and the way each was taken up and challenged, we bring into clearer focus three major conceptions of the leadership-honor dynamic that continue to inform and influence the way we understand leadership and honor. More specifically, in chapter 2, "Magnanimous Leadership," we examine the classical formulation of the leadership-honor dynamic first formulated by Plato. Ambitious leaders, according to Plato's Socrates, long to be admired by those they respect because it will assure their immortality. Honor explains the noble action (later called magnanim- ity) of the great leader and the selfless actions of the courageous patriot, but also shows its darker aspects in the tyrant with imperial designs and in the intransigence and stubborn dogmatism of the citizen who defends "our way." Plato's account was later challenged by two contending modern views of the leadership-honor dynamic, the Machiavellian and the Hobbesian. In chapter 3, "*Gloria* and Machiavelli's New Prince," we see how Machiavelli attempted to rehabilitate *gloria* and honor from its denunciation by Chris- tian piety. As the only passion that was other-regarding, Machiavelli argued that honor, directed yet untrammeled, could mediate between the few and the many who make up every community. Glory is the fair reward to the few for securing the comfort and security of the many, even if in being confined within the horizon of political excellence it is less ambitious than classical magnanimity. Yet, as we will see in chapter 4, "Dispersed Lead- ership of Thomas Hobbes," the disruptive unpredictability of Machiavelli's *gloria* convinced Hobbes that honor was a dangerous passion to be curbed or extirpated rather than encouraged or celebrated. Hobbes's critique of pride, and his innovation of amoral power as a measure of honor, was a radical attempt to reconstitute the economy of the human soul and thereby the foundations of all politics to come. Hobbes questions the role of the great leader in the name of the individual rights-bearer who, in defending his entitlements, also defends the social contract and the welfare of all. Modern leadership can be said to have been informed predominantly by both the Machiavellian "vertical" view and the Hobbesian "horizontal," each determined by its own understanding of the political force and importance of honor. Meanwhile, the classical Platonic position continues, in popular opinion if not scholarship, to challenge both, albeit sotto voce, in the name of public-spirited magnanimity.

Part 3 of the book, "Politics of the Leadership-Honor Dynamic," tests the merits of seeing leadership and honor as mutually constitutive by tracing the influence of the three approaches we have examined in significant and diverse contemporary political contests. It also allows us to see if the leadership-honor dynamic provides new insights into understanding the character of pressing contemporary political challenges. Part 3 therefore is of special interest to students of leadership studies, as well as those who are concerned with the specific political themes and questions explored in each chapter. Thus chapter 5, "Rethinking Transformative and Transactional Leadership," examines MacGregor Burns's conception of esteem to argue that the theoretical provenance of his famous transformative and transactional distinction lies not only in modern psychology, as he claims, but also in classical magnanimity. Chapter 6, "Idealistic Leadership of Lee Kuan Yew," examines the life and leadership of Lee Kuan Yew, founder of Singapore, to see if his self-proclaimed Machiavellianism and resort to Confucianism is sufficient to sustain his vision of good leadership. Chapter 7, "Flattery of Advisors," notes that, if honor matters to leaders, then their longing for it exposes them to the dangers of flattery. It focuses on the close relationship between leaders and advisors to reveal the potential dissonance between political power and knowledge. Chapter 8, "Anti-Politics of Fame and Identity," shows how modern politics is shaped by two contending trajectories of honor: fame and recognition. Fame, which is founded on honor uncoupled from excellence, results in an anti-politics of modern celebrities who challenge the authority of political leaders. Recognition, a move to counter mere fame by restoring dignity to individuals, issues in a new identity politics that in its various iterations—as dignity, recognition, and authenticity—seeks to reconstitute the terms of political debate and contestation. Chapter 9, "Patriotism and National Pride," argues that pride in one's country manifests itself in three competing notions of patriotism (classical, modern, nationalist) that present both opportunities and serious challenges to modern leaders. Taking up the case of Xi Jinping of China, it shows how Xi is forced to negotiate all three to secure his personal and national ambitions.

In part 4, the book concludes with chapter 10, "Noble Ambitions, Dangerous Passions," revisiting our initial claim that honor is both an ennobling and pernicious passion for leaders. It argues that adopting the leadership-honor dynamic provides new resources for exploring and understanding important political and moral questions. In particular, the leadership-honor dynamic provides new insights into the powerful passions that favor and impede innovation; a new approach to understanding moral leadership, allowing us to develop a more nuanced understanding of populists, dictators, and authoritarian leaders; and, finally, the extent to which modern democracies need to acknowledge and honor the noble sacrifice of good leaders.

PART 2

LEADERSHIP-HONOR DYNAMIC

CHAPTER 2

MAGNANIMOUS LEADERSHIP

Homer's portrayal of Achilles's fateful choice of a glorious short life over an undistinguished long one presented a captivating account of how leadership and honor are mutually constitutive. It was also a celebration of that glorious choice, instructing future readers on the proper disposition of leaders toward honor and thereby instituting and endorsing a magnificent new conception of the leadership-honor dynamic. Achilles as the epitome of the beautiful, brave, and heroic leader thereby became the shining example that captivated not only the Greeks, but also subsequent generations, even to the present day.[1] It was this model of leadership that confronted Socrates when he "called philosophy down from the heavens" and turned his attention to political things.[2]

Socrates's discovery of political philosophy gave rise to a "quarrel between philosophy and poetry," questioning not only Homer, but all poets concerning their conception of human excellence and their account of the gods.[3] More specifically, however, Socrates became critical of Achilles's *andreia* (as courage and manliness) and the tragic view of the world it presumed, presenting himself as the new model to be emulated.[4] Socrates's seemingly innocuous claim that the "unexamined life is not worth living" (*Apology* 38a) reveals the radical nature of his perspective, both for the meaning of a good life and as a novel standard for evaluating politics, while his famous proposal of the philosopher king brings into focus the puzzling character and far-reaching consequence of this new perspective. Socrates's challenge to Homer in the name of philosophy therefore entails a comprehensive new approach that seeks to replace both the *Iliad* and *Odyssey* with philosophy, mandating an exploration of who is a philosopher and how he is to be distinguished from those who resemble him, such as sophists, rhetoricians, and other knowers.[5] It also requires an account of the virtues such as justice, courage, temperance, and prudence; a reconsideration of the nature of statesmanship and friendship; and therefore the meaning of theology and cosmology. It is in this larger context that we explore the classical understanding of what constitutes good leadership and how it is shaped and defined by honor. We focus our discussion on the role of honor in Socrates's new psychology, how these insights into the nature and constitution of the soul are influential in determining the character of regimes, and, finally, the implications this has for Socratic soul-craft in the education of both philosophers and statesmen.

SPIRITEDNESS AND LEADERSHIP

Socrates's conversations with Plato's brothers Glaucon and Adeimantus in Plato's *Republic* are an especially valuable starting point for understanding his views on how leadership and honor are mutually constituted.[6] In deliberating on the nature and goodness of justice, Socrates, Glaucon, and Adeimantus thereby become, if only in speech, political founders of *kallipolis* or the beautiful city, disclosing along the way the nature of the human soul and how it is reflected in the character of the regime. The *Republic* therefore provides a dramatic and philosophical account of how honor with its origin in *thumos* or spiritedness moves the souls of these ambitious young men, how this is only one aspect of the soul that is also constituted by *eros* or desire and *logos* or reasoning, and finally how the struggles between these various aspects of the soul define the nature of leaders and the regime they favor.

With a powerful longing for political office, authority, and leadership, the daring and ambitious Glaucon is tempted by the tyranny endorsed by sophists and rhetors such as Thrasymachus, who claim that exceptional individuals should not defer to the laws and justice in satisfying their ambitions. Yet his good character and education inclines him to do what is right, explaining his keen interest in having Socrates explain and defend justice. Having decided that it would be easier to see justice writ large in the city, Socrates, Glaucon, Adeimantus, and other interlocutors set about to found a just city. It is not surprising, then, that the question of spirit-edness first emerges in the *Republic* after the original "healthy" city, or, in Glaucon's disparaging terms, the "city of sows," becomes a luxurious city by appropriating territory from its neighbors and is thereby compelled to defend its new acquisition. This "feverish" city, as Socrates calls it, therefore now requires guardians who are skilled in martial arts and possess spirit, making them "fearless and invincible in the face of everything" (375b).

But what is spiritedness?[7] It does not seem to be a specifically human passion, as Socrates suggests that dogs too possess it. Yet it appears to be especially dangerous and volatile politically, because a spirited guardian may potentially be savage to other guardians and citizens. This indictment of spiritedness is countered by Socrates's amusing claim that there is something philosophical about dogs. Dogs' love of learning, according to Socrates, is evident in their inclination to be well disposed to what they know and hostile to what is alien. Dogs, and by implication guardians, know and protect their masters and are wary of strangers, displaying hostility toward those they do not know. Socrates's allusion to a "philosophic" dog suggests that spiritedness is concerned with guarding or protecting, initially what is uniquely its own, its body, and, by extension or education, what it can regard as its own.[8] But as this account of philosophic dogs shows, the character and extent of the dog's openness to learning and knowledge reveal the limitations of spiritedness. Spiritedness judges or evaluates by a simple expedient—the familiar or what it knows is a friend; everything else is an enemy. Consequently, it seems indifferent to the virtues or vices of those it meets and therefore oblivious to merit, a limitation dramatically demonstrated in a dog's willingness to protect (and therefore implicitly consider as "its own") its human master.

Indignation, anger, even rage, seem to draw on the natural desire of all living things to protect themselves and, in a minimal and sometimes confused sense, what they consider to be their own. In spite of these limitations, it is not surprising that Socrates calls spiritedness an attractive affection of the soul, as it represents all those actions we praise as noble and beautiful, ranging from the protection of family and friends, to the defense of city and homeland. Indeed, our willingness to risk ourselves, even our very lives, in protecting others is the principal civic measure of our virtue, certainly an essential requirement for heroism. Yet this beautiful aspect of spiritedness seems to forget that dogs are not only guardians but are also used for hunting, revealing a more assertive or aggressive form of spiritedness that protects one's own through active acquisition.[9] Spiritedness as "getting" rather than "keeping" complicates our understanding and suggests that to comprehend its complex and morally ambiguous nature, it is necessary to examine its place in the soul. The subsequent discussion in the *Republic* reveals a composite soul constituted by *eros* or desire and *logos* or reasoning as well as by spiritedness. This more complex account reveals how spiritedness may range dangerously from the divine heights of grand nobility to the dark depths of depravity. To understand how spiritedness is shaped by both desire and reasoning, we need to consider Socrates's discussion of the constitution of the soul and the extent to which spiritedness can be said to side with justice.

Having seen the development of the city in speech and examined the place of justice within it, Socrates now turns to the individual to discern justice in the single human being, an approach he warns is less precise than the "longer road" they do not pursue (435c–d). After examining the three parts of the city—money making, auxiliary, and guardian—the question arises of whether the individual's soul is similarly constituted, that is, does the soul have three forms and dispositions?[10] The discussion commences with thirst, hunger, and *epithumia* or desires generally. Desire is a longing or neediness that makes us "embrace" what we want to become (437c). It also appears as something we have control over, something we assent to, or choose. In any case, Socrates suggests that desire is always for good things, and distinguishes between desire simply, which longs only for satisfaction, and particular desires, which seek specific satisfactions. This distinction is intended to show that any drawing back from a desire must come from some other part of the soul—the person who longs to drink, but does not, must be being checked by something other than desire. This Socrates calls calculation, subsequently concluding that the soul has two parts, the irrational that loves, hungers, and thirsts and the calculating (439d). But this distinction is less clear-cut than it first appears. Is it not possible that the desire for drink is in fact checked not by calculation but by another desire? Could the calculating part have its own desires? Still, the distinction between calculation and desire presents Socrates with a perplexing question of where spiritedness fits in this division. Is it a third part or an aspect of one of the other two?

Glaucon's initial response is that spiritedness is a desire. Socrates counters by giving three examples. The first is the story of Leontius, who, noticing corpses lying near the public executioner, desired to look but was at the same time disgusted and made himself turn away. After struggling for a while, and overcome with desire, he opened his eyes and said, "Look, you damned wretches, take your fill of the fair sight." Socrates relies on this example to suggest that anger sometimes makes war against desires. In addition, Socrates reminds Glaucon that when someone's desires overcome calculation, that person reproaches himself. The spirit is roused against what appear to be factions in his soul, suggesting that spiritedness never sides with desires against speeches declaring what must be done (440b). Finally, Socrates notes the connection between spiritedness and justice by observing that human beings are prepared to accept without anger what they perceive to be just punishment (440c–d). These three examples are meant to show that spiritedness sides with calculation against desire. And indeed, they do reveal the extent to which spiritedness allows us to overcome ourselves, and more generally, defend justice, even if it means that we sacrifice our own welfare. Spiritedness appears impressive and commendable in this light. Yet a closer examination of Socrates's story reveals a more ambiguous aspect.

It is true that spiritedness allows us to overcome desires; it presses down or silences apparently natural desires such as hunger, thirst, and in the case of Leontius, the desire to see the corpses. But such suppression is at a price: it is a sign of a divided or factious soul. Leontius's physical struggle—looking, turning away, covering his face, and finally running and yelling—is an outward expression of the conflict in his soul. But it is only because his spiritedness is inadequate and "loses" that we discover the struggle at all. The story of Leontius shows a failure of spiritedness—Leontius does not stop himself from looking. Perhaps a more spirited Leontius may not have looked. In that case, his discordant soul would have seemed whole, his unhappiness concealed by the appearance of harmony that spiritedness achieved by powerful suppression or oppression.

Confronted by the power of spiritedness, we may be comforted by the observation that it always sides with what is just. If so, how are we to understand Leontius's disgust with the sight of corpses? Certainly they are not a "fine sight"—perhaps he is ashamed of a morbid if not ghoulish curiosity that questions his gentlemanly sensibilities. Perhaps his desire to look at the way convicts are punished uncovers his secret and illicit desires for violence or injustice that will escape the city's reach. Maybe his curiosity is derived from a suspicion about the gods and their providential and retributive judgments. We do not know. What we do know is that his spiritedness sides with his opinion of what is just to limit his actions. In doing so, however, it will not interrogate what is just, but accepts justice as it finds it. It therefore appears incapable of adjudicating between what is and what appears to be just.

Finally, Leontius's exclamation in giving into desire does support the view that spiritedness is an ally of speech and therefore reasoning. But a closer look at the speech—the personification of eyes as the culprit or lawbreaker—discloses a disturbing feature of spiritedness. It shows the tendency of spiritedness to insist upon, and even create by personifying, an entity with intentionality and motive. Seemingly a means for guarding or protecting oneself, human spiritedness as indignation, anger, and in the extreme case rage has an added dimension that interprets all harm, and presumably all events, as volitional and directed. Hence the notorious and otherwise perplexing case of the Persian King Xerxes, whose attempt to bridge the Hellespont having failed because of a storm ordered the river be whipped 300 times and lowered into the sea a yoke of fetters in addition to branding it. He ordered the lashers to say, "You bitter water, our master lays this punishment upon you because you have wronged him, though he never did you any wrong. King Xerxes will cross you, whether you will or not; it is with justice that no one sacrifices to you, who are a muddy and briny river" (Herodotus 1987, 483; 7.35).

Moreover, and equally unreasoning, in the very moment of such per-sonification Leontius effectively forgets himself—he cannot blame his eyes without somehow letting go of Leontius the person. It is this self-forgetting and self-neglecting nature of spirited anger that is arguably the source of noble acts of sacrifice—and frenzied acts of rage—both of which are inexplicable in terms of clear-sighted and measured actions that seek to protect oneself. That spiritedness in humans cannot help but take things personally, that it would for some reason prefer to do so than assume that events are unintentional or accidental, may in part be due to the importance we attribute to justice. We would rather imagine, it would seem, a world of intended, or malicious, injustice, than a world of accidental or meaningless harm where we do not seem to be valuable or important. Consequently, where the spiritedness of the philosophic dog is moved by its knowledge of who is a friend and who an enemy, human spiritedness is more philosophical, taking its bearings from the legal and the just. Our attachment to justice, and therefore our sense of what is honorable and shameful, make our spiritedness unique. Nevertheless, human spiritedness seems to retain the dog-like disinclination to ask what is the legal and the just. It will necessarily speak the language of justice (and therefore of honor, shame, guilt, and punishment), even if it has a partial and approximate view of the just. This means that spiritedness may be the most powerful and intransigent enemy of the desire to look at those things proscribed by the laws, and especially the "new" things. Leontius, unlike Oedipus, finally satisfies his curiosity only after overcoming the powerful spirited guardians of shame and guilt.

TWO FACES OF HONOR

Socrates's discussion of spiritedness in the context of philosophic dogs and the drama of Leontius, a reenactment and critique of Sophocles's *Oedipus,* reveals the complex and powerful role of spiritedness in the economy of the soul.[11] But what is the precise nexus between spiritedness and honor, and how does it shape politics? To answer these questions, it is necessary to examine the role of spiritedness in Socrates's account of the dissolution of the just city. Ostensibly following Hesiod, Socrates shows how the just city degenerates into a timocracy, oligarchy, democracy, and ultimately tyranny. Consistent with the initial presupposition that a regime is an individual writ large, Socrates explores the psychology of representative individuals to see how and why each regime degenerates. For our discussion, it is helpful to focus on the transition from the just city to timocracy, the regime based on honor, and how this regime succumbs to oligarchy, the regime based on wealth.

The *timocrat* or honor lover comes into being, according to Socrates, because the influence of his philosophic father is countered by his mother, his household, and the public more generally. His mother complains that she lacks honor among other women, that her husband turns his mind to himself, neither honoring nor dishonoring her, and that he is not serious about money and will not fight for it in law courts and in public. The opinion of the domestics that the son should be "more of a man" than his father is reinforced by general opinion that calls those who mind their business simpletons. Confronted by these conflicting influences, the son eventually "came to the middle and turned over the rule in himself to the middle part, the part that loves victory and is spirited; he became a haughty-minded man who loves honour" (549c–550b). Honor, from this account, appears to be an admixture of philosophy and spiritedness. The father's indifference to politics (he does not seek office), victory (he does not care for money and will not contest it in court), and honor (he neither honors nor dishonors his wife very much) are perceived as "unmanly," lazy, or stupid. It seems that the philosopher will always appear cowardly and indolent from the perspective of the spirited because the family and the city, the essential constituents of politics, tend to favor and praise someone who wants to rule, who will protect his reputation and what is his own. The only motive and reason they can find (or understand) for someone who eschews these things is in the terms of spiritedness: laziness and lack of courage. Timocracy, it would seem, is fundamentally opposed to the philosopher, who appears mild-mannered.[12]

It is equally instructive for understanding spiritedness and its link to honor to see how the timocrat becomes an oligarch. The timocrat, a general or some other high office holder, will "blunder against the city as against a reef." The honor- and victory-loving nature of the timocrat leads him to disdain property and entangles him in litigation. As a result, he loses his property, or, even worse, is exiled or executed. When the son sees these things and loses his inheritance, he is frightened and "thrusts love of honor and spiritedness headlong out of the throne of his soul; and humbled by poverty, he turns greedily to money-making" (553a–c). The fearful oligarch, it seems, has realized something the timocrat learns at a price—the contradictory demands of spiritedness. The superiority and "haughtiness" that elevates the timocrat leads him to think that honor is sufficient to protect him. But, as the oligarch finds out, the city also praises property; spiritedness is paradoxically premised on the view that property *and* honor are the highest goods. Spiritedness will always rally in defense of what is one's own, principally as property, at its highest signification, justice. Therefore, the city is based on, and praises, acquisition and mastery. It reserves its greatest praise for, and heaps its highest honor on, those whom it deems are its great protectors. It almost seems that the city dispenses honor to guarantee property—the war hero is admired for risking life to protect what is dear to the city, above all the land that guarantees the luxuries Glaucon and others like him demand. This principle comes to permeate every struggle within the city itself, especially in the law courts. But at the extreme, when the guardians have to sacrifice all they have for the city, when blind spiritedness makes them think they are invincible, the goodness of such a sacrifice becomes questionable to the guardian. Though the city and the gods praise noble self-sacrifice, its value is always ambiguous. For the timocrat who loses all, not in war but in the domestic political struggles of the law courts, this sacrifice is stripped of its glorious reward. When it becomes evident that in any contest between honor and property the city will tend to favor property, the educated timocrat, terrified because deprived of the comfort of honor, learns his lesson and becomes an oligarch, choosing property as the only truly secure basis for life. In preferring the useful to the noble and beautiful, the timocrat abandons honor.

Socrates's account of the timocrat as a corrupted philosopher who in due course becomes an oligarch shows the significance of honor in politics. In presenting the timocrat within a larger account of the decay of regimes, Socrates reminds us that the new standard for assessing leaders and politics more generally is the philosopher. All the Platonic dialogues take this approach and in doing so seek to demonstrate the superiority of Socrates over Achilles. But the efficacy of this new perspective is questionable when we reflect on the nature of the philosopher, especially his indifference to honor. That the philosopher is to be the new model of leadership even if he perplexes, repulses, or infuriates the many is the problem at the heart of Socratic political philosophy, succinctly formulated in the concept of the "philosopher king" as the new model for leadership. Yet the timocrat is placed next to the philosopher, suggesting an affinity between them, and distance from the oligarch and democrat. What is admirable about the timocrat philosophically speaking? The answer lies in the subtle but important distinction Socrates makes between two types of honor lovers—the *philonikia* or victory lover, and the *philotimia* or honor lover. The difference is crucial and has far-reaching implications for understanding political leadership and the way it is shaped by honor.[13]

Victory loving and honor loving point to different aspects of the desire for honor and therefore different types of human beings. The core difference seems to be that one loves victory to such an extent that he is willing to risk his good name, while the other values honor so highly that he would rather lose than appear dishonorable. While honor limits and constrains the honor lover, the victory lover seems enviably independent and self-sufficient, seemingly indifferent to the judgment of others. But is the victory lover truly free of the desire for honor? Doesn't victory always presume someone vanquished or defeated, being therefore defined by the losers as much as the winners? In other words, isn't coming first, or being on top, fundamentally and necessarily moved by the desire to be and be seen as superior to another? The victory lover in his freedom or disregard of conventional notions of honor resembles the knowledge lover who shows courage and perseverance to seek knowledge, however shameful. But they differ in a fundamental respect—the goal of the victory lover is preeminence rather than knowledge.[14] But what if victory is not over others but over oneself, struggling to have our superior or better selves prevail? Are such actions still shaped by honor? As the case of Leontius demonstrates, this civil war of the soul, where our "better" selves overcome the "worse," are inevitably shaped by honor because they are always contests determined by the noble and just where someone, even if imagined, is adjudicating the struggle. It is in this context that we see the decisive difference between the victory and honor lover. Though both love honor, in the extreme case the victory lover will transgress the laws of honor and therefore justice in seeking mastery, even to the extent of reconstituting or redefining what is honorable. The victory lover therefore appears as both philosopher and tyrant—radical and innovative from one perspective and shameless, lawless, and dangerous from another. The honor lover, on the other hand, will seek to be admired for doing what is honorable. This will mean defending what is honorable, even if it incurs individual loss or sacrifice. Indeed, such sacrifice is proof of his virtue, so that the honor lover will look from one perspective as the noble and heroic patriot, and from another as the dogmatic, unreasonable, and intransigent opponent of innovation and progress.

LOVE AND LEADERSHIP

In the *Republic*, Socrates reveals the decisive importance of spiritedness in the soul, how it explains different forms of honor that influence the political ambition of leaders and thereby shape the character of regimes. Yet the focus on spiritedness appears to provide only a partial explanation of how honor shapes leadership ambition. The conversation in the *Republic*, necessarily shaped by the nature and desires of Glaucon and Adeimantus, emphasized the importance of spiritedness in the complex constitution of the soul. For a more comprehensive account of leadership and honor, we need to examine the significance of those other parts, especially *eros* or love, otherwise neglected or disparaged in the *Republic*.[15] For this reason, we turn to Socrates's account of love in Plato's *Symposium*, an encomium on the god Eros that takes place during the tragic poet Agathon's drinking party celebrating his victory at the Dionysia.[16] Of the various speeches in praise of Eros in the *Symposium*, we focus on two, the speech by Aristophanes, which seems to reduce eros to spiritedness, and Socrates's account of his conversation with Diotima, which presents a selectively beautiful eros by seemingly denying all spiritedness. Taken together, I suggest, they reveal how leaders' noble ambitions and dangerous passions are due to the unique admixture of eros and spiritedness in their soul.

Aristophanes's fantastic account of eros starts with a story of human beings as originally descended from cosmic gods and imitating their spherical shape. But the lofty ambition of these humans to overthrow the gods results in their punishment by Olympian gods who slice them into two in their image. This cutting results in a powerful longing of each human for its other half, a desire for the ancient wholeness they now lack. But because this wholeness is no longer possible, people began to perish in searching for their other halves. Consequently, Zeus rearranged their sexual organs so that in embracing, humanity can continue, and the gods will have their adherents. For Aristophanes, eros as sexual gratification therefore conceals, however briefly, true eros, our impossible and therefore tragic hopes for completion or oneness that was destroyed by human ambition and divine punishment. Eros does not look beyond itself, according to Aristophanes, because it is fundamentally love of one's own, principally as one's own body, and more extensively as one's fellow citizens and, by extension, the city. This account of eros in effect reduces it to spiritedness, the passion most concerned with securing one's own. Eros as spiritedness has two aspects: the original and the natural, which caused a vigorous but ultimately unsuccessful attack on the gods; and a character tamed or civilized by a disfiguring divine law that defends the city and gives rise to patriotism. Aristophanes's account brings out an important aspect of the human soul, our love of our own, yet in doing so it denies the possibility of eros as something that transcends one's own. Eros is thus a tragic love of one's own, established by jealous gods as punishment for hubris or desire to displace them; love is punishment for our ambition to replace divine glory. To see the implications of such a view, we need to look closely at the alternative, the opinion that eros looks beyond oneself. For this, we turn to Socrates's speech.

Socrates begins his speech by recounting a conversation he had with Diotima, a prophetess who taught him about erotic things when he was young. This erotic education marks the decisive point where the young Socrates, famously caricatured in Aristophanes's *Clouds* as the natural scientist in the "think tank" high above the concerns of the city, turns to the human things, inquiring especially about the nature of beauty, justice, and the good.[17] Diotima corrects Socrates's opinion that Eros is a god. In a mythic account of its origins, she claims eros, a progeny of Resource and Poverty, and otherwise unrelated to Aphrodite or sexuality, is not a god but a *daimonion* or demon, mediating between gods and men. All human beings desire happiness, according to Diotima, and do so by longing for money, or health, or philosophy. But eros is in truth a love of the good. Therefore it is not love of one's own. Her proof is that we will cut off our hands or feet if we think they are no good. Nor is eros love of the beautiful, as Agathon had suggested in an earlier speech. We are all pregnant, according to Diotima, and want to give birth in the beautiful; but beauty accompanies our sexual unions as generative acts and is not its end. In repudiating the claims that eros is love of one's own and of the beautiful, Diotima seems to reveal an eros untainted by spiritedness.

In the immediate sequel, however, this view of eros is complicated by the pervasive force of spiritedness that makes us long for honor and immortality. Eros, according to Diotima, is also the desire to possess the good *forever* (206a11–13). This formulation directs our attention away from the good to the lover, with the reference to forever reminding us of something that concerns us most—our longing to preserve ourselves, or in other words not to die. The desire to be immortal is therefore a spirited longing informed by eros. Spiritedness, as we have seen, makes us forget ourselves, so that animals and humans sacrifice to protect their young in the belief that they are somehow us. But spiritedness does not make animals contemplate immortality—this is the influence of eros, which teaches spiritedness to think that our children somehow make *us* immortal. Eros combines with spiritedness in humans to give birth to the possibility of immortality and specifically immortal fame due to our virtue. Eros therefore introduces a transpersonal aspect to spiritedness. An animal may be concerned with what others do, or intend to do, but it does not care about others' opinions about its "worth." Only humans contemplate the worth of others, principally because human eros raises the possibility of virtue. Eros introduces virtue and therefore excellence into human thinking, and in doing so transforms human spiritedness, making us think the good opinion of others acknowledging our virtue is somehow essential for our own well-being. Just as spiritedness makes us think that we are our children, or, rather, that they are us, spiritedness informed by eros makes us think that in the public recognition of our virtue we acquire an undying reputation for excellence, and therefore become in some sense immortal. This form of immortality, according to Diotima, is especially pursued by poets, such as Homer and Hesiod, and legislators and statesmen, such as Lycurgus and Solon. In their search for immortality, such poets, inventors, and politikos give birth to prudence and other virtues, which in the form of political arrangements, including those of cities and households, are called moderation and justice (209a5–8). Poets and statesmen are "makers" of virtue, not for the sake of virtue but for the sake of their spiritedness and erotic longing for immortal fame.[18] After revealing this aspect of eros as love of immortal fame, Diotima initiates the young Socrates into the mysteries of love, whereby the soul is purified to receive the immortal image of beauty. What later came be to be called the "Ladder of Love" starts with the love of a specific body, then is instructed to see the beauty in all bodies, is elevated to the love of beautiful souls, the love of pursuits and laws, the love of sciences, and, at its most mysterious height, contemplates the beautiful itself.[19]

This account of eros in the *Symposium* provides valuable insights for our understanding of leadership and honor. The first is the extent to which eros and therefore love of honor and immortality dominate the souls of those who display love of leadership and noble ambition. Second is the extent to which at the apex, in the contemplation of the unchanging beautiful, Diotima depicts a form of eros seemingly unadulterated with spiritedness. The gazing at the beautiful, and therefore partaking as much as humanly possible in the immortal, is her poetic account of the philosopher contemplating the good. Here Diotima seems to make love a comprehensive but disembodied good where the more we contemplate beauty, the more we leave "us" behind, until we in a sense "die." The third aspect reveals the deeper meaning of beauty for Socrates. When Diotima says that the contemplation of the beautiful gives birth to true virtue, and therefore "it is open to him to become dear to the gods and if it is open to any other human being, for him too to become immortal" (212a, 2–7), there is the suggestion, however tentative or conditional, that at the core of the beautiful in this sense is a spiritedness longing to preserve oneself, this time with the promise of divine support. What we ordinarily understand as *to kalon* or the beautiful and noble is therefore essentially an admixture of eros and spiritedness, and gains its shine from its divine promise of immortality. It is not accidental that when moved by the unalloyed beauty and awesome grandeur of nature we gain an intimation of immortality.[20] More politically, Homer's depiction of Achilles's disdain for death in avenging his beloved Patroclus is beautiful and noble because it confirms his and our deepest longings for divine support for such virtuous self-sacrifice. The *Symposium* suggests that Socrates is largely impervious to the allure of this form of beauty. His attempt at making himself beautiful for Agathon's party consists of taking a bath and wearing sandals (174a).[21] Indeed, he arrives late for the party because he is absorbed in contemplation, presumably gazing at the beautiful. But we don't know what occupies his thoughts, and in any case such deliberation confirms he has left behind or been purified of the allure of those forms of immortality that charm citizens, legislators, poets, and statesmen (175a–c).[22]

Diotima's beautiful account of eros in the *Symposium* shows its subtle and elusive character. Between the erotic love of the good and the spirited love of one's own, we find the love of the beautiful, which at its highest is an erotic and spirited interpretation or fashioning of a divine promise of immortality for virtuous actions. What her account suggests is that most humans, but leaders above all, are moved by the longing to be immortal and try to fulfil it either by having children or by seeking divine rewards for pursuing virtue and excellence in making beautiful things, such as poems and laws, or in political practice. With proper means, however, this dominance of spiritedness can be purged, yielding an eros that partakes of the only immortality that is possible for humans—gazing at the unchanging good. For Diotima, it seems a mystical enchantment is our only prospect of limited or earthly immortality.

Yet the upper reaches of beauty that we espy in our initiation into Diotima's mysteries make us wonder if our gaze on the beautiful can ever approach the intensity and pleasure we experience when we love specific and unique individuals. How viable is her teaching that seems to surmount all that we ordinarily value, including our beloved, our families, and the cities in which we live? Is love possible without the presence of both body *and* soul? And the promise of complete initiation seems beyond our grasp. In what sense is it true to say that in gazing at the unchanging we no longer think of ourselves, that is, can we ever become "unspirited," without any concern for ourselves?[23] That Socrates's presentation of Diotima's account is immediately followed by the disruptive entry of a drunken Alcibiades, Socrates's beloved, makes us wonder how much, and which part of her teaching Socrates subsequently adopted or endorsed.

SOCRATIC EDUCATION OF LEADERS

The desire to be praised or admired, and alternatively to avoid censure and shame, is according to Socrates a uniquely human passion constituted by both spiritedness and eros. It is also fundamentally social and political, to the extent that it cannot be experienced or satisfied by oneself, requiring the opinion of others, evident from their statements or actions, or in anticipation and therefore imagination. What is specifically praised or blamed will of course differ, as we know from the extraordinary diversity of what is considered honorable or shameful. Yet the passion itself, the desire to be loved, praised, or admired for doing the right thing and therefore for the virtues we possess, is present in everyone, though its strength or vehemence will vary between individuals. It is especially evident in those admirable or honorable actions that defend and thereby reveal the good and noble, always requiring courage and sometimes sacrifice. We therefore praise and honor above all the patriot who is willing to give his life for his country. The willingness to sacrifice and in the extreme give up one's life to do the honorable and right thing can in most cases trace its source to the longing for immortality. The desire to be praised, admired, and remembered even or especially after we die, and therefore the need to recall and record for the future such noble actions, explains the importance of the arts for honor. Consequently, it is in the works of the Muses—in paintings, sculptures, poetry, and music—that the honorable actions of good men and women are recorded and memorialized for posterity. This *honestas* face of honor reveals itself as a noble passion that can transmute the entrenched and self-directed desires of material gain into noble ambition to protect those individuals and ideals we love and admire.[24] It accounts for the heroism of the anonymous solitary figure who confronts and defies the tanks headed for Tiananmen Square. It is Rosa Parks who refuses to sit at the back of the bus. It is Malala Yousafzai, who wants education for Pakistani girls.

But there is a different "face" of honor that also seeks to be praised and not blamed but will seek satisfaction not in simply defending the good and noble, but in doing so in an outstanding way. In Plato's *Republic*, this is the difference between the honor lover and the victory lover. The impulse to be preeminent in virtue insinuates in the heart of the honor lover a desire to excel and therefore seek victory over others in virtue. But in some cases, the desire will turn against honor itself so that some will seek to redefine what is honorable to become preeminent, as Alexander did when he cut the Gordian knot rather than unraveling it.[25] Others who have powerful, though frustrated, longings for preeminence will even seek to satisfy it by being outstanding in any way possible, even in vice or criminality. Herostratos is said to have burned down the Temple of Artemis, one of the Seven Wonders of the ancient world, because he wanted to be famous.[26] This victory-loving face of honor, in elevating preeminence, seemed to be a dangerous passion placing the individual above all. It was also considered dangerous because it seemed without limit and therefore shameless and sacrilegious, straining against all proper bounds. Thus, honor as hubris explained the impulse toward tyranny or, even more ambitiously, empire.

Yet for Socrates a version of this passion was also the source for the *periagoge* or turning around necessary for philosophical liberation (*Republic* 518d). The two faces of honor and therefore forms of leadership accounted for the different forms of soul-craft or education proposed in the *Republic*, evident especially in the instruction of Glaucon and Adeimantus.[27] We do not know why Socrates accompanies Glaucon that day to Athens' port town of Piraeus. But Polemarchus's insistence that Socrates and Glaucon join him and others for dinner and to see the new religious procession does allow

us to evaluate Glaucon's character and his abiding concern with the need
to be just, allowing us to conjecture what Socrates and Glaucon may have
discussed in private. Glaucon, as we know from Xenophon, was keen for
political rule, having attempted to speak in public before he was legally
entitled.[28] This is confirmed by his character throughout the *Republic*. He
is spirited, daring, and politically ambitious, yet also concerned about how
to satisfy this longing. He wants to be just and to defend justice, yet he
is also spirited enough to entertain the possibility that his greatest desires
can only be satisfied through injustice. He betrays a love of cruelty and
even morbidity in testing the happiness of a just man by imagining him
blinded and crucified. Above all, he is deeply erotic, longing to be kissed.
It is therefore not accidental that the meal promised by Polemarchus never
eventuates; Glaucon, who was dissatisfied with the "healthy city" of sows
because he wanted "relishes," is nevertheless content because he becomes a
founder, even if it is a city only in speech. Adeimantus, by contrast, is the
honor lover who is not tempted by the blandishments of Thrasymachus
but rather wants to defend justice from the claim that it is only for the
advantage of the stronger. His interventions in the conversations are less
spectacular, and his concerns center on the importance of family, the distribution of property, and the communism of women. Adeimantus wants
to protect and secure rather than change and transform and is therefore
much more concerned with the everyday demands of political life, rather
than the grand ambitions of a founding. He is to this extent the serious
citizen and noble patriot who is moved by shame and praise and cares for
his family and the city.

It is in the drama of the *Republic* as the founding of the city in speech
that we see how the discovery of political philosophy inaugurates a new
conception of leadership that challenges both Glaucon and Adeimantus.
Socrates intends to educate and therefore moderate honor in its two politically influential manifestations. Consequently, Glaucon's erotic spiritedness,
which results in a commanding ambition to excel and be preeminent, is
directed toward philosophy and away from the dangers of tyranny, while
Adeimantus's noble defense of honor and justice is ennobled by a new
poetry and theology that will moderate the dangers of a blindly intransigent indignation. But this education, as we can see from the *Republic* as a
whole, necessitates a reranking and thereby depreciation of the grandeur of
political leadership and a sober reminder of the difficulty of being a leader.
The famous image of the city as a cave relegates the city and its concerns
to the dark underground while elevating the philosophical to the proximity

of the sun (517d ff). The ship of state metaphor shows ruling as a struggle among clamorous and undeserving aspirants who desperately try to influence the people portrayed as the deaf and drunken owner of the ship (488a). Ruling is shown to be necessary for the overall happiness of the city, but at significant cost to the ruler, who will have to sacrifice his happiness for the good of all (519d). The only reason to rule, according to Socrates, is to avoid being ruled by an inferior (347c). Finally, in the famous account of the philosopher king, we see that justice will be possible only if the rulers philosophize, though it becomes clear that such an ambition is at the very least questionable because of the nature of the philosopher, who will need to be persuaded to rule, and the ruled, who would not regard philosophers as obvious rulers.[29] Indeed, as Plato's *Statesman* shows, ruling is nothing like the shepherd's art because people are obviously not like sheep—they have their own judgment about their dignity and worth—and even sound decisions may be repudiated if they do not acknowledge the people through consultation, deliberation, and sharing of offices and authority (see generally Márquez 2012). The questioning of the pleasure of ruling and the honor it bestows is accompanied in the *Republic* by a redefinition of what is honorable. The poets are banished to permit a reform of theology or account of the gods, instituting a more philosophical and therefore less wrathful and punitive divinity (363a ff). The people's spirited attachment to the love of land is reformed and ennobled, with a new emphasis on the ideas or patterns discernible in the sky and the makeup of one's soul (414d ff). Finally, the stories about post-mortem justice and judgment are ameliorated by the Myth of Er that reforms the terrors of Hades and sees death as an opportunity for reeducation through rebirth (614a ff).

How feasible and efficacious is such an education for the general community and for exceptional individuals? That the citizens of even the best city will ultimately require "noble lies" and myths to ensure they are just raises questions regarding the merits of the proposed civic pedagogy (*Republic* 414b–15d; 614–21). But perhaps the most telling charge against the efficacy of Socrates's soul-craft concerns his dealings with the talented Alcibiades. Alcibiades is the most famous love of Socrates in the Platonic dialogues.[30] He is the talented, beautiful, wealthy, and well-born Athenian who seems indifferent to these advantages, suggesting a supremely erotic soul unconstrained by such conventional attachments. Alcibiades therefore seems to be that rare creature, the philosopher by nature, another Socrates.[31] But the subsequent career of Alcibiades not only questions Socrates's erotic education of spiritedness, but also makes us wonder whether there is some truth to the charge that Socrates corrupts the young.[32] As we discover from Thucydides's *Peloponnesian War*, Alcibiades, elected general when only thirty years old, advocated the hugely ambitious Athenian invasion of Sicily, then escaped Athenian censure by defecting to the Spartans, after which he returned to head the democratic party in Athens before finally taking refuge with a Persian governor in Phrygia who murdered him. Alcibiades, it seems, cannot help but restructure and transform politics wherever he goes.[33] As Thucydides indicates, the pride, self-assurance, and brilliance of someone like Alcibiades justifies his claim for preeminence and the greatest of honors. In being free from conventional restraints, such individuals assume a god-like universal perspective that comprehends and surmounts any individual city. What from Alcibiades's perspective would seem to be the natural expression of human excellence, which is surely the aim of all cities, appears from the city's view as hubris or shameless outrage, overreach, and secret ambition toward tyranny. Alcibiades longs to be honored by the best in the city, yet he also seems to reduce the city at most to a household, or an armed camp. This core tension in the hope and ambitions of both parties is nicely captured by Aristophanes in *Frogs*: "It is best not to rear a lion in the city / But if one is reared, the city must submit to its ways."

As we have seen, from a certain vantage point, rare individuals like Alcibiades seem philosophical because they appear indifferent to, or disdain the love of, gain that moves most human beings, and seem especially indifferent to the laws of propriety and the principles of honor that shame most of us into moderating our desires to know. This indifference can, however, conceal the source of such self-sufficiency, an overwhelming desire for preeminence and hence glorying. Yet this need for preeminence is also essentially other-regarding—Alcibiades needs others to defer to him. He is therefore moved as much by spiritedness of being first or foremost as by eros for the good. The unshakeable belief in his own superiority and worth explains why Alcibiades rejects conventional honor as unjust. Hence his desire to win means he will inevitably reconstitute the laws to acknowledge his true worth. This rare combination of extreme eros and spiritedness makes the victory lover a potential philosopher or a tyrant. But Alcibiades is neither, which may well explain that Socrates did, in one sense, succeed in taming Alcibiades.

Alcibiades never displays *orge* or rage, nor does he enjoy the dubious pleasures of the victor who gloats over the bodies of the defeated, as the equally ambitious young Cyrus does over the Assyrian dead in the battle-field.[34] Indeed, in each case Alcibiades seeks to use persuasion and consent to gain political advantage.[35] This may be due to the unique combination of extreme eros and spiritedness in his character that helps him avoid the terrible consequences of the tyrant as "eros incarnate." But perhaps it is also a consequence of the Socratic education he receives. Alcibiades does not become a Plato, or even Glaucon, but it is possible that, like Xenophon, his exposure to Socrates allows him to understand his spirited nature and therefore anticipate and avoid the worst excesses of victory-loving spiritedness and of the tyrannical soul.[36] Socrates's love for Alcibiades appears to be a form of the "divine madness" noted in the *Phaedrus* (255b ff) that ennobles both lover and beloved, revealing the extent to which the constitution of our soul places limits on such love.[37] Socrates's conversations, because they are unavoidably concerned with opinions and therefore what is honorable and shameful, will be especially challenging for those of his interlocutors who are most concerned with honor. In the ideal case, as we saw, Socrates shows Alcibiades what he is lacking, and Alcibiades is sufficiently erotic to listen to him, at least for a while. Yet, Alcibiades's speech in the *Symposium* reveals the limits of Socrates's ennobling love: though thoughtful and talented enough to appreciate the superiority of Socrates, Alcibiades is ultimately unwilling (or unable) to pursue the philosophical life. Consequently, he attempts to redefine their love in terms that will preserve his superiority, either as lover or benefactor. Failing even in this, the only way he can avoid the shame he feels before Socrates is by avoiding him altogether (*Symposium* 214e). In other cases, however, especially for those who make a living as rhetors or sophists, such as Thrasymachus, Protagoras, and Gorgias, Socrates will seem no different from a victory lover, and his *elenchus* a powerful new means for eristic agonism. For a few, however, Socratic *elenchus* is just punishment, a means of improving themselves.[38] The limits of such education may account for the Platonic defense of the law and constitutional rule in the *Crito*, *Statesman*, *Minos*, and *Laws*.

MAGNANIMOUS LEADERSHIP

In this chapter we have examined the origin and substance of the Socratic insight into the leadership-honor dynamic. As we have seen, Socrates counters the Homeric heroism of Achilles with a new view of leadership that takes its direction from the primacy of the "examined life" or philosophy. Socrates founds this new perspective on his new psychology that shows how spiritedness, eros, and reasoning shape the two faces of honor, and how it accounts for the hopes and aspirations of all citizens, but especially the leadership ambitions of the most promising. The leadership-honor dynamic is therefore crucial for understanding not only the ambitions of statesman and tyrants, but also the principles that animate different regimes and their citizens.

Socrates's teaching on the leadership-honor dynamic was especially influential on Plato's student Aristotle. Aristotle defines the "great souled" (*megalopsychia*) or magnanimous individual as "one who deems himself worthy of great things and *is* worthy of them" (*Nicomachean Ethics* 1123b 3–5; Aristotle 2011).[39] One of the most important great things for the magnanimous is honor because, according to Aristotle, it is what is given to the gods and conferred on the noblest people. The magnanimous therefore take pleasure in great honors, especially from serious human beings, and therefore they have complete contempt for honors from just anyone or for small honors or fame. Consequently, they are also concerned in a measured way with fortune, wealth, and political power, neither overjoyed with good fortune, nor deeply grieved with bad. They think wealth and political power are choice worthy for the honor they confer (1124a 1–18). Because the magnanimous honor few things, they will hazard only great dangers and may even throw their life away for them. They will therefore be "the sort to benefit others but be ashamed to receive benefaction" and are disposed "to return a benefaction with a great one" (1124b 5–15). Accordingly, the magnanimous individual is neither servile nor boastful and "needs nothing, or scarcely anything, but to be eager to be of service, and to be great in the presence of people of worth and good fortune, but measured toward those of middling rank." Yet in not respecting what is generally honored, the magnanimous "is idle and a procrastinator, except wherever either a great honour or a great deed is at stake; he is disposed to act in few affairs, namely, in great and notable ones" (1124b 25).

Aristotle's account of the magnanimous helps us understand the extraordinary and virtuous actions of certain individuals who are prepared to risk their welfare and sacrifice even their lives for the greatest or noblest public causes or matters of the highest public good. Yet in focusing on the crucial role honor plays in the motives and actions of such individuals, Aristotle reveals deep ambiguities in the nature of magnanimity. One important question concerns the self-sufficiency of honor and its relationship to virtue. The magnanimous is virtuous to the highest degree and therefore should be self-sufficient. But because honor seems to reside more with those who bestow it than with he who receives it, it seems to reveal a lack of self-sufficiency rather than goodness in the magnanimous (1095b 25–27).

Moreover, the magnanimous is especially concerned with great honors, but it is not clear whether he seeks honors as proof of virtue, thus conceding the primacy of virtue, or as a "prize" and reward of virtue, thereby conceding its superiority (1095b 28–29).[40] These ambiguities help us understand the rich and complicated character of those individuals who will appear noble and heroic in sacrificing for the benefit of all, yet equally seem disdainful, contemptuous and needy, listless and neglectful of virtue when not moved by great matters of state.

Our brief examination of Aristotle's account of magnanimity reveals his debt to the Socratic conception of leadership and honor. It also allows us to see the core of the concept that later proved to be so influential through the subsequent reception of Plato's writings, and especially through Aristotle's works on politics and ethics, which were to dominate Western thought and particularly scholasticism until their confrontation with modernity. Socratic insight into leadership was also directly influential in the writings and reflections of Saint Augustine and was reintroduced to the West in the renaissance through the writings of Islamic philosophers Avicenna and Averroes. As we noted, it was a touchstone for Cicero and for other Roman scholars such as Plutarch, whose *Lives*, biographies comparing the greatest Greek and Roman leaders, instructed future generations on good leadership.[41] The contemporary influence of the concept is evident in the popular notions of good leaders as individuals who are public spirited, look to the common good, and are willing to sacrifice for it. It can also be seen in the attempts to understand the nature of leadership judgment (Kane and Patapan 2006; Patapan 2016; Uhr 2015), the ambitions and character of leaders and founders (Faulkner 2007; Holloway 2008; Newell 2009), and how magnanimity may account for imperial ambition and foreign affairs more generally.[42]

CHAPTER 3

GLORIA AND MACHIAVELLI'S NEW PRINCE

The classical conception of magnanimity shows the inextricable link between leadership and honor, and how leaders' longing for honor poses both the gravest political threat and its greatest promise. It was a view that would be radically challenged by the increasing political reach and influence of those who believed in the God of Abraham, the "God of Glory" jealous of His glory (Psalm 29: 3; Acts 7: 2). According to the Old Testament, glory and honor belonged only to God, and therefore all creation declared His glory.[1] Humanity too reflected divine glory because it was made in the image of God. But in sinning, Adam and Eve realized their nakedness and felt shame, so that humility was the proper disposition for those who were no more than *humus* or "dust."[2] So much so that the "poor in spirit" were promised the Kingdom of Heaven (Matt. 5: 3). Glory was God's alone, and all claims of preeminence that did not glorify God were the capital sin of "stiff-necked" *superbia* or pride and vainglory (see Aquinas, *Summa Theologica*, II–II, Q. 132, art. 4).[3]

This new conception of glory and humility challenged classical magnanimity, which emphasized the primacy of political life and thereby inaugurated new forms of leadership. Such a reorientation was especially significant for Christianity, as it was founded on orthodoxy or on the rightness of one's inner thoughts and dispositions rather than the orthopraxy of specific and comprehensive rules of practice of Judaism and Islam.[4] Christianity therefore now had to contend with new forms of exemplary lives conceived, defined, and sustained by Jesus as Christ. Initially these consisted of the prophets,

43

martyrs, and the Apostles or Evangelists, especially Paul and Peter.[5] Subsequently, as expectations of an imminent Second Coming receded and the Church became more authoritative, saints, priests, and monks came to predominate.[6] In attempting to answer what constituted pious leadership, the Church and theologians inevitably engaged with, appropriated, and in important respects repudiated classical political thought. Christian theology therefore was profoundly shaped and influenced by classical political, ethical, and metaphysical thought, as we can see in the writings of the most influential Doctors of the Church, St. Augustine and St. Thomas. Consequently, as both the Church and imperial powers became more dominant, how Christ could and should be a model for worldly or "secular" rulers became a profound theological question with practical import. For example, the concept of "Vicar of Christ," based on the Donation of Constantine, was an attempt to reconcile the roles of emperor and pope, secular and ecclesiastical rule;[7] while the *Munus Triplex* or *tria munera*, the threefold role of Christ as prophet, teacher, and king, became influential for the Reformed Church.[8]

It is this complex world, riven by theological disputes, imperial ambition, and papal authority, that Niccoló Machiavelli confronted and attempted to reorder. Of course, Machiavelli was not alone in seeing the limitations of contemporary political thought and practice. As he notes, there was a powerful movement, later called *renascimento* or rebirth, that looked to the past, especially ancient Greek and Roman thought, to change all aspects of contemporary life.[9] But Machiavelli was unlike the scientists, philosophers, and artists who looked in an antiquarian spirit to the past to transform the future. He repudiated the past altogether on the basis of his wholly new political teaching. In *The Prince*, his most famous work, Machiavelli claims to possess the "knowledge of the actions of great men" (Dedicatory Letter). When his attention turns to "the modes and government of a prince," he announces,

> I fear that in writing of it again, I may be held presumptuous, especially since in disputing this matter I depart from the orders of others. But since my intent is to write something useful to whoever understands it, it has appeared to me more fitting to go directly to the effectual truth of the thing than to the imagination of it. (P 15, 61)

Machiavelli's "effectual truth" is complex and comprehensive, but an important part of it concerns the problem of leadership and honor. In transforming the meaning of honor, "our religion," according to Machiavelli, has "rendered the world weak and given it prey to criminal men":

> the ancient religion did not beatify men if they were not full of worldly glory, as were captains of armies and princes of republics. Our religion has glorified humble and contemplative more than active men. It has then placed the highest good in humility, abjectness, and contempt of things human; the other placed it in greatness of spirit, strength of body, and all other things capable of making men strong. (D II, 2, p. 131)[10]

Machiavelli therefore will attempt to rehabilitate worldly glory for the sake of good leadership and healthy politics. In doing so, however, he does not return to ancient religions or recover Socratic honor or Aristotelian "magnanimity." He diagnoses honor as the most dangerous passion and the origin of tyranny, violence, and all political instability. And, like all other passions, it cannot be stopped or checked by reason or exhortation. Nevertheless, he claims that properly diked, its full and powerful flow is the only way of securing political stability and republican freedom (D I, 42; III, 1; P 25, 98).[11]

Machiavelli intervenes in the profound and long-standing political debate regarding political rule by offering a radically new basis for assuming and exercising political authority. This novel understanding of leadership has at its core his new conception of glory and honor and how it reconceives the nature of leaders, their followers, and politics more generally. Machiavelli can therefore be said to initiate the first major modern approach to political leadership. In this chapter we examine the basis for Machiavelli's repudiation of previous thinkers and their insights into political leadership and honor, his advice to future leaders, before concluding with a general overview of the Machiavellian legacy of such an approach in contemporary theories of charismatic leadership and elitism studies.

THE QUESTION OF LEADERSHIP

Machiavelli does not speak of "leadership."[12] Yet his writings are crowded with extraordinary individuals, ranging from ancient founders such as Moses, Cyrus, Theseus, and Romulus; to Roman Emperors and Christian Saints; to his contemporaries, including emperors, princes, popes, and monks, whom he calls forth to substantiate his political insights. The variety and diversity of his examples drawn from a range of historical and political contexts indicates that Machiavelli's conception of leadership is founded on, or presupposes, a fixed and unchanging human nature.[13] Indeed, though there is an extraordinary variation in our individual characters—some gentle, others cruel, some cautious, others impetuous—Machiavelli argues that we all share in a fundamental disposition, a natural desire to acquire. As he puts it in *The Prince*, "And truly, it is a very natural and ordinary thing to desire to acquire, and always, when men do it who can, they will be praised or not blamed; but when they cannot, and wish to do it anyway, here lie the error and the blame" (P 3, 14–15). But it would seem that this natural desire does not have a natural end or limit:

> Nature has created men so that they are able to desire everything and unable to attain everything. So, since the desire is always greater than the power of acquiring, the result is discontent with what one possesses and a lack of satisfaction with it. (D I, 37, 78)[14]

Though all have powerful desires to acquire, Machiavelli singles out two specific forms of acquisition as politically crucial. Because of "humors" (*umori*) or "appetites" (*appetiti*), the people (*popoli*) do not want to be commanded nor oppressed by the great (*grandi*), and the great desire to command and oppress the people (P 9, 39; D I 5, 17–19). Consequently, politics is riven by violence, "since some men desire to have more, and some fear to lose what has been acquired, they come to enmities and to war, from which arise the ruin of one province and the exaltation of another" (D I 37, 78).[15] This ambition and fear of loss is, according to Machiavelli, the source of all evils in states.[16] Machiavelli therefore diagnoses bad leaders, whose lupine desires disturb the peace of the people, as the principal source of political instability. Because this difference between the *grandi* and *popoli* is crucial for Machiavelli's understanding of political leadership, it is necessary to take a closer look at the source of this difference and its implication for leaders and followers.

The first thing to note is that because the *grandi* are defined by their character and not their social standing, they can arise from any part of society, and therefore are not limited to the well born or rich.[17] Compared with the people, however, they are few in number, so that "in republics, ordered in whatever mode, never even forty or fifty citizens reach the rank of command" (D I 16, 46; P 9; 19). The distinguishing feature of the "few," as we have noted, is their "humor," an allusion to Galen's and subsequent Medieval and Renaissance theories of physiognomy and psychology that understood human nature as an admixture of four humors or "moisture" (choler, bile, spleen, phlegm). Yet it is not clear how seriously Machiavelli means for us to adopt this account, especially because he reduces these humors to two and discards their complex physiological implications.[18] More revealing is his adoption of the medical account of our faculties, such as imagination (*immaginazione*), ingenuity (*ingegno*), and memory (*memoria*) housed in the ventricles of the brain (*cervello*). Thus, innate differences in these faculties are arguably the true sources for differences between the few and the many.[19] Especially important seems to be the ability of the few to imagine and discern accurately both particulars and universals, distinguishing between appearance and reality. Unlike the many whose vehement passions limit their judgment and imagination, the few are better able to imagine and anticipate the satisfaction of their future desires. It is perhaps for this reason that the few, in attempting to satisfy their desire to acquire, reach beyond mere acquisition of property; their desire to command and oppress the many points to their ambition to acquire and shape the opinions and views of others. This more complex form of acquisition, according to Machiavelli, is driven by the logic of fear: "the order of these accidents is that when men seek not to fear, they begin to make others fear; and the injury they dispel from themselves they put upon another, as if it were necessary to offend or to be offended" (D I, 46, 95). Such ambition (*ambizione*), where men desire to have offices or seek the highest positions, aspiring to rule and govern states, will when frustrated often circumvent legal or constitutional means for illegal or violent methods (*vie straordinarie* or *modi straordinari*), advancing one's interest, rather than the common good or welfare of the state.[20] Thus we see the few desire to rule (*regnare*: D III, 4, 14), dominate (*dominare*: D I, 5, III, 6), tyrannize (*tiraneggiare*: D I, 40), command (*comandare*; P 9), and oppress (*opprimere*; P 9) the people, displaying pride or haughtiness (*superbia*; D I, 3) or insolence (*insolenzia*; P 9; D I, 2, III, 46).[21]

WHO ARE THE MANY?

Machiavelli's initial *via negative* account of the many, as all those who do not want to be commanded or oppressed, will perhaps inevitably incline us to take their side and even come to their aid.[22] Indeed, Machiavelli appears to endorse this approach in his subsequent more detailed account of the nature of the many, praising them as more pious (D I, 11), law-abiding (D I, 58), decent (P 9), and moral (D I, 7) than the few. Upon closer inspection, however, we see that the nature of the many is more complex, with significant implications for leaders. One obstacle in attempting to understand the character of the many is the term itself—as Machiavelli reminds us, all cities are founded by individuals who come together not because of a natural political impulse, as Aristotle suggested, but because each is forced by an original terror to live together (D I, 1; III, 1). As such, the many may appear as a natural whole, but is in reality a "mixed body" made up of disparate individuals. Compelled to live together, each individual sees in others their mutual weakness, making them at first contemptuous and later distrustful of each other (D I, 47, 97). Consequently, the many may act as one, "but when the spirits of men are cooled a little, each sees he has to return to his home, they begin to doubt themselves and to think of their safety, either by taking flight or by coming to accord (D I, 58; 115).[23] It would therefore seem that in almost all cases, what are said to be the actions of the many are indeed those of individual leaders who rise up by claiming to speak for them and defend their interests, a view endorsed by one of the chapter headings of the *Discourses*, "A Multitude Without a Head Is Useless" (D I, 44). An "unshackled" or disordered many is no more than "matter" on which an individual may impress a "form" (D I, 16, 17; II, 35).

Still, if the many do not directly lead, their interests and desires will nevertheless exercise a powerful influence on the few, necessitating a closer examination of those characteristics they have in common. Here the key to understanding their virtues as noted above is the primacy and ubiquity of fear, having as its source the original terror that moved them and colors every aspect of their lives. Thus, the piety of the people and their credulity derives from their fear of punitive gods and those who speak on their behalf (D I, 11; 12–13; 29; 54–56). Aware of their weakness and fearing change, the people are deeply conservative, favoring rest over movement, peace over war, old over new (D I, 48, III 6). They cling to laws to satisfy the order and stability they crave (D I 58; 39–40; III, 5). At the same time, however, eager to overcome their fear, they long for liberation and therefore change, loving grand enterprises by those who are sensational and spirited (D I, 37; III, 21). It is the weakness and vulnerability of the many that will especially dispose them to a high-minded morality, preferring leaders such as Scipio and Camillus, who show qualities of humanity, integrity, charity, kindness, mercy, and faith while rejecting those like Appius Claudius, who are proud, cruel, and lustful (D III, 20–23; I 35, 40).[24] Finally, Machiavelli notes that the desire for freedom has its source in fear: "He will find that a small part of them desires to be free to command, but all others, who are infinite, desire freedom so as to live secure" (D I, 16, 46).

As we have seen, the few and the many are identical in their desire to acquire. They also are similar in their desire to acquire property (*roba*) and in their esteem for honor. The major difference seems to lie in their disposition toward honor. Though the many do not seek glory and preeminence and therefore do not want to dominate like the few, they do seek and value honor (*onore*). How others treat us, whether we are respected or contemned for who we are, rather than what we have achieved, is an indication of our worth. Our respectability is therefore an independent assessment of our worth. This egalitarian aspect of honor means that the many are most fearful of acts that dishonor or shame, thereby revealing their relative poverty and insecurity. This sensitivity to dishonor naturally focuses on the individual. But it can also take its bearings from the treatment of those things individuals value, ranging from what we own personally to the people we love and admire, such as spouses, children, family, and most comprehensively our love of country. Women, children, and family are especially important sources of honor because they promise a continuation of our names, even after our death. Still, the concern with honor in this sense is instrumental, showing the security of our things and, above all, ourselves. This is evident in the ambiguous relationship between property and honor for the many. The many value property and honor, as is evident from Machiavelli's counsel that the prince will always avoid the hatred of the people if he "abstains from the property of his citizens and his subjects, and from their women" (P 17, 67). But where there is a tension between the two, it would seem that the "men esteem property more than honours," as the case of the Roman nobility shows (D I 37, 80). Or, as Machiavelli puts it in *The Prince*, "But above all, he must abstain from the property of others, because men forget the death of a father more quickly than the loss of a patrimony" (P 17, 67). When pressed, the many will place property above honor because it is more valuable and will seek to acquire more property because they fear that without acquisition, the little they possess will be at risk. Consequently, the many fear above all the few who want to take their property and dishonor them. They seek security through laws that restrain the insolence of the few and through leaders who will mete out just punishment to restrain their ambition.

QUESTION OF HONOR

The natural desire to acquire, and the inability to satisfy this desire, explain the ubiquity of competition and ultimately war for human beings. But as we have seen, for Machiavelli the human economy of desire is not exhausted by material acquisition because of the natural desire for glory and honor. Because of their better judgment regarding particulars and their ability to discern the loss concealed beneath the gain, the few will be less satisfied with those things that comfort the many (D I 47; 48; 53). They will therefore favor utility over goodness, look behind laws and be less constrained by them, and exploit religion (D I, 53; 45; 13–15). Self-reliant, restless, and ambitious, they are "unquiet spirits" who will seek to dominate, "like certain lesser birds of prey, in whom there is such desire to catch their prey, to which nature urges them, that they do not sense another larger bird that is above them so as to kill them" (D I, 29; 40; 55; III 6; 48). The many, on the other hand, seek to preserve their property and honor, relying on religion, laws, and those leaders who promise to protect and avenge them from the predations of the few (D I, 16). These contests for domination and hierarchy inevitably result in corruption of a virtuous state and ultimately license (*licenza*), where there is no order, rule, law, and therefore prosperity. The chaos, brutality, and rapacity that stain the pages of history have as their source the problem of ambitious leadership.[25]

What is striking about Machiavelli's political thought is not his account of the cruel and chaotic nature of politics, but his diagnosis of the pathology and thereby the radical innovation of his proposed cure. Machiavellian realism, founded on the effectual truth (*verità effetuale*), finds the answer to political discord not in piety, which exacerbates the problem, nor in reason, which is merely instrumental in satisfying passions and never sufficient to limit them, but in the passions themselves, especially the desire to acquire. Dismissing the imagined republics and principalities of his predecessors and their hopeful rather than effective solutions, he proposes to educate future leaders and secure liberty by writing "something useful to whoever understands it" (P 15).

Machiavelli's education takes into account the diversity in humors and, importantly, a fundamental inequality in human ability. Borrowing from Hesiod, he distinguishes between three kinds of "brains": "one that understands by itself, another that discerns what others understand, the third that understands neither by itself nor through others; the first is most excellent, the second excellent, and the third useless" (P 22, 92).[26]

Machiavelli therefore seeks to address above all the very few, those who have both the ambition and the "brains" to listen to his counsel. Because *ambizione* can never be cured or stopped, but only curbed or diked like a river, his solution above all is to use passion to counter passion (D I, 42; III 1; P 25, 98). Ambition that leads to greed, domination, and rapacity is also that passion that is other-regarding, that in satisfying itself does not take from others; indeed, in making the individual forget his fears and in some cases sacrifice personal gain, Machiavelli seems to replicate what the classics taught as the virtue of magnanimity.[27] Machiavelli's realistic counsel to the few leaders therefore consists in the rehabilitation of worldly glory (*mondana gloria*) or worldly recognition of memorable deeds by those who "do great things" or undertake great enterprises.[28] It is on this basis that the tension between the *grandi* and *popoli*, the source of political disunity, can nevertheless become the source of liberty for Machiavelli (D I, 4).

What is unique to glory, as well as its other aspects, such as fame and reputation, is that, unlike other forms of acquisition, it can only be conferred by others in recognition of one's merits and achievements. This has important political implications, because to the extent that personal desire for glory can only be satisfied by thinking of others, it is in a sense a moral philosopher's stone, transmuting love of one's own into a concern for others, albeit for the instrumental purpose of satisfying oneself.[29] It is for this reason that glory is acquired above all in those matters concerning the public, especially politics, as is evident from Machiavelli's ranking of those who are praised or blamed:

> Among all men praised, the most praised are those who have been heads and orderers of religions. Next, then are those who have founded either republics or kingdoms. After them are celebrated those who, placed over armies, have expanded either their kingdom or that of the fatherland. To these literary men are added; and because these are of many types, they are each of them celebrated according to rank. To any other man, the number of which if infinite, some share of praise is attributed that his art or occupation brings him. (D I 10, 31)

As this ranking shows, public benefactions, especially through politics, gain the greatest praise, while those ordinary princes who normally desire "jewels, gold, horses and other ornaments" are not even mentioned (P Dedicatory Letter). For Machiavelli, those who, to their perpetual honor, have the opportunity to "make a republic or kingdom" will be rewarded not only with fame, glory, and honor, but also with "security, quiet, with satisfaction of mind" (D I, 10, 13). Indeed, the founder of the new state has a double glory (*duplicata gloria*) (P 24). It would seem therefore that for the few, glory is a comprehensive good because as makers of the new state they in a sense own all, and in being admired, have the love of the people for the benefits they have conferred for their security. But this love promises them more—it is the only way the leader's name and reputation will continue after his death. Glory therefore secures the present and withstands the corrosive effect of time: even if their handiwork is overturned or dissolved, the names of Moses, Cyrus, Romulus, and Theseus will live on because their admirable grand achievements and benefactions continue to serve as models for other ambitious young long after they and their principalities have passed away (P 6). God-like glory, with its promise of immortal fame, therefore seems to overcome the limitations of this world. It appears to assuage our most powerful fear and original of all our longings—the desire to live, or rather not die. The few, through glory, seek the only form of immortality available *sub specie aeternitatis*—the perpetuation of one's immortal name and reputation.[30] It would therefore seem that for Machiavelli the few, though apparently disdaining material goods and courageous in their disregard of safety in their ambition, are moved not by erotic longing for noble and magnanimous acts displaying their virtue, as suggested by classical political philosophers, but by a deep and pervasive sense of fear, satisfied, albeit partially, by the contemplation of their immortal glory. This glory, the cause of all political discord, in turn becomes its own solution, sublimating the ambitions of the few for the greater good.

Machiavelli's education of leaders inevitably confronts and has to counter the Christian virtue of humility premised on the glory of God. His rehabilitation of glory therefore requires a new rhetoric that repudiates the contemporary lack of spirit (*ignavia*) and ambitious leisure (*ozio*) by liberating and celebrating the natural spirit of a daring few. *Fortuna*, according to Machiavelli, "lets herself be won more by the impetuous than by those who proceed coldly" (P 25, 101). This insight accounts in part for Machiavelli's provocative writing and his preference for shocking examples and pungent language. In addition to this rehabilitation of glory, Machiavelli's leadership education consists of a twofold education in political practice: an instruction in means (*modi*) or how to acquire rule; and how to gain and keep glory, especially through new foundations (*ordini*). The lessons on how to succeed in politics are radically new, as Machiavelli declares in

The Prince (P 15, 61). "Prudence," according to Machiavelli, "consists in knowing how to recognize the qualities of inconveniences, and in picking the less bad as good" (P 21, 91). Divorced from moral virtues, which are in any case the "orders" of those leaders and founders who preceded him, Machiavelli proposes new instructions for acquiring office. A prince who wants to maintain himself needs "to learn to be able not to be good, and to use this and not use it according to necessity" (P 15, 61). The virtues, such as liberality, piety, faithfulness, humanity, chastity, and honesty, are "very praiseworthy" qualities, but the prince "cannot have them, nor wholly observe them, since human conditions do not permit it." Therefore, the prince should be prudent in avoiding their infamy, but if unavoidable,

> one should not care incurring the fame of those vices without which it is difficult to save one's state; for if one considers everything well, one will find something appears to be virtue, which if pursued would be one's ruin, and something else appears to be vice, which if pursued results in one's security and well-being. (P 15, 62)

Hence the notorious "Machiavellianisms," such as one should be liberal with other people's property (P 16); on the good use of cruelty (P 17; 8); the contingency of honesty so that a prudent prince should model his actions on the half-man, half-beast Chiron and in using the beast imitate the lion and the fox (P 18); and, best known of all, "fortune is a woman; and it is necessary, if one wants to hold her down, to beat her and strike her down" (P 25).

This education seems shocking from the perspective of those who have taught how things should be, rather than how they are. But once one understands the natural desire to acquire that animates all human beings, and the uniquely human desire for honor and glory, their necessity becomes evident for anyone who has judgment. Machiavelli's rejection of pious and classical political practice in favor of a flexibility that takes into account circumstances is nevertheless mindful of the implications of such teaching for the many, who tend to elevate virtue over vice, and the moral, legal, and honest above the cunning, fraudulent, and expeditious. Machiavelli's suggestion, therefore, is that all leaders must as much as possible *not* appear "Machiavellian": even if one cannot always observe them, it is nevertheless useful to appear "merciful, faithful, humane, honest and religious" (P 18, 70).[31] True ability lies in not having either good or evil determine one's actions, but rather to "not depart from good, when possible, but know how to enter into evil, when forced by necessity" (P 18, 70). Thus, the means he advises are in effect attempts at preserving the moral standing of the leader, such as having "anything blameable administered by others, favors by themselves" (P 19, 75). Cesare Borgia, for example, used the Remirro de Orco, a "cruel and ready man," to bring peace and unity to Romagna and to "purge the spirit of the people and to gain them entirely to himself," subsequently blamed him for the cruelties, and had him "placed one morning in the piazza at Cesena in two pieces, with a piece of wood and a bloody knife beside him. The ferocity of this spectacle left the people at once 'satisfied and stupefied'" (P 7, 30). The application of this principle is also evident in laws and institutions, such as the Roman practice of decimation, or the office of tribune, that purge humors without tainting the leader's reputation. Yet, as we have seen, when it is not possible to conceal, Machiavelli always counsels what is necessary to keep office, rather than what would seem desirable. As he observes in *The Prince*, if one had to make a choice, "it is much safer to be feared than loved" because men love at their convenience and fear at the convenience of the prince (P 17, 68).

But it is often forgotten that he also says the ideal is "to be both one and the other," to be *both* loved and feared, which is "difficult to put together" (P 17, 66). This explains the extensive discussion and advice in *The Prince* on how to be loved and held in esteem (P 17; 21), how to avoid contempt and hatred (P 19), and how to avoid flatterers (P 23). This combination of love and fear is the new Machiavellian definition of *virtù*.[32] It is therefore the *virtuoso*, understood in the new Machiavellian sense of someone who uses prudence and judgment to conquer *Fortuna* and thereby gain and keep office, who will be rewarded with glory according to Machiavelli. As the case of Agathocles shows, the deft exploitation of political necessity may gain one security of office, but it will not result in glory (P 8, 37).[33] Machiavelli's praise of a public-spirited leader shows the importance of glory for good leadership:

> And truly, if a prince seeks the glory of the world, he ought to desire to possess a corrupted city—not to spoil it entirely as did Caesar but to reorder it as did Romulus. . . . In sum, those to whom the heavens give such an opportunity may consider that two ways have been placed before them: one that makes them live secure and after death renders them glorious; the other that makes them live in continual anxieties and after death leaves them a sempiternal infamy. (D I 10, 33)

Having shown the means to potential tyranny, Machiavelli altogether repudiates tyrants (*tiranni*) as those deceived by a "false good and a false glory," gaining instead of fame, glory and honor, "infamy, reproach, blame, danger and disquiet" (D I 10). Thus Machiavelli's advice on political means or *modi* is moderated by the ends or *ordini*, directing future leaders to a free community (*uno vivere libero*) and a "well ordered republic." Glory points to republicanism not simply because of the importance of liberty, but for the realistic insight that republics are more stable and will therefore endure longer, preserving and celebrating the glory of the founder.[34] For example, to succeed, the founder of a principality needs to change with the times, which is difficult because "he cannot deviate from what nature inclines him to or also because, when one has always flourished by walking on one path, he cannot be persuaded to depart from it" (P 25, 100). Even if the prince has such *virtù*, principalities cannot assure virtuous successors.[35] Republics, on the other hand, are founded upon laws and institutions that will allow the elevation of leaders whose character will suit the times, whether it be a humane Scipio or a cruel Manlius Torquatus (D I, II, 34). Moreover, republican liberty assures international security in relying on patriotic citizens and the abilities of suitably able military leaders.[36] The legal foundations of republics not only allow the marshaling and discharge of the humors, so that the people feel secure and their dignity defended by suitable executions, but they also allow the few to direct their ambitions through suitable offices, especially in the international arena where the potential for gain by both the few and the many allows leaders much greater latitude in displaying their *virtù* and gaining glory.[37] As founders of republics, leaders will thereby assure their glory above all as the defenders of liberty.

MACHIAVELLIAN LEGACIES: CHARISMA, ELITISM

Machiavelli provides a comprehensive modern alternative to both classical and pious conceptions of good leadership. He accepts the crucial importance of honor for leaders and therefore rejects humility as a politically defective solution to the problem of political stability. His new conception of the leader-honor dynamic therefore retains significant aspects of classical thought, for example, the difference between the glory seeker and the honor lover and therefore two types of leaders—those who seek innovation and those who want to preserve and protect. But Machiavelli's repudiation of humility does not lead him to return to or recover classical magnanimity. His approach has no room for Socratic eros and therefore the possibility that the philosophic life may be superior to noble magnanimity. Consequently, his rehabilitation of glory is on a wholly new, modern plane with the longing for glory now recognized as the only self-concerned yet mediating passion that can approximate the common advantage or common good.

We have focused on Machiavelli's modern conception of the leadership-honor dynamic because of the radical alternative it represents to the classical or magnanimous conception we examined above. Machiavelli is an important influence on the contemporary scholarship on leadership. Some of this scholarship uses Machiavelli only as a point of departure, taking up his most famous and shocking statements as guides for larger lessons for business, bureaucratic, or management leadership. Others engage with Machiavelli's teachings and advice more comprehensively, attempting to discern in his writings subtler insights into leadership practice.[38] In these concluding remarks, we trace the enduring and extensive influence of his new approach and the way his insights continue to inform and shape modern leadership studies in two specific and influential areas, the seminal concepts of "charismatic" leadership and "elitism."[39]

The idea of the charismatic leader, drawing on Weber's seminal formulation in *Economy and Society* (1978) of charisma or authority from a "gift of grace" rather than laws, office, or customs, has been deployed to understand the extraordinary and revolutionary authority conferred on exceptional individuals by their followers.[40] Yet the concept of a charismatic leader can in important respects be traced to the Machiavellian glory-seeking leader who makes things "altogether new" as it was interpreted by Nietzsche, who significantly influenced Weber.[41] Nietzsche greatly admired Machiavelli.[42] Especially important for Nietzsche was Machiavelli's *virtuoso* as the great founder, who in Nietzsche's formulation becomes the creative *ubermensch* or overman who will overcome the nihilism of "God is Dead" and the resultant "herd" mentality by creatively revaluing existing values or writing a new "table of values."[43] These Nietzschean concerns with "secularization," the dangers for humanity of the dominance of the hedonistic "last man" who lacks any sense of nobility, and the increasing influence of science were important themes taken up by Weber.[44] Weber too despairs of the "last men" who are, according to him, no more than "specialists without spirit, sensualists without heart" (1978b, 125). To recover nobility and redeem humanity, Weber, in the spirit of Machiavelli and Nietzsche, points to the need for a new aristocracy, and in particular charismatic leaders who are not elected, but rather create a new people by the power of their charisma.[45] Unlike Nietzsche, however, Weber denies as inauthentic the Nietzschean "pathos of distance" between such leaders and their followers.[46] He abjures an "ethic of conviction" in favor of a humane "ethic of responsibility" that acknowledges that "Politics is a strong and slow boring of hard boards. It takes both passion and perspective."[47] In the modern concept of the charismatic leader, we can therefore see the powerful legacy of the Machiavellian *virtuoso* prince who for Nietzsche and subsequently Weber becomes the creative savior of humanity from the nihilism and banalization of modernity.

Machiavelli's approach to leadership and honor can also be seen in the modern concept of the "elite." Elite theory claims that any society is fundamentally shaped by an "elite" or few who rule over the many.[48] It is not accidental that this approach is reminiscent of Machiavelli's view of the few and the many, and especially his claim, noted above, that fewer than forty or fifty citizens have command in republics. Classical elite theorists drew extensively on Machiavelli to counter the Marxist concept of the "ruling class." "Elite" was first used in the social sciences by the Italian engineer and later economist Vilfredo Pareto in his *A Treatise of General Sociology* (1935), where he refers to the diversity of individual abilities and proposes an index of excellence to rank them.[49] In his discussion, Pareto specifically draws on Machiavelli's distinction in *The Prince* between the lion and the fox to understand elite psychology. This approach was taken up by the other classic elite theorists. Gaetano Mosca in *The Ruling Class* (1939) noted the political importance of a superior minority, noting in particular their organizational ability as well as intellectual, moral, and material superiority, while Robert Michels in *Political Parties* (1911) posited his famous "iron law of oligarchy" to claim that the exercise of political power was inherently oligarchic, and therefore mandated the "technical indispensability of leadership." More recent works have sought to extend the concept by linking it to power, so that C. Wright Mills in *The Power Elite* (1956) combines in his concept of the "power elite" a Marxist and elitist view to evaluate American society, while Pierre Bourdieu in *State Nobility* (1989) replaces the ideas of the ruling class and elites with "field of power." Given the Machiavellian origin of the concept, it is not surprising that Machiavelli's concern with how to reconcile the rule of the few with the demands of the many has also been a central question for recent elitism scholarship, which is especially concerned with the tension between elitism and democracy.[50]

As these cases show, Machiavelli's new formulation of the leader-honor dynamic continues to have a significant influence on the contemporary understanding and debates on leadership. It also shows the larger reach of his insights, ranging from the role and influence of exceptional individuals in transforming politics to formulating the terms of contests regarding innovative institutions and political structures. Machiavellian *gloria* therefore became a formidable alternative and counter to the previously dominant view of magnanimous leadership. How they would both be challenged by the new Hobbesian leader-honor dynamic of dispersed leadership is the question we take up and explore in the next chapter.

CHAPTER 4

DISPERSED LEADERSHIP
OF THOMAS HOBBES

Magnanimous leadership and Machiavelli's glorious prince represented two major contending approaches to the leadership-honor dynamic. They were soon to confront a third alternative that would challenge both and indeed in time come to predominate. In this chapter we examine this third approach, which took its bearings from Machiavelli's innovations while radically questioning his core commitment to glory as essential for good leadership and government. Thomas Hobbes is the famous English political philosopher who significantly influenced many of our contemporary concepts such as rights, sovereignty, power, and the state. He is especially important for our examination of the leadership-honor dynamic because, as we will see, he initiates the modern attack on honor that has the effect of effacing and silencing it so that it is no longer considered relevant for understanding leadership.

Hobbes endorses and adopts many of Machiavelli's insights, including the repudiation of the classical concept of the regime, the primacy of the individual, and a depreciation of the role of reason in politics. Yet his fundamental aim of securing peace and prosperity above all leads him to reject a core element of Machiavelli's teaching, thereby inaugurating a new politics of individual rights, social contract, and state sovereignty that becomes a mainstay for subsequent liberal thought. Hobbes rejects altogether the glorious prince and therefore glory because he views it as the most dangerous political passion that cannot be educated, as the classics claimed, or manipulated, as Machiavelli suggests. His new politics is therefore founded on a new, alternative conception of honor, which in effect extirpates the glory of the "few" by celebrating the achievements of the many. To see how Hobbes initiates the dominant modern trope of dispersed leadership that rejects both the glorious prince and the magnanimous leader, it is necessary to consider why Hobbes saw glory as a political pathology, the means he used to cure this problem conclusively, and, finally, how the legacy of his approach continues to dominate contemporary approaches to leadership studies and politics more generally.

HOBBES'S UNSUNG HERO

If Machiavelli's writings are crowded with singular individuals and extraordinary leaders, Hobbes's works by contrast seem to eschew naming specific persons.[1] The notable exception is Sidney Godolphin, the English poet who died in action aged thirty-three while advancing into Devon as a member of Sir Ralph Hopton's Royalist forces during the English Civil War. Hobbes starts his most famous political work, Leviathan, with a dedication to his friend Francis Godolphin in honor and gratitude to the memory of Francis Godolphin's brother, Sidney Godolphin. Hobbes admires Sidney Godolphin as an exemplary citizen:

> For there is not any vertue that disposeth a man, either to the service of God, or the service of his Country, to Civill Society, or private Friendship, that did not manifestly appear in his conversation, not as acquired by necessity, or affected by occasion, but inhaerent, and shining in a generous constitution of his nature.[2]

Having introduced Leviathan with Sidney Godolphin, Hobbes returns to him at the very end, in his A Review, and Conclusion (L, A Review and Conclusion, 718), where he takes up the claim by some that "Civill Amity" is not possible where there is "perpetuall contention for Honor, Riches, and Authority" (L, A Review and Conclusion, 718–19). His response is that these "are indeed great difficulties, but not Impossibilities: For by Education, and Discipline, they may bee, and are sometimes reconciled" (L, Review and Conclusion, 719). To demonstrate that there is "no such Inconsistence of Humane Nature, with Civill Duties, as some think," he cites once more the example of Sidney Godolphin:

> I have known cleernesse of Judgment, and largenesse of Fancy; strength of Reason, and graceful Elocution; a Courage for the Warre, and a Fear for the Laws, and all eminently in one man; and that was my most noble and honored friend Mr. *Sidney Godolphin*; who hating no man, nor hated of any, was unfortunately slain in the beginning of the Civill warre, in the Publique quarrell, by an undiscerned, and an undiscerning hand. (L, A Review and Conclusion, 718)

Godolphin, the talented and law-abiding subject who through no fault of his own, indeed from his very sense of duty, becomes a victim of the English Civil War, is Hobbes's true hero. Hobbes's writings—his public service—are intended to save and protect the Godolphins of the world from their cruel mistreatment "occassioned by the disorders of the present time."[3] Yet Hobbes concedes that his proposed solution is novel, and in its novelty, offensive (L, A Review and Conclusion, 728–29).[4] To see what is genuinely radical in Hobbes's teaching and how it reconceives the leadership-honor dynamic, it is necessary to start with his diagnosis of the sources of war.

BELLUM OMNIUM CONTRA OMNES

A war of all against all is Hobbes's grim assessment of the human condition. And like Machiavelli, he sees religion as playing an important role in this warfare. In the context of the English Civil War, he singles out "Vicars of Christ on earth." If the Kingdom of God

> were not a Kingdome which God by his Lieutenants, or Vicars, who deliver his Commandments to the people, did exercise on Earth; there would not have been so much contention, and warre, about who it is, by whom God speaketh to us, neither would many Priests have troubled themselves with Spirituall Jurisdiction, nor any King have denied it them. (L, 35, 448)

These Vicars are aided, according to Hobbes, by the "Doctors of Schoole Divinity" who are "interested, or envious interpreters" who use the fear of powers invisible and the threat of eternal punishment after death as a means to challenge the sovereign's laws.[5] In this, universities play an important role, for they are "Fountains of Civill, and Morall Doctrine, from whence the Preachers, and the Gentry, drawing such water as they find, use to sprinkle the same (both from the Pulpit, and in their Conversation), upon the People" (L, A Review and Conclusion, 728).[6] Finally, Hobbes refers to "Popular Men" who use their patriotism to garner public support for their personal ambitions, influencing the "vulgar" or the "Common people" who are like "clean paper," ready to receive whatever the Public Authority impresses on them (L 30, 379).

Hobbes's account of the specific ways "Divine Politiques" and popular men were the source of English Civil War needs to be reconciled with his more theoretical reflections on the origin of all wars. In the *Leviathan*, Hobbes argues that the state of nature is a state of war due to three causes: competition, diffidence, and glory (L13, 185). The diffident or fearful are the "moderate" and "reasonable" who invade for "Safety" and use violence only to defend themselves and their possessions (L 11, 161; L 13, 185). The competitive are less moderate than the diffident because they use violence not just for safety but also gain, seeking mastery over "mens persons, wives, children and cattell" (L 13, 185). But because "Mastery" is no more than evidence of gain for the competitive, their need to master is circumscribed and limited by material gain. Glory poses a more intractable political problem because it seems to lack the inherent limits on violence that restrain the safety-seeking diffident and the acquisitive competitive.[7]

Glorying, according to Hobbes, is a type of "Joy," a pleasure or 'exultation of the mind" arising from "imagination of a mans own power and ability" (L 6, 122–25). Beyond the "short vehemence" of "carnall Pleasure" open to all people, contemplating one's "own power in the acts of conquest" results in intense delight (L 13, 184). Some glory seeking is to be expected of all people because even the most "moderate" person naturally demands some value be placed on their person and finds joy in "comparing himselfe with other men" and judging himself "eminent" (L 17, 226). But Hobbes also notes that glory seekers often pursue glory "farther than their security requires," so that some seek glory even at the risk of their lives (L 13, 185). For these people, glory becomes disengaged from its source in the pursuit of the power needed to preserve their vital motion. The intense nature of the pleasure of actual conquest is one reason why some place glory above security. But there are more complex forces at work, as we can see from Hobbes's assessment of the person who invades for "Reputation":

> For every man looketh that his companion should value him, at the same rate he sets upon himselfe: And upon all signes of

contempt, or undervaluing, naturally endeavours, as far as he
dares (which amongst them that have no common power, to keep
them quiet, is far enough to make them destroy each other), to
extort a greater value from his contemners, by dommage; and
from others, by example. (L 13, 185)

The foundational human problem that exacerbates our dealings with each
other is our need to have neighbors "value" us as we value ourselves. This
is compounded by our inability to construe "signs" of valuing because we
are unable to see internal motions, compelling us to attempt to read external signs, so that "trifles," such as "a word, a smile, a different opinion,"
become signs of undervalue (L 13, 184). These trifles become as important
as those gross signs of security such as mastery of people and things that
comfort the diffident and the competitive. But their subtlety and fleeting
aspect, combined with our suspicion that we are being undervalued, make
them easy to misconstrue. Finally, the glory lover can be slighted by "reflex-
ion"—by undervaluing "their Kindred, their Friends, their Nation, their
Profession, or their Name." Glory seems to enlarge beyond the individual
to an ever-expanding conception of oneself (L 13, 185). This, of course, is
part of the intense pleasure of glory, the feeling of being bigger, greater, or
more majestic. Indeed, the glorious falls in love with his reputation because
"extraordinary power" continually satisfies the never-ending desire for power.
Yet such passionate attachment to glory and its feeling of enlargement
exposes the glorious to greater risk of undervaluing and therefore anxiety,
demanding ever-increasing vigilance in appraising their glory.

The difficulties in establishing true valuation pale in comparison with
what is required to restore the joy or pleasure of glory upon being slighted.
The glory lover needs to "extort a greater value from his contemners, by
dommage; and from others, by example," which means that the glory lover
must prove his worth by publicly threatening or injuring those who have
slighted him, extracting a concession of superiority and thereby a public
display of power. In doing so, the glory lover is compelled to risk himself
to show his power. Sustaining the joy that is glory may necessitate harming
his body or undermining his power as property. In the extreme case, the
glorious may risk his own life to show his power. Therefore, the pleasure of
glory is not checked by the moderating demands of security and property in
two senses. The first is in the sense that we have noted—the glorious will
illogically sacrifice his life for his name. The second is that the pleasure of
glory seeks to ever increase its delectation—glory will in social terms seek
ever greater mastery, at the risk of security. Of the three causes of quarrel,

glory or pride as a struggle over valuing is the most dangerous because it has no reasonable stop, tends to escalate, and is essentially political. That the glorious initiate the struggles that compel the competitive and the diffident into unreasonable warfare is the principal reason pride is *the* political problem for Hobbes.[8]

"LORD OVER THE CHILDREN OF PRIDE"

Religion has of course always been critical of pride and glory. And as we have seen, honor and chivalry as pathologies of feudal life had been the subject of critique by poets, novelists, and political philosophers. Though Hobbes endorses these sentiments and is indeed unstinting in his disparagement of feudal pretensions, he also differs from them in his radical ambition. His attack is not merely on feudal honor; he means to extinguish the passion that is the source of glory, and in doing so redefine the nature of leadership and refound all of politics. Hobbes therefore agrees with Machiavelli on the dangerousness of glory and the pervasiveness of fear in politics. He rejects altogether Machiavelli's solution that sees glory as its homeopathic antidote. Glory for Hobbes is a form of madness that cannot be manipulated and therefore must be extirpated. His strategy is therefore twofold, a new way of thinking about honor and leadership, and thereby a new politics premised on fundamental equality.

The centrality of honor for Hobbes's political thought is signaled by the very title of his most famous and influential work, *Leviathan*. Hobbes's leviathan, unlike the Old Testament creature of the Lord set over the children of pride (Job 41, 34), is an artificial body, made by the "*Art* of man," whose business is *Salus Populi* (L Introduction, 81). Pride, it would seem, is not the greatest sin, but a political problem to be remedied by human ingenuity. Hobbes's solution to the problem of honor is to fundamentally transform how we think about it, as we can see from the seminal chapter in the *Leviathan*, Chapter X "*Of* Power, Worth, Dignity, *and* Worthiness." As the chapter title suggests, Hobbes's conception of honor is essentially linked to his innovation of "power." Hobbes denies the classical claim that humans are "Politcall creatures" or lovers of some "greatest Good" (L 17, 225; L 11, 160). Nature, "the Art whereby God hath made and governs the World," gives no positive directions or aims: "For there is no such *Finis ultimus*, (utmost ayme,) nor *Summum Bonum*, (greatest Good) as is spoken of in the Books of the old Morall Philosophers" (L, Introduction,

81; L 11, 160). Therefore, "The Power *of a Man*," according to Hobbes, is "his present means, to obtain some future apparent Good" (L 10, 150). Having defined power, Hobbes is in a position to redefine the meaning of "Worth," "Dignity," and "Honor." "The *Value*, or Worth of a man, is as of all other things, his Price; that is to say, so much as would be given for the use of Power: and therefore is not absolute; but a thing dependent on the need and judgment of another" (L 10, 151). Hobbes denies that we are inherently valuable—no matter how highly we value ourselves, our price is determined by the "buyer," that is, others and not us, the "seller." Consequently, "*Honourable* is whatsoever possession, action, or quality, is an argument and signe of Power" (L 10, 155). Honor as a measure of power allows Hobbes to redefine the meaning of "Dignity" and "Worthiness." Dignity is not inherent, natural, or derived by our own actions. Rather, the "publique worth of a man," according to Hobbes, "is the Value set on him by the Common-wealth" (L 10, 152). Taken together, these observations make us realize that for Hobbes, there is nothing honorable about honor. "Honorable" or honor is a "sign" of power, a measure of ability to acquire future goods. Because our power (and therefore our honor) is always changing since it derives from the will and opinion of others (the purchaser will determine the price), it is subject to the accuracy of their judgment, which inevitably relies on the appearance of power, that is, our fame or reputation of power. Consequently, as "Reputation" or "Fame," honor itself is a form of "*Instrumentall*" power.[9]

Hobbes's conception of power suggests he intends to undermine honor altogether by questioning the foundations that sustain our hopes and beliefs that we are worthy, have dignity, and therefore are honorable. Natural abilities, such as physical strength and beauty, innate ability, perspicacity, or judgment, cannot be inherently honorable because they are not reliably powerful to warrant such a claim. Just as the moral virtues, such as justice, cannot be the foundation of honor, neither can birth or nobility—Hobbes seems to relish humiliating his betters with his historical account of "Coates of Armes" and the mean and dishonorable origins of all claims to nobility.[10] Importantly, his reflections on divine preferment, of the power of saints, prophets, and priests, is telling.[11]

Hobbes's ambition to uncouple honor from excellence and reduce it to an aspect of power (as its measure and an instrument) can therefore be seen as his attempt to redefine the two faces of honor. Honor as excellence or longing for distinction is now dismissed by Hobbes as politically dangerous pride. His emphasis is therefore now on the second face of honor, those who want to do the right thing and in doing so are moved by the desire to avoid shame. His strong medicine, the depreciation of honor, is needful, he would claim, because it is the only remedy for destroying the seeds of pride or vaine-glory.

DISPERSING LEADERSHIP

This novel conception of honor provides the foundation for Hobbes's political innovations. Hobbes's debunking of honor is consistent with the ninth Law of Nature, "*That every man acknowledge other for his Equall by Nature* (L 15, 211). It is on the foundations of this law that Hobbes can inaugurate his new political solution to the problem of the children of pride, a radically new conception of political authority as a neutral and democratic "power," with honor now redefined as a sign, measure, or form of power. Relying on rhetoric, or on a Euclidian joining up of words as "reackoning," Hobbes will now make all substantive claims of honor inherently dubious or questionable, removing the shame that historically accompanied individual claims of rights. Hobbes's well-known social contract is therefore founded not on the dynamic tension between the few and the many, as Machiavelli advocates, but on the diffident and the competitive, who have foresight and want to leave the state of war to preserve themselves and secure a more "contented life" (L 17, 227).

For Hobbes, the Law of Nature, which is not in fact a law but a "precept, or generall rule," contains the "Fundamentall Law of Nature," which is "*to seek Peace, and follow it*," and the Right of Nature, which is, "*By all means we can, to defend our selves*" (L 14, 189–90). Where there is no common power to keep all in awe, the nature of man yields a condition of "such a warre, as is of every man, against every man" (L 13, 185–86). In such a state, "every man has a Right to every thing; even to one another's body" (L 14, 190). Hobbes depicts the state of nature in chapter XIII, "*Of the* NATURAL CONDITION *of Mankind, as concerning their Felicity, and Misery*." It is a state of insecurity and animosity that requires self-reliance; because there is no common power it is lawless, and therefore "Right and Wrong, Justice and Injustice have there no place"; as a state of war, the "two Cardinall vertues" of war, Force, and Fraud predominate. In such a condition, men with foresight who want to leave the "miserable condition of Warre," to preserve themselves and to secure a more "contented life," will establish a common power or sovereign to whom they will submit their will and judgment (L 17, 227). This new "*Mortall God*" will use fear of punishment to keep all in awe, making men observe their covenants and especially the Laws of Nature (L 17, 227). Fear is needed, according to Hobbes, because "without the terrour of some Power, to cause them to be observed," the Laws of Nature "are contrary to our naturall Passions, that carry us to Partiality, Pride, Revenge, and the like" (L 17, 223). Thus, Hobbes's solution to our natural condition is the institution of a new artificial entity, the *Leviathan* state, with a sovereign to ensure security and thereby prosperity.

HEROIC GEESE

We saw in the leadership-honor dynamic of both magnanimous leadership and Machiavellian glory a consistent distinction of the two faces of honor, of leaders who seek glory, even at the risk of redefining what is honorable, and others who want to preserve what is considered honorable and fear shame in not doing so. Does Hobbes transform this understanding or simply restate it? After all, isn't Hobbes's sovereign nothing more than Machiavelli's glorious prince renamed and disguised? There seem to be compelling arguments to support this view. In Hobbes's initial account, the sovereign is authorized by the many, yet, as he subsequently shows, sovereignty by conquest is also legitimate, and indeed more probable than sovereignty by institution. Hobbes's more comforting account of a public contract therefore diverts us from the grim reality of sovereignty by compulsion. Whether by conquest or by agreement, the sovereign is authorized by all and consequently, according to Hobbes, is the most powerful and therefore the most honorable. Indeed, not subject to the original agreement founding the state, the sovereign is seemingly unconstrained by legal or moral considerations, both domestically and in the international realm. Finally, Hobbes's view that the people are like "white paper," ready to be inscribed by others, seems identical to Machiavelli's notions of political founders as radical innovators.[12]

As these reflections suggest, there is enough evidence in Hobbes's writing to see him as a Machiavellian who defends the absolute authority of the sovereign. But this view needs to accommodate Hobbes's more complex account of the nature of the sovereign and the character of the Leviathan state. The sovereign is the "Artificiall *Soul*" of that "Artificiall Man," "that great LEVIATHAN called a COMMON-WEALTH, or STATE' (L Introduction,

81). As he states in his dedication to Francis Godolphin, "I speak not of the men, but (in the Abstract) of the Seat of Power, (like to those simple and unpartiall creatures in the Roman Capitol, that with their noyse defended those within it, not because they were they, but there)" (L Dedicatory Letter, 75). Hobbes's amusing paean to the noble leadership of geese is intended to show that for him institutions, rather than individuals, are the true solution for political discord. Where you are, it seems, is more important than who you are for Hobbes.[13] This view is supported by his debunking of the Aristotelian understanding that some should command because they are more prudent and wiser.[14] Hobbes's response is that "For there are very few so foolish, that had not rather governe themselves, than be governed by others" (L 15, 211). Natural equality means equality in prudence: "A plain husband-man is more Prudent in affaires of his own house, then a Privy Counseller in the affaires of another man" (L, 8, 138).[15] Perhaps nowhere else is this made clearer than in Hobbes's account of the "Generation of a Commonwealth," which is silent as to the character of the sovereign, only requiring the reduction of many "Wills" unto one "Will" (L 17, 227). The Hobbesian sovereign should be seen in the larger context of the institutional machinery that is intended to be self-sustaining precisely because it is moved and maintained by the economy of fear and the manipulation of power. It is for this reason that for Hobbes the sovereign can be one, few, or many, though for reasons of expeditiousness, resoluteness, and efficacy he prefers a single sovereign (L 19, 239).

In any case, even if Hobbes's formulation does not impose specific legal obligations or duties on the sovereign regarding its subjects, he is at pains to show the sovereign's more general rights and duties.[16] He also reminds the sovereign that the identity of interests between the sovereign and his subjects means good policy is in the interest of the sovereign as much as that of the subjects because it redounds to the prosperity of the state. Sensible sovereigns do not take "any delight, or profit they can expect in the dammage, or weakening of their Subjects, in whose vigor, consisteth their own strength and glory" (L 18, 238). In the extreme, bad decisions by the sovereign would undermine his ability to enforce the law, exposing him to the dangers of being overthrown by another who can assure stability.[17] These circumstances pertain especially in international affairs, where sovereigns may be tempted to overreach. Hobbes debunks foreign relations as gladiatorial contests, reminding the sovereign that few succeed in that realm.[18] In any case, the raison d'etre of having a sovereign, the enforcement of laws, means that the idea of the sovereign is a more specific concept for

Hobbes. And it is here that we come to Hobbes's fundamental repudiation of the Machiavellian glorious prince.

Hobbes's sovereign may be powerful and therefore honorable above all, but this honor is not personal but institutional—it is the focal point of the collected and refracted glory of the power of all the individuals who have authorized the sovereign. The actions of the sovereign matter only because they have been authorized by subjects; the sovereign is only the executor and enforcer of the laws. There is no possibility for the Hobbesian sovereign to claim the glory of a founder or innovator, because all honor can be traced to its source in its true founders, those individuals who exist in the state of nature and bring the state into being. Hobbes defines the "Right" of nature as the "Liberty each man hath, to use his own power, as he will himselfe, for the preservation of his own Nature; that is to say, of his own Life; and consequently, of doing any thing, which in his Judgment, and Reason, hee shall conceive to be the aptest means thereto" (L 189). Such an extraordinary elevation of the individual is admittedly limited by laws.[19] But the Laws of Nature, the "true Morall Philosophy," which are eternal and always bind in conscience, are no more than a "Precept, or generall Rule" that do not bind in practice if there is no security. This decision, according to Hobbes, can only be made by the individual. Hobbes therefore makes the historically radical claim that natural rights endow the individual with supreme authority. This authority is confirmed in the political role Hobbes assigns to each person. As maker and author of the state, the subject is above all a founder; the shameful origins of the state, founded on fear and necessity, are now obscured and salved with the knowledge that every individual should be honored as the author of peace and prosperity. Hobbes's reinterpretation of natural law and natural right allows him to democratize Machiavelli's *gloria* by distributing it to everyone.

But this will not be the dangerous glory and pride Hobbes seeks to extinguish. On the contrary, the state is founded by the diffident and competitive who reject altogether such madness. Hobbes's subjects accept their fundamental equality as the basis for assuring their common security. Importantly, in asserting and protecting their personal rights, Hobbesian subjects defend the state and thereby the rights of all—Hobbes solves all potential conflicts between self-interest and duty by making self-interest the foundation and guardian of public good. Subjects will never again feel shame in asserting their personal claims—what may seem self-interested and partial is in effect a public face of an individual's valiant defense of the state. In defending one's right, the Hobbesian subject defends the rights of all.

DOMINANCE OF HOBBES'S
LEADERSHIP-HONOR DYNAMIC

Hobbes rejects Machiavelli's conception of glory as the only passion that can remedy the irreconcilable humors of the few and the many. He attacks honor with all means at his disposal, diagnosing it as a pathological madness and redefining it out of existence as nothing more than the measure of what is common to all—the search for power after power. This Hobbesian approach yields the concept of power and the novel political arrangement that legalizes politics to guarantee peace and prosperity. The wholly modern state is now founded on individuals who are not, however, unique or distinctive in any important respect. Hobbes democratizes Machiavelli's unique founder, making everyone a maker and defender of the new constitutional order. Hobbes's specific insights into human nature, and his overall approach to politics more generally, have had a profound and far-reaching influence on the way we think about both honor and leadership. The leadership-honor dynamic he institutes is arguably the preeminent and predominant one in contemporary political thought and practice, whose legacy can be usefully summarized as the forgetting of honor and the forgetting of leadership.

Hobbes's debunking of honor can be seen in the common modern approach that denies honor any role in understanding politics. The emphasis on power and the assumption of the self-evident nature of individual "interest" has come to dominate important aspects of political science.[20] The influence of rational choice theories, founded on notions of power and calculation, gives rise to dominant game-theoretic approaches to individual judgment and conflict resolution in politics.[21] The price of such an approach is the puzzling anomaly of prisoners' dilemmas and the general debunking of any form of self-sacrifice as a concealed form of interest aggrandizement. The Hobbesian minimalist conception of honor as a measure of instrumental power to be calculated, preserved, and deployed continues to exercise an extraordinary influence, from the international relations idea of honor as "prestige" or "soft power," to economics where it remains unassailed, to its deployment in marketing and public relations, especially in the study of fame, celebrity, and "brand" marketing.[22]

The forgetting of leadership, a consequence of Hobbes's delineation of the problem of honor and his solution in the form of egalitarian constitutionalism, is manifest in the views that dominate contemporary leadership studies and the neglect of political leadership in political science more generally. The view that everyone, but especially leaders, are power seekers—so that it is safer to assume they are "knaves" who cannot be educated but only managed by the proper construction and implementation of institutions—has the effect of undermining any significant role for leaders. Much of modern constitutionalism, for example, emphasizes structures and processes while depreciating the role of founders and innovators.[23] Related to this is an approach that denies individual leaders any significant political agency—the forgetting of leaders and leadership is complete when the focus shifts, for example, to some transhistorical impulses and drivers such as "spirit" or material causes or even the "state" to account for political changes. Finally, the Hobbesian denial that individuals have variable abilities in discretion and judgment assumes parity in deliberation and inevitably points to the demand for arrangements that counter the limited vision of individual self-interested calculation in favor of the "wisdom of the crowds."[24] Deliberative and associative democrats therefore celebrate horizontal structures where no "one" leads and no one follows. The leadership of all means in effect that all are leaders, and therefore the concept of "leadership" can safely be consigned to an atavistic politics that unjustifiably—and dangerously—elevated any one individual over the hopes and desires of the many.[25] It is not surprising, therefore, that the major focus in modern leadership studies has turned to the role of "followership."[26]

As this brief overview suggests, the influence of Hobbes's approach to honor and leadership has been widespread and significant. Indeed, it may be said that Hobbes's denial of honor, his democratic preferences, and his psychology of power account in large measure for the depreciation of leadership and the forgetting of the question of honor in modern leadership studies.

PART 3

POLITICS OF THE
LEADERSHIP-HONOR DYNAMIC

CHAPTER 5

RETHINKING TRANSFORMATIVE AND TRANSACTIONAL LEADERSHIP

The core argument of this book is that leadership and honor are mutually constitutive. To examine the nature of this leadership-honor dynamic, we explored in part 1 the relative neglect of the question of honor in contemporary leadership studies, and in part 2 the three influential and competing conceptions of the leadership-honor dynamic—classical magnanimity, Machiavellian glory, and Hobbesian dispersed leadership. In this third part, we examine the politics of the leadership-honor dynamic, evaluating its efficacy in yielding greater clarity and new insights into contemporary political debates and challenges. In the following chapters, we therefore explore the diverse ways this dynamic manifests itself in contemporary politics, from the glory and ambition of political founders, to the use of flattery by political advisors, how anti-politics is sustained by both fame and identity politics, and, finally, the powerful allure and pervasive influence of nationalism and patriotism. Before we do so, however, it is appropriate to begin with perhaps the most influential contemporary theoretical framework for understanding leadership—James MacGregor Burns's distinction between transformative and transactional leadership. Accordingly, in this chapter we examine whether the leadership-honor dynamic we have delineated provides new insights into the theoretical origins of the distinction between transformative and transactional leadership and in doing so provides the theoretical foundations for a richer understanding of moral leadership.

Everyone is and can be a leader. Possessing different yet valuable skills and abilities, each one of us can through deliberation and consensus take part in decisions that are better informed, more inclusive, and more legitimate.

This popular and influential view of leadership can be found in a range of disciplines, from democratic thought to leadership studies to business and management. Often unstated and implicit in this approach is the darker alternative that it seeks to counter and repudiate, the "strong" or "toxic" leader who will use divisive rhetoric to exploit political weaknesses and manipulate and distort institutions to seek and maintain power.[1] Together, these perspectives unintentionally present a formidable challenge to the study of leadership. Egalitarian leadership by presuming parity in ability and aptitude seems to deny unique and exemplary judgment to any single individual, so that all are indistinguishably leaders and followers. The presumption of *animus domandi*, on the other hand, appears to retain a role for leaders, but does so by characterizing all leadership as a struggle for individual gain, making the tyrant indistinguishable from the "rational actor." These views leave out altogether the possibility of an outstanding individual who pursues leadership for the common good. Their practical effect is to endorse a tragic view of leadership and politics, where leadership that is not collective or participatory—typically most leadership in modern political institutions—is inevitably defined as immoral, exploitative, and therefore illegitimate.

The disheartening prospect of being at the mercy of ambitiously predatory leaders, and a yearning for leadership that was resolute yet moral and public spirited, became the powerful motive for some to restore dignity to leaders and to political life. They yearned for outstanding and inspirational individuals who had noble and grand ambitions, willing to deploy their considerable talents not just for their own benefit but for the larger good, even willing to sacrifice for others. It was this longing for good leadership, and the desire to recover and teach creative leadership, that moved James MacGregor Burns to write *Leadership* (1978). It also accounts for the extraordinary success and far-reaching influence of a book that reintroduced to contemporary political science the importance of studying leaders and leadership. Burns had worked with the Kennedys and in his earlier book on Roosevelt described a form of leadership that he now regarded as necessary but seemingly impossible to find. Having endured the Nixon presidency and taken part in the Johnson administration, he wanted to recover a public-spirited leadership he considered essential for the future of American politics. *Leadership* was his attempt to make readers see the possibility of such noble leadership, and indeed through his writing to foster and sustain it against what he saw as powerful forces that favored mercenary and occasionally lupine leaders.

At the theoretical heart of Burns's entire enterprise is his influential distinction between "transformative" and "transactional" leadership. Given the significance of this distinction, it is instructive to see whether the leadership-honor dynamic we have elaborated in the second part of this book may yield useful insights into its theoretical foundations and political scope. Accordingly, in this chapter we undertake a close reading of Burns's account of types of leadership to see the extent to which they are founded on a notion of honor. As we will see, Burns correctly intuited the need to acknowledge the importance of esteem for innovative or founding leaders that prevailing theories of leadership had dismissed. Yet his theoretical framework, drawing on Adlerian and Maslowian psychology, did not allow him to see the form of leadership he envisaged and desired, which I contend was in effect a form of magnanimity. The leader-honor dynamic therefore reveals the core ambiguities and limitations of Burns's insights into transformative and transactional leaders. The chapter concludes by exploring the implications of these insights for a new conception of moral leadership.

MacGREGOR BURNS ON LEADERSHIP AND PRESTIGE

James MacGregor Burns's *Leadership* (1978) was preceded by his earlier *Roosevelt: The Lion and the Fox* (1956), an admiring biography of Roosevelt as a leader who had transformed America. At the end of *Roosevelt*, Burns appended "A Note on the Study of Political Leadership," where he observed recent developments in leadership studies that shifted away from the individual's hereditary and innate traits toward environmental factors and the reciprocal relationship between personality and culture. The increased emphasis on the context in which leaders operate "is all the more welcome," according to Burns, "in an era when democratic peoples seek to understand the difficulties and possibilities of political leadership both in order to handle social and economic problems and to meet certain psychological needs of the people." In the *Note* (1956, 481), which is no more than seven pages, Burns turns to the case of Franklin D. Roosevelt to illustrate some of these increased complexities to better understand political leadership in democratic societies, thus anticipating the direction he will later take in *Leadership* (1978).

Written in the wake of the Watergate scandals, President Nixon's resignation, and the Ford presidency, Burns begins *Leadership* with the observation that "One of the most universal cravings of our time is a hunger for compelling and creative leadership," noting that "The crisis of leadership today is the mediocrity or irresponsibility of so many of the men and women in power, but leadership rarely rises to the full need for it" (1).[2] The book is a paean to past great leaders such as Roosevelt, and has as its ambition to "teach leadership" (448). It seeks to "fashion a general theory of leadership" that will allow us to distinguish between "transactional" leaders, those who take the initiative in making contact with others for the purpose of an exchange of valued things, and "transforming" leaders who "engage with others in such a way that leaders and followers raise one another to higher levels of motivation and morality" (1978, 19, 20). The test of leadership for Burns is real social change, in attitude, norms, institutions, and behavior (382, 403, 413). Transactional leadership is concerned with "modal values" or values of "means" such as "honesty, responsibility, fairness, the honoring of commitments," while transformational leadership is more concerned with "end-values," "such as liberty, justice, equality" (426). "Transforming leadership," according to Burns, "ultimately becomes moral in that it raises the level of human conduct and ethical aspiration of both leader and led, and thus has a transforming effect on both" (20). Burns is aware that such transformational leaders exercise extraordinary influence on their followers. It is for this reason that he wishes to distinguish them from base "manipulators" and especially Weber's "charismatic" leader, whom he calls "heroic" yet inauthentic because there is no true relationship and no lasting influence (246). His emphasis on morality also allows him to set aside those ostensibly transformational leaders such as Hitler and Mao by denying that they are leaders at all.

Burns's formulation has been especially influential not only in political leadership studies, but also in related fields of management and organizational theory.[3] Its strength is to go beyond the previous trait theory to pose a simple yet compelling dichotomy of two types of leaders, those who lead for change and others who seek to conserve.[4] He also introduces the leader-follower dynamic, showing the importance of context and followers for understanding leadership authority. In doing so, he poses the question of what it means to be a moral leader, reintroducing to the study of leadership the question of morality and ethics.[5] Yet important questions remain regarding his approach, especially ambiguities in the meaning of transformative and transactional leadership.[6] It is not clear, for example, whether these forms of leadership are distinct and opposite ends of the spectrum, are independent but not mutually exclusive, or whether one is an extension of the other.[7] Questions also remain regarding the specific nature of transformative leadership, whether transformative leaders are inherently moral or simply inaugurate change, irrespective of its ethical aspects.[8] To see if the leadership-honor dynamic can help in addressing some of these questions, we begin by examining Burns's account of the theoretical source of the distinction between transformative and transactional leaders. We are especially interested to see if his explanation acknowledges a role for honor as an essential aspect of the relationship between leaders and followers, and whether it can provide a foundation for moral leadership.

LEADERSHIP AND ESTEEM

Because Burns emphasizes the importance of the relationship between leaders and followers, one would expect an extensive part of the book to be devoted to what leaders and followers think of each other and how these perspectives shape their relationship. In this light, it seems that the question of honor—the mutual respect and admiration of leaders and followers—is neglected by Burns. Upon closer examination, however, we see that the question is discussed as the problem of "esteem" in part II, "Origins of Leadership," especially in chapter 3, "The Psychological Matrix of Leadership"; chapter 4, "The Social Sources of Leadership"; and chapter 5, "The Crucibles of Leadership." This discussion reveals a complicated and ambiguous view of honor or what Burns calls variously status, prestige, and esteem. Burns recognizes that his new focus on leaders and followers necessitates an understanding of the complex nature of this relationship. Though aware of the extensive political, philosophical, and historical scholarship that had engaged with the question of good leadership, "The key to understanding leadership," according to Burns, "lies in recent findings and concepts in psychology" (49).[9] Burns does consider Freud and Jung but ultimately rejects both Freudianism and B. F. Skinner's behaviorism as inadequate (35, 63), turning instead to Alfred Adler and his student, Abraham Maslow, to provide the theoretical foundation for his understanding of leadership.

Adler's "Individual Psychology" rejects Freudian psychology to claim that, though all individuals are unique, there is nevertheless a common and lifelong drive in all of us to fulfil our potential. Our aim at "self-actualization," a conscious and subconscious endeavor toward "fictional finalism," is shaped by our social context, giving rise to "inferiority" and "superiority" complexes. Adler distinguishes between types of individuals, but his focus is on the "socially useful" type who value having control over their lives to do good things for the sake of society (Adler 1924). Like his teacher Adler, Maslow too rejects Freudianism and behaviorism to focus on what makes people happy and psychically healthy. His "Third Force" approach advocates a humanistic psychology that studies positive moments and constructive people or "self-actualizers" to understand the uplifting aspects of human existence. Self-actualizers for Maslow live to their full potential, bringing their best selves into being. As he puts it succinctly, "what a man can be, he must be" (Maslow 1943, 91). Self-actualizing individuals are not motivated by greed or self-interest but are socially responsible and devoted to advancing humanity. His insight into the nature of self-actualization explains his famous hierarchy or pyramid of needs, where he ranks needs (starting with basic physical needs, then love, followed by esteem and finally self-actualization) and argues for a direction in satisfaction so that lower needs must be met before the satisfaction of the higher. Thus Adler and Maslow in general can be said to reintroduce into modern psychology a Thomistic natural law ranking of human desires, albeit with a modern Nietzschean "creative" individual who wills himself into being as the new exemplar.[10]

Burns turns to Adler and Maslow to understand how leaders come into being. Adler explains for Burns how two separate influential factors—the need for self-esteem and perception of esteem by others and the need and capacity for social role taking—work in harmony to bring out the potential for leadership (94–95). Maslow shows Burns how the need for self-esteem ("a high individual valuation of one's own worth") is affected by the desire to be esteemed by others, noting the twofold nature of the need as a form of mastery and competence and the "desire for reputation or prestige" (95). This difference between the "desire for skill" and "desire for fame" (112), as Burns puts it, is used by him in his subsequent discussion of "the crucial distinction" between the "quest for *individual recognition and self-advancement*" irrespective of social and political consequences, and the "quest for the kind of status and power that can be used to *advance collective purposes* that transcend the need and ambitions of individuals" (106). Or, as he notes subsequently, "the crucial question becomes the nature of the linkage between their attempts at self-gratification or other gratification, their achievement of gratification, and their consequent impact on history" (114). The problem, as he later observes, is that leadership can become a matter of "all-too-human motivation and goals, of conflict and competition that seem to be dominated by the petty quest for esteem and prestige" (33). The quest for esteem and prestige can lead to conflict due to struggles over esteem itself, or to the disparity between one's own sense of self-esteem and status and the esteem accorded by others (298, 294). Burns relies on Maslow's distinction between the need to acquire power and the need for status and recognition to argue that a key element for political ambition is unfulfilled esteem needs:

> One generalization seems safe on the basis of both systemic and casual observation: *the most potent sources of political motivation—the key elements of political ambition—are unfulfilled esteem needs* (both self-esteem and esteem by others). (113; emphasis in original)

Though these needs for "esteem, for prestige, for reputation, for admiration" are powerful according to Burns, self-esteem "is not simply a generalized force" but relates to specific expectations and contexts (114). Self-esteem can be a source for leadership but in two very different ways, with high self-confidence and self-esteem linked to successful leadership, while low self-esteem, which may be disabling for some, "may compel others to seek fame and glory in order to overcome doubts about one's worth" (100, 104). It is self-esteem that allows Burns to understand Woodrow Wilson's character and presidency: "the need to compensate for damaged self-esteem lay at the source of Wilson's moralistic, messianic dogmatism and his quest for personal power in his later years" (102). It also allows him to understand Lyndon B. Johnson, whose need for social esteem was so voracious that he wanted to be loved by everyone (34).

This discussion of esteem is especially valuable for Burns because it permits him to explain how individual desires can be reconciled with collective goods, distinguishing between Gandhi, Hitler, Lenin, and Roosevelt (106–12). The crucial concept here is Maslow's "self-actualization," one of those "higher" needs that are "more healthy psychologically, tending toward more creativity and a better balance between individual and collective aims, a continuing striving for efficacy in a series of challenges and tasks" (116). This form of development, which proceeds from within, is flexible, looks to oneself and others, and is open minded, leading to successful leadership (116). The concept of self-actualization therefore explains how personal ambition can be reconciled with public good, but only if Maslow's emphasis on *self*-actualization can be rectified to recognize "mutual actualization with others." Burns therefore corrects Maslow to argue that, beyond self-actualization, leaders have a capacity to learn and to be taught and therefore the ability to listen and be guided by others so that "Self-actualization ultimately means the ability '*to lead by being led*'" (117). Such leaders "rise with their followers, usually one step ahead of them, to respond to their transformed needs and thus to help followers move into self-actualization processes" so that in time the expression of needs becomes more related to socially sanctioned aims and collective goals and values, allowing leaders to "help transform followers' needs into positive *hopes* and *aspirations*" (117).

In emphasizing interpersonal relationships, especially in the higher ranking of social needs such as love and esteem, in the importance accorded to public-spirited action and above all, in its account of "self-actualization," Adlerian and Maslowian psychology provides important theoretical support for Burns's understanding of transformational leadership. Yet in relying on these modern humanistic psychological theories, Burns necessarily adopts or incorporates their limitations into his approach. This is evident in the ranking of esteem in Maslow's hierarchy, placed above physical needs yet located between love and self-actualization, suggesting it is both inherently desirable and instrumental for attaining self-actualization.[11] The directional nature of the hierarchy also denies the possibility that some may be willing to sacrifice the satisfaction of physical needs to defend their self-esteem or what they think is honorable and right. Though this approach provides a valuable focus on needs and passions, especially the importance of esteem, the complexity of the passion—manifesting itself variously as noble ambition, desire for domination, or longing for mere fame—remains unexplored.

We can see this in Burns's dissatisfaction with the individualistic "self" in Maslow's formulation, which is not only seemingly indifferent to others, but also fundamentally disengaged from political or moral aspects of leadership. Burns's "to lead by being led" shows what he longs for, but without explaining exactly what it is that distinguishes such public-spirited leaders from the "idolatrous form of heroic leadership" he finds in transitional or developing societies. In these, "idols are usually motivated by powerful need for affection, esteem, and self-actualization" to satisfy the needs of followers, including "their need for esteem from performers who bestow recognition and flattery on them—and thus by their need for self-esteem."[12] The problem seems to be the absence of a transcending purpose so that "While emotional needs in hero and spectator may be deeply involved, no central purpose, no collective intent other than short-run psychic dependency and gratification unites performer and spectator" (246, 248). Burns's requirement for "authentic" leadership therefore raises larger questions regarding the link between esteem and what he calls the "vital need for qualities of integrity, authenticity, initiative, and moral resolve" (25). We are therefore left with the impression that Burns is interested in the question of honor only incidentally, to the extent that it is deployed in modern humanistic psychology to provide theoretical justification for his longed-for transformational leaders, those with noble ambition who will look to the greater good, sacrificing for what they think is right and thus displaying what was once called magnanimity. Self-actualization, duly corrected by Burns, comes close to providing such an account, yet the lack of clarity regarding how individual ambition and the public good are actually reconciled, and how the pathologies of domination and fame can be mitigated, show the limitations of this psychological approach to leadership.

Burns's desire for good leadership and his focus on prestige, though innovative for contemporary political science, is not novel in the larger context of political studies. His distinction between transformative and transactional leadership in particular exists and was anticipated, as we have seen, in the classical or Socratic insight into the difference between the victory and honor lover, where the desire for preeminence characterizes the transformative leader, while the transactional leader is most concerned with doing the right or honorable thing and thereby avoiding shame. Though both want to pursue virtuous action, their desire for honor can lead to tyrannical impulses for the transformative, and unreasoning intransigence in the transactional. This distinction also exists in the modern or Machiavellian insight into the grim struggles between the few and many that can be resolved and elevated, not by an education in virtue, as suggested by magnanimous leadership, but by directing the few to the distinction of being glorious founders. Burns therefore in effect recalls and reanimates the larger debate between classical magnanimous and Machiavellian glorious leadership. But to the extent that he rejects the desire for mutual pandering of passions by leaders and followers, and aspires for an elevation in both, relying on a notion of a greater good to allow good leadership and even sacrifice, he implicitly favors the classical conception of magnanimous leadership.[13] Whether this view reflects his own hopes and desires or a clear-sighted assessment of the nature of transformational leadership remains unresolved.

MORAL LEADERSHIP

Our examination of the leadership-honor dynamic has given us deeper insights into Burns's conception of transformation and transactional leadership. In these concluding comments, I would like to outline how these insights can help us better understand an important aspect concerning transformative and transactional leaders that warrants closer examination—the meaning of moral leadership and its implications for education and innovation.[14]

As we have seen, Burns implicitly acknowledges that the distinction between transformational and transactional leadership has its source in the way honor shapes leadership ambition. Yet his turn to modern psychology occludes the deeper debate that informs his understanding and his own ambition to educate new creative leaders. From the perspective of the leadership-honor dynamic, Burns can be said to combine Machiavellian and Hobbesian approaches. He admires the Machiavellian transformational leaders, but, aware of their anti-egalitarian impulses (especially evident in his suspicion of the charismatic leader), he wants to incorporate Hobbesian moderation by insisting that transformative leaders must educate not only followers, but also themselves, thereby reconciling the tension between the "few" and "many" we discerned in Machiavelli. In doing so, he wants to reconceptualize the modern leaders as creative and moral, which means that he really seeks to recover the classical conception of magnanimity and locate it within a modern egalitarian constitutionalism. Magnanimous leadership is therefore the implicit goal and model for Burns, even if it is appraised and justified in terms of modern psychology and from a modern demo-cratic perspective. Such a classical perspective and approach would explicate and justify the moral leadership that is at the heart of Burns's overarching enterprise and is an increasingly important theme of contemporary politics. It is the absence of this approach that accounts for Burns's difficulty in explaining the nature of moral leadership. Burns celebrates transformative leaders such as Roosevelt and Gandhi as moral leaders, especially because they are "educators" who lead themselves and others to new perspectives. He thereby endorses these leaders *because* they are moral innovators. But the question of what exactly is moral innovation presents a challenge for Burns, evident in his unwillingness to list Hitler and Mao as leaders pre-sumably because he regards them as unethical or immoral. Our examination of the theoretical origins of transactional and transformational leadership from the perspective of the leadership-honor dynamic allows us to see more precisely the link between morality education and innovation that Burns has difficulty specifying.

The leadership-honor dynamic shows a twofold aspect to moral lead-ership. One important feature, not acknowledged by Burns, is of morality as codes of honor that define and inform transactional leaders, who are in effect guardians of these codes and in their defense appear as exemplars and thereby public models for what is moral and just. This form of leadership is to be contrasted with the moral leadership recognized by Burns, the transformative leader who seeks to change these codes, appearing as founders or reformers. As transformers of rules of justice and definers of what is noble and honorable, transformative leaders become the preeminent moral leaders. This twofold aspect challenges the idea of moral leadership that informs Burns's distinction between transformative and transactional leaders, allowing us to think more expansively in three important ways regarding the meaning of moral leadership and the role of political and moral innovation. First, in showing a link between what is moral and what is honorable, we see the important role of honor in innovation—honor and the force of shame can defend the ethical status quo but in doing so limit innovation. Equally, however, for those who seek preeminence, glory is a major reason for innovation and change, with the potential for subversion and corruption as well as progress. Second, this approach allows us to evaluate some leaders as morally innovative and transformative without insisting on a specific moral code as a prerequisite for defining their transformative leadership. Finally, such an approach reveals to us transactional leaders as moral leaders, expanding our conceptualization of moral leadership. In this way, the leadership-honor dynamic enlarges our understanding of moral leadership and in doing so underlines the crucial role of honor in both sustaining and limiting innovation and change.

CHAPTER 6

IDEALISTIC LEADERSHIP OF LEE KUAN YEW

The most celebrated leaders are those who found new nations and states. Their thoughts and actions in politically momentous circumstances warrant our close attention because of their far-reaching significance, and especially because they reveal with exceptional clarity the opportunities and challenges of political leadership. But who are these leaders and what are their ambitions? This is an important question not only for evaluating their character, allowing us to distinguish between statesman and tyrant, but more generally for understanding the nexus between such leadership ambitions and the nature of the political regimes they inaugurate. As we have seen, contemporary leadership studies have attempted to answer this question by distinguishing between transformative and transactional leaders. In this chapter we see whether the leadership-honor dynamic and more specifically classical magnanimity or Machiavellian glory provide new insights into this type of leadership. We do so by focusing on the leadership of Lee Kuan Yew, founder of Singapore. Lee is a suitable case for study because he actually defends his actions as founder and political leader in Machiavellian terms, suggesting that Machiavellian glory provides a profound insight into the character and ambitions of such contemporary founders. Yet, as our detailed examination of Lee's thoughts, speeches, and actions shows, Lee also defends an "idealistic leadership" and turns to Confucianism to consolidate and secure his legacy. Whether Lee's conception of idealistic leadership can be understood as Machiavellian glory, or, as in the case of James MacGregor Burns's understanding of transformative and transactional leadership, magnanimity appears to provide a more persuasive account of Lee's political ambitions and leadership is the core question we explore in this chapter.[1]

LEE KUAN YEW AND HIS FOUNDING AMBITION

Lee Kuan Yew is celebrated for guiding Singapore to independence from Britain and separation from Malaysia, cofounding the People's Action Party (PAP), which has governed Singapore since 1959, and transforming Singapore into one of the most prosperous states in Asia. On his death in 2015 at the ripe age of ninety-one, Singaporeans waited in line for up to seven hours to pay their last respects.[2] By any account, he was a transformative leader and will be remembered as the founding father of Singapore. Lee as political leader warrants our closer attention because he adopted a "modern" approach to his politics and eschewed the demands of "ideology." Singapore is arguably a modern prosperous Asian state that has at its core a simple bargain between the government and the people—the state and therefore the government is allowed to retain power and authority as long as it fulfils its promise of stability and prosperity. And it seems this bargain has been successfully kept. Singapore's continuing prosperity guaranteed Lee's authority: he ruled Singapore as its founder and first and longest-serving prime minister, the longest-serving head of government in Asia, and the longest-serving prime minister in the Commonwealth. He continued in office as minister mentor until his resignation in 2011.

A general overview of Lee's life and political achievements is useful for understanding his conception of leadership. Lee Kuan Yew was born on September 16, 1923, a fourth-generation Peranakan Chinese Singaporean. Lee, generally known as Harry Lee and the first-born male of the family, was educated to be the "equal of any Englishmen."[3] He was a talented student who was accepted into the exclusive Raffles Institution, after which he was awarded top Malayan boy in the Senior Cambridge examinations. His plans to become a lawyer in England immediately after matriculating were disrupted, however, by the fall of Singapore to the Japanese Imperial Army in February 1942.[4] After the Japanese surrender in August 1945 and the return of the British in September 1945, Lee resumed his education in England. He was admitted to the London School of Economics, but soon moved to Cambridge University, where he excelled in law. Lee returned to Singapore in 1950 and became a lawyer, gaining public attention with his defense of trade unions. He won his seat as a founding member of the PAP in the first Singapore general election in 1955, when the Labour Front's David Marshall became Singapore's chief minister. In the period of 1955 to 1959, Lee and his largely English-educated colleagues fought the Communists to retain the leadership of the PAP. In the 1959 election, the PAP won a landslide victory, capturing forty-three of the fifty-one seats and installing Lee as Singapore's first prime minister. But in 1961 a large majority of the PAP's rank and file left to join a new party, *Barisan Sosialis* (Socialist Front). Lee marginalized the pro-Communist party with his strategic use of a referendum on a merger with Malaya, partisan use of campaign laws, and finally "Operation Cold Store," where in 1963 more than one hundred opposition leaders were imprisoned before the election.[5] For a brief period between 1963 and 1965 Singapore merged with Malaya, only to be separated and become an independent nation on August 9, 1965. For the subsequent twenty-five years, Lee would dominate Singapore, transforming it into one of the most prosperous states in the world. Lee stepped down as prime minister in 1990, though serving as senior minister in the administration of Singapore's second prime minister, Goh Chok Tong, and as minister mentor, a post created when his son, Lee Hsien Loong, became the nation's third prime minister on August 12, 2004. On May 15, 2011, the eighty-seven-year-old Lee formally announced his retirement from Cabinet. He died on March 23, 2015.

This brief account of Lee's life and achievements shows him to be a formidable, often ruthless, but pragmatic leader. Yet throughout the course of his political life, Lee also displays a self-reflective awareness of what it takes to be a good leader. In an early speech to school principals in 1966, Lee outlined how the entire government was based on a "thin crust" of 150 people:

> This government at the moment—the whole of this administration—is running on I would say the ability and drive and dedication—not on the basis of what they get in salaries—of about 150 people. You remove these 150 people, if you can identify the 150; whoever wants to destroy this society, identifies these 150 people and kills them, the push will be gone. This is a very thin crust of leadership.[6]

Because of the diversity in physical stamina, mental capacity, and character, society is inevitably structured into a "pyramid," according to Lee. The exceptional leaders, a very small number, are the "spearhead" of society. This apex is supported by the larger middle strata of high-quality executives to help carry out ideas, thinking, and planning. Finally, there is the "broad base," the average person who must be nurtured because "the quality of your privates determines the quality of your army as much as the quality of the general does" (394). By 1971, in a speech at a seminar on communism and democracy, Lee had doubled the number of exceptional leaders in Singapore to 300. Though all parts of the society are important for Lee, leaders play a crucial role:

> It is strange, but true, that the fate of millions often turns around the quality, strength and foresight of the key digits in a country. They decide whether a country gains cohesion and strength in orderly progress, or disintegrates and degenerates in chaos.[7]

As these speeches reveal, a fundamental idea for Lee is the unequal natural distribution of excellence, with few having exceptional ability. Consequently, good government requires authority to be given to these talented few, for the benefit of all. "Singapore is a meritocracy," Lee proudly announces in his 1971 speech.[8] He does not think these insights into leadership are specifically Asian—he regards them as universal, to be found in every country. All nations strive to have a meritocracy, where the talented few are elevated to positions of power and authority, but not all succeed. It is this key insight that allows us to understand almost all major political measures Lee introduces into Singapore.[9]

Lee's understanding of the importance of leadership explains his reluctance to adopt liberal democratic constitutionalism. Leadership, not institutions, is necessary for good government, according to Lee. Though institutions are important, he does not think they are sufficient. Contrasting the views of "American liberals" who think separation of powers and checks and balances will yield good government "even if weak or not so good men win elections and take charge," Lee responds in a speech in Parliament on a White Paper on ministerial salaries:

> My experience in Asia has led me to a different conclusion. To get good government, you must have good men in charge of government. I have observed in the last 40 years that even with a poor system of government, but with good strong men in charge, people get passable government with decent progress.[10]

Because he values the knowledge and expertise of leaders, Lee is wary of representative democracy: "So when people say, 'Oh, ask the people!' it's childish rubbish. We are leaders. We know the consequences. You mean the ice-water man knows the consequences of his vote? Don't tell me that. That's what the Western journalists write."[11] To be judged by the people is especially difficult in a developing country where the majority of the population is semi-literate and sacrifice is demanded from the people. In such cases, the people

> respond more to the carrot than to the stick, and politicians at election time cannot use the stick. So . . . he who bids the highest wins. . . . At a time when you want harder work with less return and more capital investment, one-man-one-vote produces just the opposite.[12]

In a speech on leadership to public servants in 1962, Lee argues that one-man-one-vote, especially in inexperienced or unsophisticated electorates, would produce a bidding war where the highest bidder wins.[13] It is on this basis that Lee suggests economic development must precede democracy in Singapore and emerging countries. Legitimacy was gained as much by effective meeting of people's aspirations for a better life as by elections. The three essential elements for a successful transformation of any society, according to Lee, are: "First, a determined leadership, an effective determined leadership; two, an administration which is efficient; and three, social discipline. If you don't have those three, nothing will be achieved."[14]

Lee's conception of leadership defines the way he deals with the base of the pyramid, the people. It inevitably leads to the need for a Machiavellianism in politics:

> Between being loved and being feared, I have always believed Machiavelli was right. If nobody is afraid of me, I'm meaningless. When I say "please don't do that," you do it, I have to punish you because I was not joking when I said that. And when I punish, it's to punish publicly. And people will know next time, if you want to do that when he said "no, don't do it," you must be prepared for a brutal encounter.[15]

And an unflinching ruthlessness. In discussing the critical commentaries by Singapore writer Dr. Catherine Lim on Goh Chok Tong, Lee's successor as prime minister, Lee observes:

> Supposing Catherine Lim was writing about me and not the prime minister. . . . She would not dare, right? Because my posture, my response has been such that nobody doubts that if you take me on, I will put on knuckle-dusters and catch you in a cul-de-sac. . . . Anybody who decides to take me on needs to put on knuckle-dusters. If you think you can harm me more than I can hurt you, try. There is no other way to govern a Chinese society.[16]

The "business of the leader," according to Lee, is "not to follow the crowd. That's a washout. The country will go down the drain."[17] Such disregard for popular sentiment includes a willingness not to reveal everything to the people: "My job is to persuade my flock, my people, that that's the right way. And sometimes it may be necessary not to tell them all the facts because you will scare them."[18] Indeed, it would seem that the people can be a hindrance to good government. In an interview in 1962, Lee argues:

> if I were in authority in Singapore indefinitely, without having to ask those who are governed whether they like what is being done, then I have not the slightest doubt that I could govern much more effectively in their own interests. That is a fact which the educated understand, but we are all caught in this system which the British—I do not know what the French do in their colonies in Africa—export all over the place, hoping that somewhere it will take root.[19]

Finally, Lee's merit-based system requires a constant attempt to recruit the best into politics and public service more generally. This is for the obvious reason that the best are essential for good government. But it has another aspect. As Lee notes, if the best are not accepted, they may pose a challenge to the government.

> If we reject people who are natural activists with ideas, with ability, with dedication, then PAP is inviting breakdown of the system. It cannot reject people who are committed with ideas and ability. It must absorb and allow change to take place from within because the party cannot have the foresight to incorporate in its programme and its policies all the changes that are going to happen in the world.[20]

Or, as he puts it subsequently, "the smarter a man is, the more harm he will do society."[21] For this reason the Singapore model, given the country's small population and talent pool, may have limited application in countries that are substantially more populous. In a country of 30 or 300 million people where the number eligible to form a Cabinet may multiply by ten or one hundred, it may be impossible to include all the best people in government.[22] In addition to recruitment, Lee emphasizes the need for good education, at high schools and universities, as the first step in meritocratic selection. The academically best are then selected by PAP leaders with a systematic round of "tea sessions" and interviews, including psychological testing. This form of recruitment resembles corporate recruitment for chief executives rather than traditional political leadership contests found in other countries.[23]

Good leaders, however, are not decided solely by IQ but also by character. In a 1967 speech at a conference on youth and leadership, Lee observes: "And it is this as yet unmeasurable quality called "character" which, plus your mental capacity or knowledge or discipline, makes for leadership."[24] Lee frequently refers to "helicopter qualities" of leadership, a reference to the Shell Corporation system of selection. Shell had switched from forty attributes of good leaders to four, which they called "helicopter qualities" and on which they judged their executives worldwide.[25] Based on these qualities, Lee sought the best leaders:

> Singapore must get some of its best in each year's crop of graduates into government. When I say best, I don't mean just academic results. His "O" levels, "A" levels, university degree will only tell you his powers of analysis. That is only one-third of the helicopter quality. You've then got to assess him for his sense of reality, his imagination, his quality of leadership, his dynamism. But most of all, his character and motivations, because the smarter a man is, the more harm he will do society.[26]

Our brief account of Lee's conception of leadership—a pyramid of authority—is regarded as typically "Asian." Thus Pye (1985, 329–36), in his survey of the cultural aspects of power in Asia, argues that paternalistic authority dominates Asian politics. The features of paternalism include strong leadership aided by technocratic advisors, the insistence on "tidiness and order," an emphasis on loyalty to the collectivity, and weak institutional constraints. It is certainly true, for example, that respect for education and knowledge, meritocracy, and therefore paternalism were important aspects of

Confucianism, as is evident from the examinations for civil servants insti-
tuted in Imperial China and subsequently adopted by other countries in the
region.[27] Yet even a cursory examination of the leadership scholarship shows
that there is nothing specifically "Asian" about this model of leadership. As
we have seen, Lee's actions can be accounted for in terms of Machiavelli
(whom he quotes), not only his view of the few and many, a theme taken
up by elite theorists as we noted, but also the importance of fear in politics.

LEE KUAN YEW AND ASIAN VALUES

Lee's conception of politics and leadership we have outlined needs to be
reconciled with his subsequent endorsement of "Asian values." In 1982 he
initiated his Confucian Ethics campaign, with the Singapore government
announcing that Confucian Ethics would be offered as an optional subject
for moral education in secondary schools. The second phase in 1983 focused
on higher education, with the new Institute of East Asian Philosophies
within the National University of Singapore to define Confucianism for the
citizens of Singapore. This was followed by a media campaign encouraging
Confucian Ethics as an appropriate social philosophy for modern Singapore.
Despite these initiatives, the campaign was unsuccessful. Consequently, in
1991 the government issued a set of five "Shared Values"—nation before
community and society above self; the family as a basic unity of society;
respect and community support for the individual; consensus before conflict;
and racial and religious harmony. In 1994 Lee condemned the Western
liberal tradition, announcing, "Singapore [is] a Confucian society which
place[s] the interests of the community above those of the individual."[28]

Lee's endorsement of Asian values, specifically Confucianism, is unexpected, in part because a number of his closest associates questioned such
an approach. There were, in any case, obstacles to adopting Confucianism.
Foremost is the fact that Confucianism was long held in disrepute because
it was seen as an obstacle to progress.[29] Moreover, Lee's recourse to ideas,
ideology, and cultural claims was in tension with his pragmatism. He had
always been described as highly intelligent but not philosophical; ideas were
important merely for solving pressing practical problems.[30] If so, what was the
practical problem Lee wanted to solve with Confucianism? Finally, from the
first days of Singapore, Lee had avoided Malay and Chinese chauvinism—
Singapore was to be a multiracial society. In 1972 Lee expressed concerns
that the majority ethnic Chinese in Singapore would see themselves as

Chinese and not Singaporean. The future of Singapore, according to Lee, depended on the majority seeing itself as Singaporean.[31] He had promoted religious tolerance by enacting the *Religious Harmony Act*. Why was he now emphasising one nationality—the Chinese—over others?

Lee's Confucian initiative has been seen as an attempt to stem the sharp decline of PAP electoral support after the election of an opposition MP in 1981. Others have judged it as a form of religious ideology to manipulate the public, a sort of Platonic "noble lie," even an Aristotelian "endoxa" to secure the state against the West's moral decay.[32] An important aspect of it has been to counter Western claims that Singapore is not democratic by pointing to the economic and social achievements of developmental states.[33] It certainly has been criticized by other Asian leaders.[34] While these assessments have considerable force, my suggestion is that we should take seriously the possibility that Lee's Confucian initiative was also intended to secure "idealistic" leaders.

In addition to his Machiavellian view of leadership noted above, Lee also has a more comprehensive conception that he calls "idealistic" leadership. Lee claims that extreme situations give rise to idealistic leaders who will put to one side their personal considerations of safety, security, and wealth for the sake of their commitment to the people and ideals.[35] But in times of tranquility, such leadership is harder to find. I would argue that Lee regards Asian values, and specifically Confucianism, as an important means for ensuring such leadership, an initiative he pursues not only for the future prosperity of Singapore but also, importantly, for his own legacy. If true, this suggests that at least for Lee, the continual survival (if not the founding) of modern states requires more than a simple notion of "performance." What is needed is some larger conception, whether philosophical, ideological, or cultural, that justifies and defends the regime as a whole.

To see what Lee means by idealistic leadership, it is necessary to examine the significant problem Lee the founder confronted. As we have seen, Lee thought it essential for Singapore to have the best people in charge, necessitating a systematic selection process. But in time he realized he faced a serious problem in getting good leaders. Lee had already anticipated and identified this issue in the 1960s but took it up in earnest in the 1990s. In an interview in 1966, Lee identified it as the problem of succession: "how do we, over the next ten years, allow a new generation to emerge to take over from us? This is important. We are not getting younger. We cannot go on forever."[36] There were two related problems in the selection of future leaders. The first was the many new career options now available to the best, resulting in the second problem, of careerists rather than idealists dominating politics.

> My problem is there are so many career opportunities now that unless we do something to make politics more attractive incentive-wise, your best men are going into executive and managerial careers. This will leave your second-best careerist . . . any party faces it. They faced it all along in Eastern Europe. The second generation communist is more of a careerist than an idealist. The first generation [communists] who were captured by Hitler and put into concentration camps all along—I have met them—they are the first generation. They emerged naturally *just as we emerged*, and the process of selection was natural.[37]

Lee describes himself as an "idealist." But what is an idealist?

> Either you felt strongly about the colonial system and you wanted a better society enough to take the risk of being locked up or being clobbered by the British and then of being shot and killed or murdered by communists. . . . Unless you feel strongly enough, you don't emerge; you just subside beneath the broad mass.[38]

In a speech in 1994, he put it in these terms:

> The fate of the country, when it's a matter of life and death, you throw up people who put personal considerations of safety and security and wealth aside. But that's when you have a revolutionary situation, when a whole people depend on the actions of a few. . . .
>
> So it is crucial when you have a tranquil Singapore that you recognise that politics demands that extra of a person, a commitment to people and ideals. You are not just doing a job. This is a vocation; not unlike the priesthood. You must feel for people, you must want to change society and make lives better. And if I had done that and got no satisfaction out of it, then I would be a fool doing it because I could have gone back to Lee & Lee umpteen years ago and ridden the boom and sat back,

probably at least as rich as my brother or my two brothers—one
is a doctor, another a lawyer.[39]

Unique circumstances, such as the instability and danger of foundings, *natu-rally* bring out or reveal idealist leaders. Lee describes himself and all idealist leaders as exceptional individuals who are willing to sacrifice themselves for the common good. This sacrifice included risking his life and, it would seem, substantial wealth in not pursuing a career in the private sector.[40] But why? What is the satisfaction he gained for his idealistic leadership?

Lee sees the Japanese invasion of Singapore as a decisive moment in his political education. As a Peranakan or Straits Chinese, he saw himself as a British subject. But the ease with which the Japanese invaded Singapore made Lee question British colonial authority, a view confirmed when completing his studies at LSE and later Cambridge. Lee the talented legal scholar resented colonialism: "And I saw no reason why they should be governing me; they're not superior. I decided, when I got back, I was going to put an end to this."[41] In one of his earliest political speeches in January 1950 at the Malayan Forum in London, the twenty-six-year-old Lee explains his strategic assessment: the English-educated Malaysian students, especially those who had studied in England, and not the Chinese who were drawn into the communist movement, were best placed to take over the British administration in a smooth transfer of power.[42] His return to Singapore in 1950 and his crafty manipulation of the fraught politics, first countering the Communists in the PAP, then negotiating a union with Malaysia in 1963 that ultimately ended in Singapore's precarious independence in 1965, saw Lee as prime minister and founder of a new political entity, Singapore. Lee in effect is forced to create and nurture Singapore out of nothing:

> Remember, when we started, we were not even one society, never mind a nation. We were several different separate societies brought together under the British, an accident of history. Our loyalties and roots were in different parts of China, India and the Malay archipelago.[43]

The satisfaction Lee gets from idealistic leadership is therefore the honor and glory of being a founder. Lee can claim preeminence as a founder of a unique city-state that is not a product of the decolonization movements in the region.[44] He can also claim the glory of all founders, who give of themselves to benefit others on the greatest scale possible. Finally, it is the glory of an "Asian" who shows the West that they are not superior. Lee's success with Singapore, evident in the benefits he confers on those who are less able or talented, becomes a living, glorious testimony to his own sacrifice, ability, and vision. Lee loves Singapore; Singapore's continuing prosperity and grandeur honor Lee.

It is in this context of honor that we gain a better appreciation of the significance of succession for Lee. Holding onto office is no longer sufficient for Lee. It is essential for his continuing, perhaps immortal, glory that Singapore should prosper. Hence the need for new leadership to sustain his founding and pursue his vision. But tranquil times do not produce idealistic leaders. The future Lees who will take over will inevitably follow in his footsteps—in nurturing Singapore and his memory, they can never outdo him because there can only be one founder. It seems unavoidable, then, that without idealistic leaders, Lee's efforts may be short-lived. His entire cause and the sacrifices he believes he has endured now rely on the critical question of how to maintain his legacy.

Lee seeks to solve this problem of leadership as his final act of leadership. His solution takes three forms. The first is commonplace in Asia and, indeed, in many parts of the world—the appointment of a family member to succeed the leader.[45] Many reasons recommend such a solution, ranging from the continuation of the family name to the reliance on the strength and reliability of family ties, enhancing the legitimacy of the regime by transforming it into a type of hereditary monarchy, and finally, the possibility of maintaining influence and control, albeit indirectly. The appointment of Lee's son Lee Hsien Loong as prime minister in 2004 seemed to solve Lee's succession problem. Yet it also challenged his views on merit. Was Lee Hsien Loong's appointment simply another case of nepotism and patrimonialism? Lee claimed that his son should succeed on merit and not simply inherit office. His genetics arguments naturally pointed to his family members as suitable candidates. As the oldest of Lee's three sons, Lee Hsien Loong had won both the president's and the Singapore Armed Forces scholarships and had studied at Cambridge, graduating with first class honors in mathematics in 1974. He has a postgraduate degree in computer science and a master's in public administration from Harvard University and had spent a year at the US Army Command and General Staff College at Fort Leavenworth in Kansas.[46] Though Lee Hsien Loong entered politics in 1984, he did not become prime minister until 2004. In the interim, Goh Chok Tong was prime minister from 1990, with Lee Hsien Loong as his deputy. When asked if he was a transitional prime minister, like Taiwan's Yen Chia-kan, who ruled for three years after Chiang Kai-shek and before Chiang Kai-shek's son Chiang Ching-kuo took over, Goh denied being a "seat warmer."[47] In this light, Lee Hsien Loong's educational background and fourteen-year term as deputy may support Lee's claim that he was in training and being tested for merit. For others, however, the reason for Lee Hsien Loong's long tenure as deputy prime minister was his ill health—he was diagnosed with cancer in 1993 and had to clear a critical five-year period before he could be considered cured. This suggests that Lee is no different from other Asian leaders. But such a solution still left the problem of succession—who would succeed Lee Hsien Loong?

The second solution Lee proposed is the use of financial incentives to draw the best and brightest into government. This initiative had the added advantage of preventing official corruption, which is rampant in the region.[48] In 1995 Singapore introduced a new pay rate for ministers, based on a formula benchmarking them to the highest paid in six private sectors (banking, manufacturing, accountancy, engineering, law, and multinational corporations).[49] The argument seems clear—the best should not have to sacrifice their personal welfare and the welfare of their families for public office. But there is another, more important aspect to this payment. To the extent that wealth is honorable, Lee was conferring greater honor to future leaders. He was in effect conceding that after his founding, in "tranquil" times, politics had become less honorable to those with exceptional ambitions, the "idealistic" leaders. But Lee must also have known that such a solution would not satisfy the idealists precisely because to them honor cannot be bought. Idealists, like Lee, were less interested in money; they wanted to sacrifice for a great cause, for the common good, to be honored and remembered for doing great things. The fiscal measure may have solved one problem—making politics financially competitive with commerce—but it did not solve the problem of how to recruit idealists because it seemed to encourage the careerists. It was to address this problem, I suggest, that Lee turned to "Asian values."

The need to secure idealistic leaders had two aspects for Lee. The increasing prosperity of Singapore had exposed it to new and potentially fatal problems. The energy, thrift, and hard work of the founding generation had resulted in greater prosperity. Naturally, parents wanted to shield their children from harsh experiences. Consequently, the new generation led a much more comfortable but "soft" life. Related to this general softness, and contributing to it, was a Western "atomism" or individualism, a product of

Singapore's open economy, that was dissolving family ties and thereby all aspects of social life. Though this "biculturalism" was a particular problem at the top, it would inevitably affect the entire society.[50] Confucianism was therefore Lee's attempt to counter these trends. It would provide a sort of "cultural ballast" for Singapore.[51]

Chinese core values, according to Lee, are derived from basic human relationships. These were Confucius's five critical relationships. "Father and son, ruler and subject, husband and wife, old over young, faith between friends. In other words, the family is absolutely the fundamental unit in society. From family, to extended family, to clan, to nation."[52] As Lee indicates, his intention is to protect and nurture the family unit as the foundation for the entire nation. In doing so, he clearly wants to protect society generally from the pernicious influence of wealth and Western liberal individualism. But Lee also hopes to accomplish something much greater. To the extent that it is the people at the top who matter, his Confucianism is intended to invigorate not only society at large, but future leaders. Confucianism will certainly encourage the thrift and hard work of the many. But its moral teaching about good rule and of the *junxi* or "gentlemen" will have even more important consequences for society. Its teachings that the leader must consider the common good and the welfare of all, and not exploit his position to advantage himself, will replenish and repair what is missing from future leaders—their sense of sacrifice and public good, in short, their idealism.

But why turn to Confucianism? Surely there are other Asian traditions, such as the Indian and Malay, that would have been equally useful? Was it simply the fact that the majority in Singapore are Chinese? As we have seen, Lee was born Straits Chinese and, though exposed to Chinese traditions when young, he spoke only English and pidgin Malay at home. He began to learn Mandarin during the Japanese occupation and, by 1955, he "started learning in zest not just the [Chinese] language, but the diction, the slang, the style, the idiom, the proverbs and with it went the mythology of Chinese civilisation and culture and its traditional values" so that he could "strike a responsive chord" with the Chinese electorate.[53] It is possible that by acquiring this knowledge of Chinese literature and culture, he came to realize the usefulness of what he had discovered in the Chinese classics. Yet it was not just a matter of personal preference. He thought that for cultural and genetic reasons the Chinese were superior. In a 1994 interview with *Foreign Affairs* he noted: "If you have a culture that doesn't place much value on learning and scholarship and hard work and thrift and deferment of present enjoyment for future gain, the going will be much slower."[54]

Lee demarcated Asian culture into East, South, and Southeast Asia. He traced the influence of China in East Asia—Korea, Japan, and Vietnam. Chinese culture, and perhaps genetic makeup ("intense types, hard-driving, hard-striving people"[55]), predisposed the Chinese to success.[56] The contrast with India showed, according to Lee, an otherworldly culture: "The Indians have a more tolerant and forgiving approach to life. More next-worldly. If you do good, then in the next world you'll get rewarded."[57] This was typical of Malays, too, who did not want to renounce traditions for wealth and economic advancement.[58] As he had said in an early speech, "I have said openly that if we were 100 per cent Chinese, we would do better. But we are not and never will be, so we live with what we have."[59]

Singapore's success was due to the Chinese, who formed the majority of the population. But it was the Chinese who were most susceptible to the changes wrought by prosperity and liberal individualism—the Indians and the Malays, relying on their customs, traditions, and religion, had not changed as much.[60] Therefore the remedy for idealistic leadership, and for a continuing vigor in society, was to sustain its source, Chinese culture. Chinese culture, in addition to its support of family relations and its moral and ethical virtues, was religiously "this-worldly" and more tolerant. Lee could introduce this "Chinese" remedy because Chinese chauvinism and communism were no longer a threat. Indeed, such a Chinese solution would benefit Singapore with the future rise of China, which he anticipated.

IDEALISTIC LEADERSHIP AS MAGNANIMITY

We started by asking what are the nature and ambitions of those leaders who found new states? Our examination of Lee's life and his reflections on leadership reveals the importance of idealistic leaders. But what exactly is idealistic leadership, and can the leadership-honor dynamic explain its core features? Lee's success as founder of Singapore seems to confirm in general terms the efficacy of a Machiavellian approach to politics, where a few rule for their benefit, especially their glory, while the many are satisfied by being left alone and provided for in wealth and comfort. In other words, Machiavellian glory as "performance legitimacy" sufficiently accounts for Lee's ambition, the honor he seeks, and the difficulties he endures as founder of Singapore.[61] Upon closer inspection, however, we see a different picture emerge, questioning the efficacy of Machiavellian glory for understanding Lee and his endorsement of idealistic leadership. It is not clear how Lee's claims that he sacrificed for Singapore, giving up substantial wealth in order to exercise political leadership, can be accommodated within this Machiavellian framework. Moreover, Lee's hope to secure an idealistic leadership suggests that the Machiavellian grand compact exchanging glory for security may be insufficient for ensuring subsequent leaders of his caliber will continue to rise in Singapore, securing his own glory and achievements. His turn to Asian values is therefore an admission that Machiavellianism many not be sufficient, that it may need to be repaired by a Confucian *junxi*, an Asian version of classical magnanimity. Lee's actions therefore suggest that, though endorsing a pragmatic Machiavellianism, his greater ambitions required a more comprehensive account of leadership that accommodated notions of self-sacrifice and virtue. In other words, Lee's avowed Machiavellianism and his pursuit of idealistic leadership is founded on his recognition of the need for a more comprehensive notion of a leadership-honor dynamic, a version of magnanimity that is sustained by a larger sense of the common good. Idealistic leadership therefore confirms the importance of classical magnanimity for understanding the character and ambitions of political leaders, both for those who found regimes and those who preserve them.

CHAPTER 7

FLATTERY OF ADVISORS

H enry Kissinger, President Richard Nixon's national security advisor and later secretary of state, regularly recorded his conversations with colleagues, associates, and especially Nixon.[1] The recent release of the Kissinger tapes, combined with the extant recordings by Nixon of his discussions with aides, advisors, and others, provides a new and welcome opportunity to reconsider the unique relationship between Nixon and Kissinger.[2] It also allows us an unprecedented access to the private, candid, and necessarily secret conversations and exchanges between political leaders and their counselors, relationships that by their very nature are tantalizingly out of reach and inaccessible to outsiders. What the Kissinger and Nixon tapes reveal is the nuance, tone, and color of this complicated relationship between a powerful president who seeks out counsel and a dependent advisor who considers himself intellectually superior. The disparity in power and authority is implicit in their dealings, though as Nixon increasingly confronts political challenges and a crisis of legitimacy, this balance seemed to shift in Kissinger's favor, until in the end he emerges relatively unscathed from the Watergate scandal that claimed Nixon's presidency. That they both need each other, the one for advice, the other for the office, yet regard themselves as intrinsically superior to the other shows the delicate, finely wrought, and fluctuating nature of their relative authority.

In his book *The White House Years*, where Kissinger (1979, 299) provides a public account of this relationship, the closest we come to an assessment of Nixon's character is Kissinger's observation that Nixon was "too insecure and, in a strange way, too vulnerable." Certainly, Kissinger admires Nixon for being "very decisive." Yet even as he praises, Kissinger

attempts to distance himself from these "strong" decisions, hinting at the
complex relationship between president and advisors:

> Almost invariably during his Presidency his decisions were
> courageous and strong and often taken in loneliness against all
> expert advice. But wherever possible Nixon made these decisions
> in solitude on the basis of memoranda or with a few intimate
> aids. He abhorred confronting colleagues with whom he dis-
> agreed, and he could not bring himself to face a disapproving
> friend. (1979, 45)

Missing from Kissinger's book but evident in these tapes is Kissinger's
frequent recourse to flattery to secure his position and counter Nixon's
authority. Kissinger was notorious both for his consuming ambition and for
being a "suck-up" both at Harvard where he was on the faculty and later
in his public service career.[3] Yet his frequent and fulsome praise of Nixon
as revealed in these tapes is remarkable for showing how susceptible Nixon
was to such flattery, and how shameless Kissinger was in deploying it. Nixon
longed to be praised, and Kissinger was more than willing to oblige.[4] So
much so that flattery was one of Kissinger's principal tools in winning over
Nixon. For example, a transcript of the phone conversation after a 1971
presidential address on the economy gives us a taste of Kissinger's sycophancy
and obsequiousness: "It was absolutely spectacular! The thing that's so interesting about your style of leadership is that you never make little news, it
is always big news. You are a man of tremendous moves!"[5] Similarly, after
another speech in July 1971, Kissinger phones Nixon to advise, "This was
the best speech you've delivered since you came into office." He concludes,
"You are saving this country!"[6]

Leaders, because they're especially concerned with honor, derive great
pleasure from praise by close associates and advisors. They therefore become
particularly vulnerable to flattery—complimentary words that benefit the
flatterer. Flatterers typically magnify, exaggerate, or even fabricate some
aspect of the flattered in order to please them, and thereby gain an advantage. But because flattery assumes an advantage to the flatterer, telling the
truth for gain would also qualify as flattery, and indeed may be its most
insidious form. Flattery therefore is to be distinguished from tact, which is
a restraint in noting an aspect of someone's character to spare them pain,
and obsequiousness or servility, which flatters but with no evident benefit
to the servile.[7] The danger of flattery was a familiar theme, as we can see

from Aesop's salutary lesson of the crow who is praised by the wily fox for its beautiful plumage and the promise of being called "Queens of Birds" if its singing could match its appearance. Flattered, the crow begins singing, dropping the food from its beak into the fox's open mouth.[8]

Given the perniciousness of flattery and the susceptibility of leaders to its charms, a comprehensive insight into the nature of flattery and how it shapes the relationship between leaders and advisors is essential for understanding good leadership. The increasingly powerful role of advisors in contemporary politics would suggest that flattery should be a prominent theme of modern scholarship on political advisors.[9] Appointed by the executive and exempt from the impartiality requirements that apply to the permanent public service, political advisors present a challenge to modern bureaucracies founded on principles of political neutrality and democratic accountability.[10] Attempts to understand the evolving and complex nature of advisors, or how they "whisper to princes," have focused on various types of advisory roles.[11] Until recently, less attention has been paid to the specific dealings between the executive and advisors, in part because a relatively simple principal-agency model was used to account for the relationship.[12] Though more recent or "second wave" scholarship has taken a theoretical turn, providing a new framework for understanding this relationship, the importance of honor and therefore flattery continues to be neglected.[13]

In this chapter we examine the extent to which the different conceptions of the leadership-honor dynamic we have delineated can explain why modern scholarship has neglected this question, and provide new insights into the way flattery shapes the relationship between leaders and advisors. In the discussion that follows, we examine the fundamentally different ways the classical magnanimity, Machiavellian glory, and Hobbes's dispersed leadership approaches understand and address the problem of flattery. In doing so, we argue that the contemporary neglect of flattery can be traced to the influence of dispersed leadership that considers flattery something that can be ameliorated institutionally. Our examination of the two other major approaches reveals profound differences. Magnanimous leadership recognizes the dangers of flattery and recommends education in virtue and good judgment as well as *parrhesia* or truth telling within a larger context of public interest to counter its pernicious influence. Machiavellian glory, by contrast, shows what happens when we abandon these larger overarching concepts such as common good and magnanimity. Anticipating and rejecting the Hobbesian institutional and contractual solution, Machiavelli demonstrates how flattery is an irresistible and therefore a formidable weapon in able hands, confirming the fundamentally irreconcilable struggle between rulers and advisors, politics and philosophy.

HOBBES AND FLATTERY

Our examination of flattery starts with Hobbes's dispersed leadership because it is arguably the theoretical source of the "principal-agent" dichotomy that dominates contemporary scholarship on political advisors. As we have seen, "Honor" according to Hobbes "consisteth onely in opinion of Power" (L 10, 155). This debunking of honor is intended to undermine the malign political influence of glorying that is especially appealing to those who aspire to leadership. The new psychology of humans as power-seeking individuals, where the "power of man" is "his present means, to obtain some future apparent good" (L 10, 150), means that we are constantly attempting to gauge our power, so that we are essentially honor-judging and honor-measuring creatures. Consequently, we will be especially susceptible to what others think of us and will constantly seek their approbation, not principally as a measure of our goodness, excellence, or virtue but instrumentally, as a sign or indication of how others may be able to advance our search for some future apparent good. This means that Hobbes's new account of power and honor does not do away with flattery, but places it centrally in our dealings with others.[14]

Hobbes understands the dangers posed by flattery, but because of his rejection of *summum bonum*, so that there is no greater common good to unite us in political societies, and his denial that some are superior in prudence, he is unable to appeal to the classical remedies of education in virtue or truth telling for ameliorating the dangers of flattery. Instead, Hobbes turns to institutions to mitigate if not solve the problem of flattery. We can see this in his preference for monarchy over other executive forms, and in the specific institutional arrangements he proposes that will govern the dealings between the sovereign and his counselors.

The dangers of flattery are so significant for Hobbes that it may even be said that it provides one of the major reasons for his critique of democracy and aristocracy and his preference for monarchy. Hobbes rejects Aristotle's understanding of regimes by viewing monarchy, aristocracy, and democracy as merely forms of government (L 19, 239–40). Yet he is not equally disposed to all three, primarily because monarchy appears less susceptible to the vice of flattery that inevitably undermines the other regimes. Hobbes's argument here is that, though all these institutions will be susceptible to flattery, monarchy is most immune from its dangers. The reasons for this can be traced to the public form of deliberation in aristocracies and democracies and therefore the extent to which they replace counsel with eloquence. An "Assembly of many," according to Hobbes, provides a forum for public counsel that inevitably favors eloquence and persuasion over reasoning and advice. It therefore will always reward those who rely on orations to inflame passions and pander to the people (L 25, 309). Public assemblies in effect use honor and shame to force individuals to agree with the most powerful or eloquent (L 25, 309). By contrast, monarchies limit the extent to which counselors can publicly vie with each other in eloquence and therefore flattery, and thereby undermine the use of sycophantic speech. The doubts, indecisions, and contending wills that give rise to flattery in democracies do not affect the monarch, whose decision is determinative and final, and unites in one natural person and will the individual and public interest (L 19, 241).

But this does not mean that monarchies are immune from flattery. It is for this reason that Hobbes suggests institutional solutions that are specific to monarchy to limit the danger of flattery. Hobbes redefines and therefore enfeebles the role of advisor or counselor. We have already seen that Hobbes denies superiority in prudence. He goes on to distinguish between command and exhortation, so that an "*apt*" counselor is now nothing more than someone who will serve the sovereign "in the place of Memory, and Mentall Discourse" (L 25, 306). Moreover, the monarch will determine how this counsel is given. Hobbes suggests that the monarch should consult experts individually and never in an "Assembly." These private meetings will limit the potential for advisors to compete with each other and resort to flattery to gain an advantage over each other. It will also allow the sovereign to ask questions, limiting the eloquence of the advisor. Such counselors are limited to "firm ratiocination" and not improper inferences, and metaphorical speeches (L 25, 306–7). Finally, these consultations will allow the monarch the privacy to be moved by fear as much as courage, leading to sound political judgment that would otherwise be undermined by public flattery and use of shame by counselors.[15]

It is not clear the extent to which Hobbes's institutional solutions could avert the dangers of flattery. Though the sovereign is the most powerful and therefore most honorable, did this not mean that he was especially vigilant on signs of diminution of power through disrespect, and therefore very sensitive to flattery? And did the redefinition of the role of counselor and recourse to private meetings really do away with flattery, or rather accentuate and exacerbate its force and potential in the hands of able advisors? Leaving these questions to one side, the Hobbesian and later liberal responses did promise a simple institutional means for overcoming flattery. It was not surprising then that much of subsequent scholarship was tempted with such an efficient solution, forgetting the source of the problem of flattery and seeing the relationship between monarch and counselor as one of principal and agent. From this perspective, the provision of rewards and punishments conclusively addressed the danger of flattery. In doing so, however, it had little to say about flattery that surmounts any institutional arrangements between leader and advisor because it is founded on a nuanced and fluid relationship where the advisor has the skill to flatter and the leader is susceptible to flattery.

FLATTERY AND MAGNANIMITY

Given the limitations of the Hobbesian approach, it is instructive to consider the way classical magnanimous leadership understood the problem of flattery. As we have seen, the danger of flattery is an important theme in classical political thought. Socrates rejects flattery because in appealing to the pleasure derived from the admiration of others, it undermines the promise of praise, which is the due appreciation and acknowledgment of the good. Flattery therefore distorts the recognition of the good by separating the pleasant from the good and thereby corrupting both the flatterer and the flattered. It is evident above all in oratory, according to Plato, but is similar to cosmetics, pastry cooking, and sophistry, which are the false counterparts to the true arts of gymnastics, medicine, and legislation.[16] Similarly, Aristotle, distinguishing friendliness from the extremes of obsequiousness and surliness, defines the *kolax* or flatterer as someone who aims at being pleasant in order "to gain some benefit for himself, in money and all that comes from money." In democracies, where the principle of equality predominates, *kolakeia* or flattery becomes the vice of the demagogue who seeks to persuade the *demos*. In other regimes, especially monarchies, where the court or the entourage includes political advisors or counselors, flattery exposes rulers to the dangers of the ingratiating courtier who, as *parasitos*, became a threat to good rule (NE 1127 a7; 1108a, 27–29). Such an understanding of flattery came to dominate subsequent thought. For example, when Thomas Aquinas confronts the problem of flattery, he follows in important ways the Aristotelian view of the flatterer or adulator as one who praised for gain, justifying his conclusion that flattery is a venial and not a mortal sin (*Summa* II, IIa Q 115, Art. 1, 2).

Having discerned the political dangers of flattery, magnanimous leadership proposed two different solutions to counter it. The first was education, of both rulers and the people. Rulers in particular would be taught virtues of character to make them impervious to the blandishments of flatterers, with an emphasis on philosophical inquiry, as well as historical lessons derived from lives of eminent leaders.[17] The other was the attempt to show the difference between true friends and flatterers by noting the importance of *parrhesia* or "saying everything," a form of honesty or candor in speech between friends. Frank advice revealed true friends, gained the ruler good counsel, while thwarting the pleasing lies and exaggerations of the flatterer.[18] These teachings were especially evident in the "mirror to princes" works that sought to counsel princes on good rule. Thus, Machiavelli's contemporary Erasmus in his *The Education of a Christian Prince* (1514) devotes an entire chapter to how princes must avoid flatterers, who are described as "the most dangerous tame animal."[19] The main emphasis here is on the education of the prince, with special attention paid to the selection of nurses, companions, attendants, and tutors. Dangers of flattery implicit in portraits, statues, inscriptions, and honorary titles are also noted by Erasmus. Young princes are to be taught to think of the welfare of the people and not to believe that they can do anything they want. An education in philosophy and especially the reading of books (because they are honest and candid and therefore do not flatter) is recommended to develop character and judgment (Erasmus 1997, 54–65).

MODERN FLATTERY

We now turn to Machiavellian glory to see whether this approach provides new insights into the challenge flattery poses to leaders. We do so because Machiavelli's most famous book, *The Prince*, itself a work seeking to advise princes, has been endorsed by a number of contemporary political advisors, who argue that their roles are best understood in Machiavellian terms.[20] Moreover, Machiavelli's succinct yet rich account of flattery in *The Prince* yields insights that are especially valuable as they present a radical challenge to both the Hobbesian and magnanimous leadership approaches.[21] Provocatively, Machiavelli claims that flattery is an irresistible weapon in the hands of the able advisor, that the absence of a common good means that the relationship between leaders and advisors will always be defined by conflict, and, anticipating yet ultimately rejecting the Hobbesian solution, that various attempts to remedy this conflict institutionally will end in failure because at a deeper level there is an intractable dissonance or tension between those who wield power and those who know. His discussion of flattery therefore leads to the profound claim that there is inevitable contest between politics and philosophy that can never be mitigated, repaired, or reconciled.

Machiavelli writes *The Prince* soon after the fall of the Florentine Republic in 1512, when he is dismissed from office as first secretary in the Florentine Republic and banished by the new Medici regime to San Casciano in the countryside. As he makes clear from the first lines of the *Dedicatory Letter* to *The Prince*, he is offering it as a "small gift" to "acquire favor" from Magnificent Lorenzo de' Medici (D, 3). In doing so, he admits his neediness, due to "a great and continuous malignity of fortune," and his hope that Lorenzo will raise him by employing him as an advisor. This very personal introduction to *The Prince* reminds us that the question of advisors is an especially important one for Machiavelli. It is one that he addresses in a sense twice, first from the perspective of an ambitious Machiavelli seeking patronage from Lorenzo, and second as a wise advisor counseling not just this prince, but all future readers and leaders. It is this double aspect of the book, of the specific relationship between Machiavelli and Lorenzo, and the more fundamental tension between all advisors and princes, that determines the structure and rhetoric of *The Prince* as a whole. We will have to be sensitive to both aspects and accounts to gain a comprehensive understanding of Machiavelli's insights into the nature of the relationship between leaders and advisors.

The *Dedicatory Letter* appears to be conventional praise of a patron or future benefactor. Yet its substance shows the significance of the relationship between advisor and leader for Machiavelli, and anticipates the important themes that he will subsequently take up in *The Prince*. Taking the perspective of a potential advisor, it immediately shows an inescapable fact about the relative disparity in power between advisors and princes. Princes are "high atop the mountains," while advisors are in "low places." Princes are self-sufficient, even great, while advisors are needy, hoping to please princes to acquire favor. The next notable difference, in addition to their disparity in authority, is the differences in interests of princes and advisors. Most princes tend to admire "horses, arms, cloth of gold, precious stones and similar ornaments worthy of their greatness" (*Dedicatory Letter*, 3). But advisors like Machiavelli value above all "knowledge of the actions of great men" that can only be learned by "long experience with modern things and continuous reading of ancient ones" (DL, 3). One may infer from this that Machiavelli, in possessing such knowledge, is in an important respect superior to Lorenzo. Yet it is not clear that princes like Lorenzo believe they are deficient in this respect, or, if they did, whether they thought such deficiency mattered. Therefore the disparity in power, interest, and ability between princes and advisors would seem unbridgeable if it were not for one notable weakness of princes. That princes want greatness and need to be constantly assured of their superiority means that they long for honor. But this desire opens them up to flattery, praise, and compliments that will please them but will be to the advantage of the flatterer. Susceptibility to flattery is therefore a significant weakness of princes and possibly the only weapon at the disposal of advisors to redress or remedy their abiding weakness. Machiavelli in the *Dedicatory Letter* claims that in giving a gift that pleases him rather than Lorenzo, and in not filling *The Prince* with "fulsome phrases nor with pompous or magnificent words," he shows he does not flatter and therefore can be trusted. Yet in saying so, he immediately reminds the prince of such a danger and makes us wonder if it is possible to distinguish between flattery and praise when the only difference between the two is the advantage of the flatterer. He also implicitly raises questions about his own intentions and the deeper problem concerning the very possibility of a common good that unites leaders and advisors.

These reflections on the nature of princes and advisors, from the perspective of a weak yet knowledgeable advisor, introduce and frame their subsequent discussion in *The Prince*. Because *The Prince* as a whole consists of advice to future princes, in a sense the entire work is a meditation on the relationship between rulers and advisors, those who have power and those who know. But the nerve of Machiavelli's argument regarding the role of advisors and the problem of flattery is found in two separate chapters toward the end of *The Prince*. Chapter XXII, "Of those Whom Princes Have as Secretaries," and Chapter XXIII, "In What Mode Flatterers Are to Be Avoided," ostensibly address separate topics, but on closer inspection appear to provide a comprehensive and self-sufficient essay on the relationship between the prince and advisors. Yet it is only when they are read in this way that we see that Machiavelli contradicts his own counsel in the space of a few pages, initially extolling the merits of advisors and subsequently denying their usefulness. To see the nature of this argument, and the implication of such a contradiction for our contemporary understanding of political advisors, it is necessary to pay close attention to the subtle argumentation of each chapter before finally reflecting on the work as a whole.

ON SECRETARIES

Chapter XXII, "Of those Whom Princes Have as Secretaries," starts provocatively: "The choice of ministers is of no small importance to a prince;
they are good or not according to the prudence of the prince" (P 22, 9).
Provocatively because it establishes prudence as an essential aspect of princely
or political rule, and because it suggests that the goodness or otherwise of
advisors is subject to this prudence rather than being innate to the character
of the advisor. There is, it would seem, an ambiguity regarding the goodness
of advisors, based not on their virtue, but on their usefulness and loyalty
to the prince. Machiavelli follows this remark by appealing to the prince's
vanity: "the first conjecture that is to be made of the brain (*cervello*) of the
lord is to see the men he has around him." Distinguishing between *sufficienti*
or "capable" and *fedeli* or "faithful" ministers, Machiavelli seems to exploit
a prince's love of honor with his observation that a prince's reputation for
wisdom is determined by his entourage, and especially by his ability to
recognize competence and to keep advisors faithful. The prince's incapacity
in this respect exposes him to "unfavorable judgment," and importantly,
"the first error he makes, he makes in this choice." Advisors seem like the
"ornaments" that Machiavelli in the *Dedicatory Letter* said pleased princes
and reflected their greatness, in this case for wisdom, but, unlike these
ornaments, their goodness depends on the nature of the prince.

Machiavelli seeks to demonstrate this argument with the example
of Pandolfo Petrucci, who is described here as a prince of Siena, and his
minister, Messer Antonio da Venafro. Pandolfo was judged a "most worthy
man" according to Machiavelli because of Venafro.[22] Yet this judgment is
quickly challenged with Machiavelli's account of the "three brains":

> And since there are three kinds of brains (*cervelli*): the one that
> understands by itself, another that discerns what others under-
> stand, the third that understands neither by itself nor through
> others; the first is most excellent, the second excellent, and the
> third useless—it follows, therefore, of necessity that, if Pandolfo
> was not in the first rank, he was in the second. (P 22, 92)[23]

Following Machiavelli's argument, we presumably know of "prince" Pandolfo's
excellence because of our judgment of Venafro, his advisor. Yet does not this
assessment also permit another possibility where Venafro could be a first
brain, "the one that understands by itself," while Pandolfo "discerns what

others understand"? Can the minister's excellence say anything about the worthiness of the prince? After all, the most excellent advisor may well be minister to the third brain, the one that is useless. Machiavelli's appeal to the prince's vanity and pride therefore reveals a complexity in the relationship between prince and minister that was not evident in his initial formulation, when he suggested the prince recognized the ability and determined the faithfulness of the minister. It now seems possible that an excellent minister may have more influence, if not dominance.

Aware of this implication, Machiavelli now quickly seeks to comfort the potential "second brain" princes. Even if such a prince does not have "inventiveness by himself," as long as he has judgment to recognize the good or evil someone does and says, and extols the one while correcting the other, "the minister cannot hope to deceive him and remains good himself" (P 22, 92). The problem of disparity of brains and the danger of deception can be overcome by the simple expedient of judging the goodness of deeds. These comments are intended to calm the fears of the second brain prince with a first brain minister, though in doing so the third brain prince is implicitly abandoned to the mercy of the first brain minister, unless one can argue that a bad deed is evident even to those with the meanest capacities. But clearly Machiavelli thinks this may not be sufficient, because he immediately continues, "But as to how a prince can know his minister, here is a mode that never fails" (P 22, 93). Yet as the tone of his discussion indicates, Machiavelli's helpful advice, which is in effect a permanent solution to the problem of the prince-minister relationship, is directed to the second brains, who may now see in ministers not a means to augment their reputation for wisdom, but rather a danger to their rule. The irony is that Machiavelli's comforting advice takes the form of a "rule," an order he will be giving to all future princes who are not inventive.

What then is the "mode that never fails"? The first thing to note is that the goodness of the minister is now no longer to be judged by the prudence of the advice. This has been silently dropped because of the obvious assumption regarding the differing excellences of the prince and minister. The new test concerns the faithfulness of ministers: is a minister "thinking more of himself than of you"? The problem, it would seem, is that such a minister can never be trusted and will never be a good minister because "he who has someone's state in his hands should never think of himself but always of the prince" (P 22, 93). This familiar problem of partiality and private interest could be simply resolved by having such ministers replaced by others who are virtuous, show integrity, and look to the common good.

Machiavelli's "mode that never fails" does not even mention this possibility. On the contrary, he seems to assume (or perhaps thinks it is more reliable to presume) that all ministers (or indeed everyone) are unavoidably partial and self-regarding. Hence his proposed solution to making a minister always think of the prince, that is, "to keep him good," is not to persuade or educate but rather bestow so much honor, wealth, and obligations that the minister will not desire more of these, but in realizing "he cannot stand without the prince," he will fear changes. Goodness or faithfulness is to be achieved by concord of interest rather than an appeal to an idea or principle that transcends both prince and advisor. Machiavelli finishes this discussion (and the chapter) with the chilling observation, "When, therefore, ministers and princes in relation to ministers are so constituted, they can trust one another; when it is otherwise, the end is always damaging for either for one or the other" (P 22, 93). Trust, it seems, is not founded on mutual respect and confidence, or a common commitment to some higher good, but on a subtle calculation of the advantages that outweigh the costs of mutually beneficial relationships.

The theme of secretaries, which was initiated as an important question for the prince and subject to his prudent management, and promised to burnish his reputation for wisdom, is now revealed to be an intractable problem of a struggle between princes and secretaries caused by differences in interest and the excellence of their "brains." This problem, according to Machiavelli, cannot reliably be resolved by a turn to a middle or common ground in wisdom, patriotism, or religion to mediate and resolve the necessarily divergent ambitions of the princely and ministerial "brains." Rather, the only dependable means is the institutional use of rewards and punishments, the calculated dispensation of honor, wealth, and fear by the prince to make the minister "good."[24]

ON FLATTERERS

Chapter XXII seems to be Machiavelli's conclusive advice on how to manage secretaries. Yet the next chapter, Chapter XXIII, "In What Mode Flatterers Are to Be Avoided," which is ostensibly about a different question, in effect reopens the discussion concerning advisors and in fact seems to offer completely different counsel. Machiavelli introduces Chapter XXIII almost as an afterthought, prompted by the discussion in the previous chapter: "I do not want to leave out an important point and an error from which princes defend themselves with difficulty, unless they are very prudent or make good choices" (P 23, 93). All princes need to "defend" themselves from the "plague" of flattery and flatterers that crowd the courts. Yet the source of this problem lies not with the deficient character of the flatterer, but in humanity itself. Because "men take such pleasure in their own affairs" they deceive themselves so that powerful self-love makes princes seek the pleasure of praise, while blinding them to its truth. Consequently, they look needy and contemptible. Though he speaks of the "plague" of flattery, Machiavelli's focus is not on the flatterer but on the deficiencies of character in princes that makes flattery possible. Such a diagnosis would suggest the conventional remedies for such a problem, such as an education in virtue to make princes impervious to such flattery. But Machiavelli does not take this opportunity to advocate a classical conception of magnanimity to moderate the prince's love of honor, nor does he remind the prince that pride is a sin and humility or meekness one of the foremost Christian virtues. The reason is twofold. By the time we have reached chapters XXII and XXIII Machiavelli has already provided an education that in effect "departs from the orders of others" as he claimed in Chapter XV. This includes a teaching on how "to be able not to be good," (P 15, 61); on being liberal by spending other people's money (P 16, 62); on the safety of being feared rather than loved (P 17, 65); on how to appear, rather than be "all mercy, all faith, all honesty, all humanity, all religion" and use laws as weapons (P 18, 69–70). In the light of this education it would be difficult for Machiavelli to deny the usefulness of flattery as a political tool. Moreover, as the discussions in Chapter XIX "Of Avoiding Contempt and Hatred," and Chapter XXI "What a Prince Should Do to be Held in Esteem" indicate, Machiavelli seeks to rehabilitate honor from the ignominy it has endured under "our religion." For these reasons, he denies any role to the classical or pious education in virtue: "For there is no other way to guard oneself from flattery unless men understand that they do not offend you in telling the truth" (P 23, 94). With this remark Machiavelli appears to endorse the other well-known solution, *parrhesia* or frankness, as the only means of countering flattery. Yet as we will see, the subsequent discussion reveals formidable problems with this solution to the extent that one is left with the impression that there may be no solution to the problem of flattery.

The main difficulty with such truth telling is that if everyone tells you the truth, "they lack reverence for you." The danger is that the prince will look contemptible in seeking honest advice. But why would seeking the truth from advisors lead to lack of respect? Is it because open discussion presumes a form of parity between interlocutors and therefore unavoidably depreciates the authority of the prince? Perhaps because it is public acknowledgment by the prince of a deficiency (he does not know or lacks judgment) so that regular deference to the opinion of advisors would perhaps confirm to everyone that the real rulers are those who know and advise? Honesty and truth telling may overcome flattery, but seemingly at the expense of the dignity and therefore authority of the prince.

Having noted the significant obstacles associated with what Machiavelli stresses is the *only* solution to the problem of flattery, he now proposes a "third mode" ostensibly an attempt to retain truth telling while remedying its potential threat to the dignity of the prince. Addressing the "prudent" prince, this mode starts by dividing people into two groups, the "wise men in his state" and the "others." Only the wise should be given freedom to speak the truth to the prince, but even in this case, not about everything—only about those matters that the prince has asked about and nothing else. Yet even this restriction on the wise is soon removed: "But he should ask them about everything and listen to their opinions; then he should decide by himself, in his own mode; and with these councils and with each member of them he should behave in such a mode that everyone knows that the more freely he speaks, the more he will be accepted" (P 23, 94). As for the "others," the advice is simple: "he should not want to hear anyone," and once having decided he should be "obstinate in his decisions." Where this mode is not adopted, according to Machiavelli, the prince is exploited by flatterers or in changing views constantly is seen to be indecisive and therefore contemptible. With this advice we see that one major source of being contemptible is indecisiveness, due no doubt to the different advice a prince will receive. The price of frankness is contradictory advice, to be remedied by seeking advice only from the wise, and then by deliberating not in their company. To demonstrate this case, Machiavelli refers to Emperor Maximilian.

Before turning to this example to see how it supports Machiavelli's claim, it is necessary to see the consistency of this "third mode" with the advice he had given in the previous chapter on secretaries. In the emphasis on wisdom, this approach certainly reinforces what Machiavelli had said previously about the necessity of prudence in politics, moving away from the other test, whether a minister is thinking of the prince or his own welfare. Indeed, it seems to go further in advocating a sort of deliberative council of the wise at the apex of political authority. But the solution he proposes seems to neglect altogether the problem of the "three brains" and the tension between prince and advisor he identified in the previous chapter as well as the solution he proposed in terms of making advisors "good" by a combination of reward and fear. Why should a "first brain" prince be counselled, even by the "wise"? Is there not a danger in the second, or even the third "useless" brains in being advised, and therefore controlled by the wise? Who exactly are the "wise"—after all, is there not an extraordinary range in human excellence, from the philosophically profound to the practically prudent? Finally, what about the problem of self-regard that distorts the prince's judgment and makes possible the plague of flattery? Will the prince's opinion of who is wise be inevitably distorted by this passion? If so, doesn't this third mode simply ignore the problem of flattery?

With these thoughts in mind, we turn to Machiavelli's "modern" example, that of Emperor Maximilian. In doing so, however, we are struck by Machiavelli's passing remark that everything Machiavelli knows about Maximilian he has gained from Father Luca, "a man of the present emperor Maximilian." Whatever the subsequent discussion of the emperor, this comment starkly confirms the problem of a secretary or advisor who is at best indiscreet, at worst treacherous in revealing the strengths and weaknesses of the emperor's character. It reminds us, in other words, of the problem of faithful advisors that was raised in the previous chapter on secretaries and apparently forgotten in this discussion of flattery. As for the emperor himself, Machiavelli sees him as someone who opposes his "third mode" and, in his ineffectiveness, proof of the need for the specific form of frank deliberation Machiavelli counsels. Maximilian, because he is a secretive man, "does not communicate his plans to anyone, nor seek their views." Consequently, in implementing them, they are contradicted by those around him, who dissuade him from his plans because he is an "agreeable person." As a result, "the things he does on one day he destroys on another, that no one ever understands what he wants or plans to do, and that one cannot found oneself on his decisions" (P 23, 94–95). On one level, this example supports Machiavelli's "third mode" because in the extremes of taking no advice and then listening to all, Maximilian becomes indecisive and looks contemptible before his court. Yet in other respects the example seems to undermine Machiavelli's "third mode." There is no indication that Maximilian's initial judgment is unsound, even though it was formed without discussion or advice of anyone. Rather, the problems arose later, when he sought to implement his plans. If Maximilian could implement his judgment unwaveringly, by not being agreeable and accommodating, or by not taking counsel in implementation, then it may be possible for him to be decisive. Because it is unlikely for him to change his character, perhaps he is better off, contrary to Machiavelli's advice, to reject counsel altogether in implementation (as he did in formulation) to avoid the charge of vacillation. Maximilian's example therefore seems to suggest that both flattery and contempt can be overcome by taking no counsel and relying on one's own judgment. Yet this solution also seems to be exposed to a grave problem. It is true that there are questions regarding Maximilian's prudence. The choice of the unreliable Father Luca tells against his judgment, if we are to rely on Machiavelli's first measure of the prince's excellence. He also seems to lack the ability to discern good and bad counsel when it is time to implement his decision. But, above all, Maximilian seems to raise a more complex question regarding the importance of character in shaping judgment. His agreeable nature—his desire to be liked—seems to undermine his judgment. It would seem that Maximilian's secretiveness and agreeable nature—and not his judgment—are the root cause of his failure. Is prudence a hostage to character and disposition? Put somewhat differently, to what extent is the question of "brains" and the exercise of prudence subject to the princes' and the secretaries' nature? To what extent is Machiavelli's "third mode," relying on prudence and frankness, subject to chance and particular circumstances?

After the ambiguous example of Maximilian, Machiavelli seemingly summarizes and restates his "third mode" suggestion. But the restatement is a reformulation because it abandons important aspects of the third mode. It is as if the example of Maximilian has forced Machiavelli to move away from his former position. In his summary, Machiavelli states that the prince should always take counsel but only when he wants it, and "he should discourage everyone from counselling him about anything unless he asks it of them." Yet he should be a "a very broad questioner" and a "patient listener to the truth," going so far as to say "he should become angry when he learns that anyone has any hesitation in speaking to him" (P 23, 95). The distinction between the "wise men" and others is now abandoned. The prince will now take counsel from everyone, the only limit being that he will initiate the discussion. It is as if Machiavelli wants to change the nature of the prince himself, for, after all, isn't "a very broad questioner" and a "patient listener to the truth" a practical definition of a philosopher? Does this mean that the "third mode" presupposes a "first brain" or a "philosopher-prince"? Perhaps it is not accidental that we have raised these questions. Machiavelli follows his summary or review with what appears to be a new theme. Yet it soon becomes evident that this discussion goes to the core of the questions we have posed:

And since many esteem that any prince who establishes an opinion of himself as prudent is so considered not because of his nature but because of the good counsel he has around him, without doubt they are deceived. For this is a general rule that never fails: that a prince who is not wise by himself cannot be counselled well, unless indeed by chance he should submit himself to one person alone to govern him in everything, who is a very prudent man (P 23, 95).

Of course it was Machiavelli who had proposed at the very beginning of Chapter XXII, "Of Those Whom Princes Have as Secretaries," that "the first conjecture that is to be made of the brain of the lord is to see the men he has around him" (P 22, 92). It is difficult to account for such a repudiation of his initial formulation within the space of three pages.[25] Was he simply appealing to the vanity of princes to direct their attention on the question of secretaries? The subsequent discussion focused on the various ways of managing the relationship between princes and secretaries, ranging from taking counsel, as in the case of Pandolfo, to the mode that never fails in judging the counselor ("is he thinking of himself more than you?"), to how to keep them "good" (the judicious use of reward and punishment, and not appealing to the common good), and in the chapter on flattery, on the "third mode," taking counsel from the wise, and finally, counsel from anyone as long as the prince does the asking. Now it seems that this entire discussion has ended in a complete repudiation of its starting point and its replacement with "a new rule that never fails": "a prince who is not wise by himself cannot be counselled well." It is in particular the inability to overcome the problems with truth telling, the only means of countering flattery that seems to decide the issue. *Parrhesia* may solve the plague of flattery but at the price of undermining the authority of princes by elevating counselors, by instituting a diversity of contradictory advice, and by not overcoming the character of the prince (who may be prudent but is too needy for the affection of others). The rule that never fails, "a prince who is not wise by himself cannot be counselled well," seems to question the usefulness of advisors altogether—why would a wise prince seek counsel at all, except in the most trivial sense of being provided with facts and detailed circumstances?

It is true that Machiavelli acknowledges an exception to this rule: "unless indeed by chance he should submit himself to one person alone to govern him in everything, who is a very prudent man." Yet this exception proves to be fatal for the prince: "In this case he could well be [counseled well], but it would not last long because the governor would in a short time take away his state" (P 23, 95). With this observation, Machiavelli outlines how this situation cannot be remedied. A prince who is not wise, according to Machiavelli, cannot usefully take counsel from many, assuming that one can have many "very prudent" counselors because such a prince will "never have united counsel, nor know by himself how to unite them." Moreover, each counselor will "think of his own interest," and the prince will be unable to "know how to correct them or understand them." The reason for this is that "men will always turn out bad for you unless they have been made good by necessity." Thus Machiavelli denies the possibility of disinterested, "scientific," or even public-spirited advice—all, and perhaps especially the "very prudent," cannot help but seek rule and authority. Machiavelli concludes the chapter with a position that denies what he asserted in his chapter on secretaries that initiated his assessment of how princes should deal with advisors: "So one concludes that good counsel, from wherever it comes, must arise from the prudence of the prince, and not the prudence of the prince from good counsel" (P 23, 95).

MACHIAVELLIAN ADVICE

Machiavelli's attempt to rehabilitate honor for the benefit of leaders and politics more generally confronts a potentially fatal weakness in the susceptibility of leaders to flattery. His discussion of flattery is therefore an essential aspect of his larger teaching of modern leadership. Yet the lessons we are to take from Machiavelli remain unclear because of the perplexing contradiction in his account, where he seems to endorse advisors as useful and important, while in the very next chapter regarding them as useless and even dangerous. It is possible that Machiavelli simply made a mistake, though the care and subtlety of his writing suggests that such an apparent contradiction in the space of a few pages is not accidental. Rather, in presenting such a contradictory account, and making us think about how to resolve these tensions, Machiavelli in the first instance seeks to present an amusing lesson and practical demonstration of the power of flattery and the inability of truth telling to counter it. That few if any readers of Machiavelli have seen the contradictory position he adopts in the space of a few pages is testimony to his view that either leaders are simply deficient "third brains" or that their vanity or lack of ability will mean they will hear the advice that pleases them, rather than the advice they are offered. In the context of the specific chapters we have examined, leaders who will take the trouble to read these passages will always assume they are first brains, disregarding Machiavelli's view that at best they are "second" brains who understand the first, but much more likely they are the "infinite" others who are useless. They will therefore never take seriously or disregard the dangers advisors may present. Machiavelli thereby shows how *parrhesia* or truthfulness makes little difference if one can skillfully tell the offending truth in a way that vanity will interpret it as justified praise.

We can see this especially in the *Dedicatory Letter*, where Machiavelli shows in practice how he will tell the truth, denigrating Lorenzo while appearing to praise him. As we have seen, though adopting the tone of praise and flattery typical of such dedications, Machiavelli avows that the work does not flatter. But how can he please a prince to "acquire favor" while telling the truth? It is not just the subtle ambiguity of claims such as "I judge this work undeserving of our presence" or even "no greater gift could be made by me than to give you the capacity to be able to understand." Machiavelli's true assessment of Lorenzo becomes clear when we return to his flattering portrayal of Lorenzo's superiority high on a mountain, while Machiavelli is in low places. Machiavelli uses the imagery of Renaissance landscape painting to defend his apparent presumptuousness in giving rules to princes—those who sketch landscapes will be in plains to consider the nature of mountains, and high atop mountains to consider low places, so "to know well the nature of peoples one needs to be prince, and to know well the nature of princes one need to be of the people." Should Lorenzo reflect on this statement, he would see that the claim that only the people know the nature of princes implies that as a prince he does not know his own nature. But it seems that Lorenzo does not know the nature of the people either, because he is unaware of Machiavelli's plight: "And if your Magnificence will at some time turn your eyes from the summit of height to the low places, you will learn how undeservedly I endure a great and continuous malignity of fortune." Lorenzo knows neither the high nor the low—he is one of the "infinite" number of useless brains who knows nothing. What such a disinterested reading of the *Dedicatory Letter* reveals is Machiavelli's amusing demonstration of how he can appear to flatter, and indeed seems to be willing to use it to his advantage, while also telling the harsh truth, albeit in such a way that only those readers who are attentive to his advice and counsel will understand. Machiavelli's suggestion that flattery cannot be overcome by education in virtue, or by the traditional remedy of *parrhesia* if used by the capable advisor, reveals its force in those exceptional or unusual cases where leaders can even become the executors of the will and judgment of advisors who are in effect hidden rulers. Machiavelli's discussion therefore compels us to ask whether the limits to "speaking truth to power" lie not in lack of courage or the integrity of advisors, but rather in the nature of the relationship itself.[26] In doing so, he suggests that flattery may be the subtle source of "groupthink," the perennial danger that shadows all closed or limited advisory assemblies.[27] It therefore poses a profound challenge to those contemporary scholars who think debate, deliberation, and discussion in groups yields good judgment.[28]

But Machiavelli's contradictory discussion of flattery has a deeper lesson to offer. Having reviewed his advice on the dangers flattery poses to leaders, we cannot help but wonder if it is wise or even safe to be counseled by him. The reason for our wariness and reluctance is Machiavelli's clear-sighted assessment of the fundamental tension between power and prudence in politics. Machiavelli shows that the relationship between leaders and advisors even or especially at the highest level is defined by a fundamental disjunction between authority and wisdom, or power and brains—those who have power may not have the brains, and, conversely, those who have brains may not have power. It is this discrepancy, according to Machiavelli, that gives rise to the need for advisors, and all the complexities and problems that ensue in this relationship. It is the disjunction between power and brains that is the basis of Machiavelli's view that advisors are always partisan or can never be disinterested, raising concerns for leaders regarding their reliability. Thus Machiavelli suggests that institutional attempts to rectify deviations from neutrality by enforcing loyalty through bargains and rewards are an inevitable consequence of this disjunction. The implication for contemporary politics is that New Public Management attempts to control senior bureaucrats, and the rise of political advisors, are not simply due to the complexity of modern policy making or ministerial workloads, but are in a sense an inevitable consequence of the asymmetry between power and brains in the relationship between leaders and advisors. Machiavelli's discussion of how to keep someone "good" therefore anticipates and explains Hobbes's solution and the modern "agency bargains" of modern policy advisors.[29] In doing so, he indicates that there is no natural basis for a unity of interest between leaders and advisors, and politics may not be amenable to prudence, thereby challenging whether such contemporary institutional remedies implicitly repudiate as unreliable the "trustee" concepts drawing on personal integrity, the law, and notions of the public good.[30]

The disparity of power and brains also accounts, according to Machiavelli, for the different ways advisors attempt to counter the authority of leaders. The institutional remedies Machiavelli outlines, the pragmatic or agency bargains of contemporary scholarship, will always be vulnerable to the powerful weapon of flattery wielded by otherwise weak advisors. The need to see how flattery is ever present in the relationships between leaders and their advisors, and how it can undermine these institutional remedies, is therefore an important Machiavellian lesson for contemporary scholarship.

Finally, having laid bare the conflict between political leaders and prudent counselors, Machiavelli suggests that the true source of this contest lies elsewhere, in the intractable struggle between the wise themselves. In his consideration of advisors, Machiavelli seems to suggest there is no reliable way of protecting oneself from a "first brain" advisor, so that these individuals should either be avoided, or be acknowledged and deferred to as true princes and rulers. But who exactly are these excellent "first brains," and how can we recognize them? In *The Prince*, Machiavelli praises Moses, Cyrus, Romulus, and Theseus as admirable leaders who became princes by their virtue and not fortune (P 6, 22). He also notes that leaders imitate others, so that "Alexander the Great imitated Achilles, Caesar, Alexander; Scipio, Cyrus." But it soon becomes clear that such imitation is not of leaders, but of what others have written about these leaders:

> And whoever reads the life of Cyrus written by Xenophon will then recognize in the life of Scipio how much glory that imitation brought him, how much in chastity, affability, humanity, and liberality Scipio conformed to what had been written of Cyrus by Xenophon. (P 14, 60 cf P 17, 68)

When Scipio imitated Cyrus, he was in effect doing Xenophon's bidding, just as Achilles, who was in effect a creation of Homer, became a model for Alexander, who in turn was copied by Caesar. Machiavelli here indicates how Homer and Xenophon are the "first brains" who have influenced the lives of some of the most famous leaders. And they have done so not through direct political action, but by writing books that became influential models and instructive works of education for future princes. These then are the "first brains" who, in ruling indirectly, govern the prince "in everything" and in effect are the true princes. Machiavelli, in his famous account in Chapter 15 of how he will "write something useful to whoever understands it," "departs from the orders of others" who write about "imagined republics and principalities" to claim to teach a wholly new teaching: "Hence it is necessary to a prince, if he wants to maintain himself, to learn to be able to be good, and to use this and not use it according to necessity" (P 15, 61). The first brains, such as Homer and Xenophon, as well as those who write about "imaginary republics" such as Plato and Augustine, are the true political masters who rule over all other brains through their books and ideas. In this sense, all second brains are servants and soldiers of first brains in their overarching struggle over the highest principles. In contemporary terms, political leaders who are not themselves "first brains" will always be implementing some "ideology" that they have acquired from their readings or education.[31] Machiavelli's comments on first brains are therefore a reminder of the other type of advisor, not the second brain who will provide immediate and strategic advice, but those who provide a comprehensive account of politics and thereby what it means to rule, not for now, but for all time. In showing the power of philosophic leaders, he also underlines the fundamental discord or struggle that animates them. At the highest level, therefore, we find a contest between first brains over primacy and preeminence. Philosophy, Machiavelli seems to intimate, can never rid itself of the desire for glory.

CHAPTER 8

ANTI-POLITICS OF FAME
AND IDENTITY

D on Quixote, Knight of the Sorrowful Countenance on his old nag,
resplendent with homemade buckler, pot helmet, makeshift lance, on
a chivalrous mission for the fair Dulcinea the farm girl—few can match,
let alone outdo, Cervantes's coruscating satire of the fancies and pretensions
of chivalric and feudal honor. Of course, Cervantes was not alone in questioning the nature of romantic love and aristocratic honor, and the force of
this general critique has culminated in the view that claims for honor are
at least quaint, if not atavistic. That one would duel to defend one's honor
is now considered so strange as to be incomprehensible.[1]

We are all now Don Quixotes, according to Peter Berger (1984), who,
in "On the Obsolescence of the Concept of Honour," argues that the new
world is liberated from the charms and mystifications of honor:

> Modern man is Don Quixote on his deathbed, denuded of the
> multicoloured banners that previously enveloped the self and
> revealed to be *nothing but man*: "I was mad, but I am now in
> my senses; I was once Don Quixote of La Mancha, but I am
> now, as I said before, Alonso Quixoan the Good." The same
> self, deprived, or if one prefers, freed from the mystifications
> of honour is hailed in Falstaff's "catechism": Honour is a mere
> scutcheon. (Berger 1984, 152; footnotes removed)

This new world is in important respects informed by the approach that sought to solve the problem of leaders who were moved by the desire to seek glory and honor. The solution proposed, a form of Hobbesian dispersed leadership that we have discussed above, has been remarkably successful in inaugurating a new politics of peace and prosperity. Yet its very success, evident in all aspects of modern life, reveals with greater clarity the larger implications of such initiatives, especially its unintended effects that reintroduce honor into contemporary politics, albeit in new terms.

In this chapter we examine two of these major unintended consequences—fame and identity politics—to see the challenges they present to modern leaders. Fame is a form of honor uncoupled from excellence or virtue, or, in contemporary terms, "all publicity is good publicity." Of course, fame was known in classical thought, where it was considered a mercurial, feverish, and contemptable perversion or shadow of true honor. Fame without excellence that gave it weight, measure, and proportion was nothing more than the infinite reflections in a house of mirrors.[2] The contemporary world, by contrast, because of the demystification and democratization of honor, is less censorious of fame. In accommodating fame, however, it has given rise to new leaders such as the celebrity who competes with and challenges modern political leaders.

The second unintended consequence of Hobbes's dispersed leadership has been "identity politics" that complicates the way leaders and followers understand, communicate, and show respect to each other. The origin of this form of politics can be traced to the political elevation of the individual that is the distinctive feature of dispersed leadership. But this elevation came at the cost of stripping away or denying any inherent worth or dignity to individuals. Consequently, in the various attempts to ennoble individualism, in the form of Kantian "dignity" and "respect," Hegelian "recognition," and existentialist "authenticity," we find an important source of modern identity politics as a new politics of honor. Yet as we will see, each of these attempts repudiated the previous, and did so by resorting to the transpolitical principles to defend individual worth and dignity.

Though fame and identity politics represent opposing trajectories in modern politics, neither has been able to extinguish the other, so that both coexist and, in their confrontations, complicate modern leadership. Indeed, in important respects, they have combined to reinforce certain modern impulses, such as the questioning of excellence, the role of reason in public deliberation, and the importance of leadership, with a common terminus in modern anti-politics.

FAME AND CELEBRITY

The modern celebrity is in important respects a creature of Hobbesian dispersed leadership that effaced the classical distinctions between the *politikos* or statesman, *demagogos* or demagogue, and *tyrannos* or tyrant. As we have seen, in classical thought, the statesman was a magnanimous leader with exceptional abilities who eschewed small advantages to perform great public acts for the distinction bestowed by citizens who admired his virtue, excellence, and public service. Hobbes's hero, on the other hand, appears to be everyone who authorized the founding of the new state. Hobbes questions magnanimity altogether with his suggestion that tyranny is merely a term of personal disapprobation, so that there may be no real or substantive distinction between the tyrant and the statesman. As he observes, "And when the same men shall be displeased with those that have the administration of Democracy, or Aristocracy, they are not to seek for disgraceful names to express their anger in; but call readily the one Anarchy, and the other, Oligarchy, or the Tyranny of the Few" (L 699).[3] Such an approach questions the motives of anyone who wants to pursue public service or political office. It is a short step from such doubts or suspicions to the contemporary "anti-politician" sentiment that "they're all alike" and that "all politicians are in it for themselves."[4]

Such a reevaluation of the magnanimous is achieved, as we have seen, by reconceiving honor as an "opinion of Power" (L 10, 156). But to the extent that the value of power was determined by the "buyer"—everyone else—rather than the "seller," one's power and therefore honor was ever changeable and uncertain. As fluidity or flux characterized power and honor, both were now in effect uncoupled from virtue or excellence, denying the classical distinction between honor as reputation for excellence and fame as mere reputation or being notable for its own sake (as the ambiguous term "notoriety" suggested). The liberation of fame from its bad reputation—because there is no bad publicity—was accompanied by its elevation as perhaps the preeminent source of power. Power as the present means of acquiring future apparent goods was derived from "Natural Power," such as "eminence of the faculties of body and mind." More significant was "Instrumental power," such as "riches, reputation, friends and the secret workings of God, which men call good luck," and, above all, other individuals who combined were the greatest source of power. "Reputation of power is power," according to Hobbes, "because it draweth with it the adhaerence of those that need protection" (L 10, 150). Moreover, as an instrumental power, it "is in this point, like to Fame, increasing as it proceeds" (L 10, 150). But if the worth of someone is his "Price," "a thing dependent on the need and judgment of another," then perceptions, however well founded or ill, are more important than any sense of "true" power. This means all power now had a twofold aspect, specific sources such as natural and instrumental power (faculties of body and mind, as well as power acquired from these such as riches, reputation, and friends), and *opinions* about these powers. And, to the extent that opinions do not necessarily have to be correct or accurate assessments of power (because there is no "absolute" price), fame now had the potential to be the greatest source of power, albeit of a fleeting or mercurial nature. Fame, how to get, keep, and augment it, was therefore the new game in town.

Fame's new authority, because of its liberation from shame, was accompanied by a concerted attempt to question and thereby undermine the importance and dignity of politics altogether. Hobbes's entire project can indeed be described as the most far reaching and ambitious initiative to depoliticize politics. He does so in a number of interrelated and mutually reinforcing ways. Above all, he removes moral debates about the good life from the province of politics. The question of the nature and justice of the regime in classical politics, the perennial struggle between rich, poor, and virtuous diagnosed by Aristotle as the essence of political contests, is now undermined and defused by redefining it as a subsidiary consideration of the size of the executive (one, few, many) (L 19, 239–40). This approach transforms the state into an uncontested locus of authority that is endorsed by all to secure political peace and stability. Consequently, the state can no longer be a forum for contests over the good life; indeed, it is tempting to say that politics is now a matter of administration, a well-oiled machine whose purpose is a technical exercise in ensuring a contented life. Hobbes's proposal to fix the authority of the state in contract and agreement means, as we will see in our subsequent discussion of patriotism and nationalism, that politics will no longer have any close connection to land, language, ethnos, or history, denying patriotic commitments to defend and sacrifice for one's country. Finally, Hobbes's comprehensive attempts to modify, limit, and redefine theology is in effect his endeavor to remove any transcendent aspects from political life. The Leviathan state is a sort of god, and therefore there is no pious or theological foothold outside the state to challenge its sanctity and legitimacy. Taken together, all these initiatives deny politics and political life any specific honor, dignity, or grandeur. When combined with anti-politician sentiments, this approach makes politics questionable, a source of instability and danger rather than a stage to display human excellence. Such a depreciation and ultimately deprecation of politics is completed by Hobbes's elevation of other contending lives. As Hobbes notes in his famous account of the penury and danger of the state of war, almost all the good things in life derive not from politics but from science, farming, and industry (L 13, 186). Such a focus on industry accounts for Hobbes's attempt to rehabilitate trade, commerce, and exchange from its traditionally low place. Money and therefore commerce, according to Hobbes, is the "lifeblood" of the Leviathan, allowing him implicitly to elevate it over the martial and political that have historically claimed the apex of all societies. As a result, Hobbes's anti-politician and anti-politics approach becomes the new lodestar for subsequent modern liberalism and constitutionalism. It informs, for example, Montesquieu's teaching on republicanism, and Locke's endorsement of comfortable self-preservation, and *The Federalist Papers'* attempt to channel individual ambition through a constitutional architecture to animate and energize the modern commercial republic.

DODOS AND DEMOCRATIC EQUALITY

The egalitarianism implicit in Hobbes's dispersed leadership was in time reinforced by the increasing political salience and influence of democracy with the result that both combined and transformed the way leaders and leadership were acknowledged and deployed in modern liberal democracies. To see how democracy in particular transformed honor and therefore leadership, it is instructive to turn to Tocqueville, a preeminent theorist of modern democracy. In *Democracy in America*, Tocqueville (2000) compares honor in feudal and aristocratic Europe, and especially France, with honor in democratic America. Though honor is found in democracies and aristocracies, Tocqueville argues that it "presents another face" in democracies: "Not only are its prescriptions different; we are going to see that they are less numerous and less clear and that one follows its laws more loosely" (Tocqueville 2000, 596). Aristocratic honor is a complete and detailed code in which all was foreseen and ordered in advance; a fixed and always visible rule for human actions. Because it represented particular needs and was felt by fewer people, honor was peculiar and powerful (598). In contrast, in democracies, all citizens are always on the move, and society modifies itself every day and therefore constantly changes its opinions and needs. As a result, "In such country one glimpses the rule of honor; one rarely has the leisure to consider it" (596). Because of such mixture, ranks are confused, and society, a single mass, can never agree on what is permitted or not in advance. True, there are common opinions, but they never present themselves at the same time, in the same manner and with equal force. "The law of honor exists," according to Tocqueville, "but it often lacks interpreters" (596). Being ill defined, and therefore imperfectly known, it is difficult to apply firmly and certainly. Public opinion pronounces with hesitation; "sometimes it comes to contradict itself; often it holds itself immobile and lets things be" (597). Though ranks differ in aristocracies, they are fixed, with each person occupying a place he cannot leave. There is no hope not to be seen, and therefore blame or praise is unavoidable. By contrast, in a democratic state all citizens are confused in the same crowd and constantly act on each other, so that public opinion has no hold; its object disappears at each instant and escapes it. Honor will therefore always be less imperious and less pressing there, for honor only acts in public view (598). Thus, Tocqueville's assessment of honor in democracies in a "single formula": "it is the dissimilarities and inequalities of man that have created honor; it is weakened insofar as these differences are effaced, and it should disappear with them" (599). Tocqueville therefore suggests that democratic equality is instrumental in destroying the extreme, passionately held, and fundamentally hierarchic notions of aristocratic honor that allowed individuals the means to judge and evaluate each other. The fragmentation in democracies of the common understanding of what is proper for each office and therefore what duties, responsibilities, and manners are required of each person means that what should be praised or blamed, or indeed what is expected, becomes fundamentally uncertain.[5] The consequence of this uncertainty is a residual conception of honor, a weak, confused, and protean expression of democratic praise and blame destined perhaps for oblivion as equality assumes ever-greater influence in democratic life.

Still, democracy does have a conception of honor that has important consequences for modern leaders. Relieved of the ossified codes, rules, and expectations of aristocratic honor, democrats are free to act as they wish, unconstrained by imposed duties and obligations. Democracy therefore allows individuals to be truly themselves, without affectation, pose, or pretense. The democratic dislike of form and formality—the casualness of democracy—is the natural expression of the democratic freedom that is shared equally by all. Because it does not insist on honor and ceremony, it permits, and indeed requires, a certain honesty or authenticity from all citizens. The result is a paradoxical view regarding honor. Honor is acknowledged and considered to be valuable, so that in a democratic spirit it is mandated that all should share it equally. Yet to share equally something that is valuable only when possessed unequally depreciates its worth. This democratic puzzle has been described as the Dodo principle. In Lewis Carroll's (1976) *Alice's Adventures in Wonderland*, Alice and her bird colleagues try to dry themselves after their swim by racing around a lake. After half an hour, when they are quite dry again, the Dodo Bird suddenly calls out,

> "The race is over!" and they all crowded round it, panting, and asking, "But who has won?" This question the Dodo could not answer without a great deal of thought, and it sat for a long time with one finger pressed upon its forehead (the position in which you usually see Shakespeare, in the pictures of him), while the rest waited in silence. At last the Dodo said, "Everybody has won, and all must have prizes." (Carroll 1976, Ch. 3)

To require a race and yet to insist everyone is a winner is democracy's honor dilemma. At its source is the question of whether honor can be uncoupled from excellence. Competition reveals difference in ability and thereby presumably excellence, so that all contests will acclaim participants but inevitably distinguish and thereby honor winners over losers. But the principle of equality denies such distinctions, assuming (at best) that everyone is excellent. Democracies seek to resolve this tension by making all winners. But such a solution, giving predominance to the democratic principle of equality, tends to conceal rather than conclusively resolve the core question, as we can see in all aspects of modern democratic life. It is especially prominent in the major public policy debates that presume or are designed to foster excellence.[6] It also accounts for a curious proliferation of awards and prizes in modern democracies.[7] It is especially important, however, for political leadership in democracies.

MODERN CELEBRITY

The democratic ambiguity regarding honor, valuing it as recognition of excellence yet demanding its equal distribution, reinforced in subtle yet important ways by the anti-politician and anti-politics impulse of dispersed leadership, sustains modern fame. The predominance of fame has influentially shaped the language and concepts for understanding the nature of leadership and the relationship between leaders and followers. As a form of power, it has in effect effaced the possibility of seeing honor as an acknowledgment of leadership excellence and sacrifice for the common good. Fame has also given greater authority to new forms of leadership that vie with modern political leaders. It has dignified those who are merely "famous," making possible the new leader, the "celebrity."[8] A celebrity is a personification of fame—someone who is famous for being famous. The celebrity thereby inverts all aspects of honor as founded on excellence. Though a "star" far removed from the common public, a celebrity is "popular" and therefore a close, even familiar and intimate presence in our lives. True, the celebrity as "A-lister" may lapse into haughtiness and contempt, seemingly returning to or reviving the pernicious hierarchies modern honor sought to replace. Yet celebrity is everything feudal honor is not. Its sparkle and fluidity signal its transient insecurity. And its very precariousness seems generous and democratic—promising everyone the chance of a place in the sun, even if briefly. Though seemingly denying excellence, celebrity is more accurately and generously indifferent to it because its gaze is actually drawn to novelty. It will therefore be easily bored, celebrating the unusual and distinct rather than the excellent. It will instantly bestow the promise of international reputation, and just as quickly relegate one to yesterday's news. For some the noise, flux, and blindness to excellence of modern fame is a product of modern technology fueled and sustained by commercial society and therefore can be safely consigned and limited to the gossip columns and entertainment industry where it thrives.[9]

Yet the ubiquity and influence of modern celebrities are such that political leaders now have to compete with individuals who are better known and often more popular. They therefore have no choice but to accommodate celebrities as an unavoidable fact of modern politics. The close links between Hollywood and Washington are well known, and being a celebrity has proven to be a political asset, as the careers of Ronald Reagan, Arnold Schwarzenegger, and Donald Trump attest. But the phenomenon is not unique to democracies. Venezuela's President Hugo Chavez befriended US filmmaker Oliver Stone and actor and activist Sean Penn, who celebrated his achievements, while funding a film factory and production house *Ville de Cine* or Cinema City to break the "dictatorship of Hollywood."[10] The rise and influence of the modern celebrity has meant that techniques employed by them—the principles of marketing—have in effect come to dominate, if not oust, politics understood as the royal art. Modern product marketing, including "brand" management and advertising, have increasingly been adopted as essential for political success. "Messaging," "signaling," and various forms of marketing campaigns in a world of "optics," "image," "look," "signals," and "narrative" point to political marketing and the consequent personalization of politics, where individual "brands" become much more powerful, and newsworthy, commodities. Advertising and marketing thereby become the mainstay of political campaigning in modern politics, constituting the bulk of the ever-increasing costs of political campaigns, with its attendant challenges to political transparency, accountability, and risks of political manipulation.

POLITICS OF IDENTITY

Dispersed leadership and democratic egalitarianism have made fame a powerful force in contemporary politics. Yet the distinctive aspects of dispersed leadership that justified fame also provoked attempts to rehabilitate a more substantial notion of individual honor that countered it. As became clear to succeeding thinkers, there was something unattractive in the Hobbesian individual whose honor or worth had no inherent source and absolute value, so that its price was determined by others. This sere conception of the individual that sustained fame therefore prompted a series of initiatives to retrieve human dignity and rehabilitate individual worth. Consequently, different aspects of humanity—the ability to be a lawmaker, the idea of mutual recognition, and even the potential for radical authenticity—became the new foundations for both individualism and modern honor. But an unintended consequence of these attempts was a new form of "identity politics" that political leaders now confronted in addition to the politics of fame. We examine the influential concepts of "autonomy," "recognition," and "authenticity" that have come to shape the language of identity politics to see how they sought to repair the diminution of individual honor, dignity, and worth that was the price paid for Hobbes's defense of the primacy of the individual. In doing so, we see how identity politics presents new rhetorical challenges to modern leadership.

RECOVERING AUTONOMY AND DIGNITY

The increasingly powerful calls to respect and recognize the autonomy and dignity of individuals and groups testify to the primacy and political salience of "identity" in modern politics. Though the question of identity has always been essential and unavoidable in politics, there seems to be something fundamentally different about contemporary identity politics.[11] For some, identity has been too often ignored and is therefore an important and missing aspect of contemporary politics that needs to be acknowledged to remedy injustices.[12] Yet for others identity politics poses profound challenges to the success and commendable achievements of modernity.[13] The specific concepts of autonomy and dignity, recognition and authenticity have been influential in contemporary identity politics.[14] To understand their political salience, especially for leaders who need to persuade their followers, it is instructive to turn in the first instance to their origin in modernity, where we find the new conception of the individual.[15] As we have seen, Hobbes's elevation of the subject comes with the high price of the denial of inherent honor, dignity, or worth. Confronted with this grim assessment of individual worth, subsequent thinkers attempted to recover a richer notion of individual worth. One of the earliest and most influential of these was Kant's restoration of individual dignity and autonomy. Kant agrees in important respects with Hobbes's political thought, acknowledging in the *Groundwork for the Metaphysics of Morals* that most people are driven by their inclinations to seek happiness, and to that extent they use each other (and sometimes themselves) as means to their ends, so that everything has a worth determined by their exchange price.[16] Yet this undeniably heteronomous, hypothetical world of necessity could not accommodate Kant's deepest longing confirmed by his experience that rational beings had a sense of duty and therefore morality that pointed to a deeper sense of human freedom. "There have always been philosophers," according to Kant, who have "ascribed everything to a more or less refined self-love" (406, 19). Indeed, he says it is impossible to rely on experience to demonstrate that all actions are not based on self-love, because motives are based on inner principles that are not seen (407, 19). Yet he found it intolerable to think that rational beings were not free to be moral. He therefore proposed a specific use of rationality to show how rational beings are free to choose duty and therefore "good will" over inclination and happiness. Kant's formulation of the categorical imperative defends individual "autonomy" to legislate a universal moral law, thereby confirming the infinite worth and dignity of rational beings who always treat each other as ends and not means.

Kant in the *Groundwork* argues that morality requires that we follow rules or "imperatives" that are "categorical" or "pure," based on a priori reasoning, rather than hypothetical reasoning that relies on "anthropology" or specific circumstances of individuals.[17] There is for Kant only one categorical imperative, namely, "Act only according to that maxim whereby you can at the same time will that it should become a universal law" (421,

30). He then provides in the *Groundwork* three separate representations of the categorical imperative, intended to "bring an idea of reason closer to intuition . . . and thereby closer to feeling" (436, 41).[18] The first is the suggestion that the categorical imperative, because it requires maxims that are to be willed as universal laws, is sufficient as a moral principle. An examination of the subsequent formulation based on humanity as an end in itself shows how Kant implicitly confronts and repudiates Hobbes's insight into the nature of honor as a measure of power, and the worth of individuals as being determined by their usefulness to others.[19]

The argument based on humanity draws on Kant's distinction between subjective ends that rest on incentives, and objective ends that depend on motives valid for every rational being. Subjective ends, because they are determined by the character of the individual, are relative and hypothetical, incapable of providing any universal principles. In searching for an objective end that can be a categorical imperative, Kant argues that man and every rational being "exists as an end in himself and not merely as a means to be arbitrarily used by this or that will" (428, 35). Therefore, unlike objects that have only relative value as means, there are limits on the arbitrary use of rational beings who are ends in themselves and therefore objects of respect. "Persons," according to Kant, "are therefore, not merely subjective ends, whose existence as an effect of our actions has a value for us; but such beings are objective ends, i.e., exist as ends in themselves" (428, 36). That rational nature exists by itself therefore gives rise to the practical imperative "Act in such a way that you treat humanity, whether in your own person or in the person of another, always at the same time as an end and never simply as a means" (429, 36). This principle, which is a "supreme limiting condition of every man's freedom of action," is for Kant derived from pure reason and not experience (431, 38). Kant outlines how all previous attempts at discovering the principle of morality failed because obedience to law, to the extent that it is tied to an interest or constraining force, meant that all actions were due to interest (one's own or another's) rather than duty. Contrary to these approaches, Kant calls his categorical imperative "the principle of the autonomy of the will, in contrast with every other principle, which I accordingly count under heteronomy" (433, 39). With this concept of "autonomy," Kant repudiates Hobbes's core argument that there is no inherent dignity in anyone, or that one's worth is determined by others.

Kant concedes that there is a fundamental truth to the Hobbesian insight into politics and, importantly, his view of the nature of honor. At the same time, he finds this Hobbesian world intolerable—because it denies freedom, morality, and the possibility of immortality. As we have seen, Kant's response is to turn to human reason to determine nonempirical or "pure" insights not only for humans but for all rational beings. This yields the categorical imperative, which demonstrates our autonomy and therefore the infinite dignity and worth of individuals, who should not be treated only as means but as ends. But perhaps what is most telling in Kant's rehabilitation of individual dignity and honor is that it is a "transcendental" claim. Kant concedes that the entire moral edifice of autonomy, of dignity and respect, and its political consequences presuppose or are founded on a notion of two worlds, a phenomenal world of necessity and a noumenal world of freedom whose existence can only be asserted or postulated and not demonstrated.[20] It would therefore seem that Kant's defense of human morality and dignity by means of his conceptualization of autonomy requires a commitment to a world beyond this phenomenal world, a commitment to *transcendental* freedom that can only be hoped for or desired.

RECOGNITION

Recognition is another key concept used in identity politics. Its theoretical provenance can be traced to seminal formulations of Hegel, who makes recognition central to his thought.[21] Significantly for our discussion, in developing his concept of recognition, Hegel confronted and repudiated important aspects of Kant's moral and ethical thought. We can see this especially in the two different critiques of Kant that justified Hegel's new conception of recognition.[22] The first is a direct challenge to the categorical imperative that founds Kant's conception of an individual autonomy that warrants dignity and respect. The categorical imperative, according to Hegel, if it is to avoid the charge of abstract formalism, needs to consider the "alien" or variable and contingent inclinations that give moral decisions their substance and meaning. The unconditional necessity of acting on moral laws can only amount to a form of preaching if it is not given substance and context by institutional and individual circumstances.[23] Related to this is Hegel's challenge to Kant's epistemological claim that we can only know appearances or the phenomenal world and never the "thing-in-itself" or the noumenal. Hegel rejects such limitation of knowledge as "subjectivism." For Hegel, the individual's perception of the world is not merely a subjectivist construction, as Kant suggested, but is always reciprocal and mutually constitutive of the subject's consciousness.[24] Apperception of objects informs the self-consciousness of the subject and in doing so reveals the complex and manifold relations between all things. For these moral and epistemological reasons, Hegel replaces Kant's individualistic *Moralität* with his concept of *Sittlichkeit* or "ethical life."

For Hegel, the rehabilitation of a richer notion of individual honor took the form of recognition. Subjects in seeking to satisfy their desires consume objects, canceling the independence of objects and confirming their inner nullity. Such a process yields short-lived satisfaction and as an expression of individuality does not realize freedom. Consciousness of freedom is only achieved, according to Hegel (1977), when consciousness, in seeking to satisfy desire yet unable to control another consciousness, results in mutual renouncing of coercion and in reciprocal recognition: "*Self-consciousness achieves its satisfaction only in another self-consciousness.*"[25] This is the "Notion of *Spirit*" according to Hegel, so that "What still lies ahead for consciousness is the experience of what Spirit is—this absolute substance which is the unity of the different independent self-consciousnesses which, in their opposition enjoy perfect freedom and independence: 'I' that is 'We' and 'We' that is 'I.' "[26]

These insights into self-consciousness are examined in detail in Hegel's famous discussion of struggle between the lord and bondsman or master and slave in *Phenomenology of Spirit* (B IV, A, 178–96). Hegel's recognition therefore acknowledges the truth of the Hobbesian struggle for honor that requires a checking of its violence. Yet with the dialectic of mutual recognition, Hegel answers Hobbes's denial of honor and Kant's subjectivist recovery of autonomy and dignity. In doing so, he justifies the comprehensive ethical state that provides the conclusive solution to the need of individuals for dignity while acknowledging the supreme dignity of the state.

AUTHENTICITY

As we have seen, the primacy of the individual in modern thought has resulted in repeated attempts at redefining who or what is an individual. Hobbes's protean individual whose worth is determined by others is replaced with Kant's universal rational individual whose autonomy justifies infinite dignity and worth in the noumenal world, who is in turn supplanted by the Hegelian individual whose worth depends on mutual recognition and the ethical state. The final such attempt at redefinition we examine is the authentic individual. Authenticity brings to mind familiar formulations of being "real" or not fake and therefore being true to oneself, sincere, honest, whole, showing integrity.[27] Yet modern authenticity is fundamentally different from these descriptors precisely because it claims to transcend social and ethical codes. To be authentic is rather to find one's own way, to be spontaneously creative in devising one's own self and life. Consequently authenticity is characterized by becoming, self-transcendence, and self-creation.[28] Unlike power, autonomy, and recognition, which can be traced to seminal or unique formulations, the idea of authenticity can be found in a range of thinkers but especially in the writings of the "existentialist" philosophers, who rejected any essentialist or foundational conception of the individual self.[29] Rousseau's seminal critique of the bourgeois as someone always in contradiction with himself, floating between his inclinations and duties—a "nothing"—inaugurated more radical critiques of modern individualism, especially evident in the writings of Kierkegaard, Nietzsche, Heidegger, and Sartre.[30]

But the uniqueness of the individual and the impossibility of devising rules or principles for being authentic meant these authors were compelled to understand authenticity through a *via negativa*, that is, by exploring inauthentic forms of being.[31] Though the Hobbesian subject's struggles over power appeared to resemble the creativity of authentic individualism, the seemingly limitless deference to power and consequent definition by others made such an individual essentially inauthentic. Similarly, to the extent that Kantian individualism endorsed autonomy, it appeared to approximate self-constitutive authenticity. But at its core, the universalism of the categorical imperative denied essential individual uniqueness and therefore rejected individual authenticity. Finally, though agreeing with Hegel that the honest individuals who deferred to the prevailing *Sittlichkeit* subjected themselves to self-alienation, they denied that authenticity could be achieved through Hegel's recognition. Recognition denied authenticity by subjecting creativity and identity to the authority of the "Other."

Authenticity is therefore the extreme end point or radical conclusion to a trajectory in modernity that seeks to preserve the primacy of the individual while recovering or returning to it the dignity and honor it lost but deserves. It culminates in the seeming apotheosis of the ineluctably sui generis individual who at the same time, and in the spirit of Hume, does not seem to exist as an "I." Yet it is not simply the opacity of each individual that makes it difficult to recognize when someone is being authentic. More pressing is the way individual authenticity appears ever susceptible to disfigurement by its unavoidable entanglement with others, so that the apparent uniqueness of each seems to defy any moral, institutional, or organizational structures to encourage and sustain it. How can authentic individuals live in society? Inconclusive answers to these questions mean that, though authenticity is the final articulation of the modern attempt to ennoble the individual, in practice it seems to endorse a tragic view of life where "hell is other people."[32]

RHETORIC AND THE POLITICS OF IDENTITY

Our review of the conceptual provenance of autonomy, recognition, authenticity—those influential ideas of identity politics—reveals important aspects about the theory and practice of contemporary identity politics. Theoretically it shows that at the heart of modern identity politics is a core commitment to the primacy of the individual. In each instance we thus find that, where confronted with a limited conception of the individual, each thinker has sought to repair or renovate its character rather than questioning the primacy of the individual itself. Moreover, as is evident from our discussion above, each such attempt to reconceive individualism to endow it with a richer conception of honor has proven inadequate, vulnerable to a subsequent formulation that has in turn been subjected to critique. This trajectory can also be described as destructive, so that autonomy is a repudiation of power, just as recognition is a rejection of autonomy, and authenticity is a refutation of all previous attempts. The modern attempt to redefine individualism to endow it with honor therefore has not only resulted in contending notions of autonomy, recognition, and authenticity, but each attempt at a more comprehensive formulation has resorted to new metaphysical and epistemological resources to substantiate its critique and insight. Autonomy has required the noumenal world or recognition Spirit, while authenticity has posited a radical *existenz*. In each such attempt to elevate the individual, there has been a commensurate depreciation of politics so that the move from autonomy to recognition and finally to authenticity has resulted in a radically unique individual whose self-creation seems oblivious to others and to political orders and institutions more generally.[33]

The practical import of these theoretical tensions has been an impoverishment in the language and terms of contemporary political contests and therefore new limitations on both leaders and followers. It is not just the way concepts of power, dignity, recognition, and authenticity are used in contemporary politics interchangeably or in combinations, with seeming disregard or lack of appreciation of their theoretical provenance. After all, political struggles will use and improvise tools as they come to hand.[34] But both in scholarly formulations and practical political deployment, the interchangeable use of these terms reveals a deeper political problem with modern identity politics: the significant disproportion between the language and theoretical architecture of individualism and the onerous work it has to do to achieve political change and reform.[35] Identity politics seems to be the constricted modern vocabulary and armature we now use to contest much bigger and more complex questions that range from the epistemological and metaphysical attempts in understanding who I am, to the political debates about who is a citizen, to larger questions concerning the character of politics and what it says about our notions of justice. To see the nature of the challenge identity politics presents to contemporary political leaders, consider, for example, the way authenticity redefines the role of persuasive speech in politics. Leadership requires respecting the honor and dignity of followers, especially by persuading them rather than simply ordering and directing, so that persuasion and rhetoric can be seen to be essential aspects of leadership.[36] An investigation into the way authenticity reconceives the role of speaker and audience in public deliberations and how it depreciates the role of reason and judgment in evaluating rhetoric shows how identity politics complicates leadership rhetoric.

The first and most obvious challenge authenticity presents to leadership rhetoric concerns the striking contrast between the privacy of authenticity and the very public nature of persuasive speech. Authenticity, as we saw, seeks sustenance from the individual and the private. In contrast, all rhetoric is by definition public speech and, in seeking to persuade, will necessarily look outside the self, taking its bearing from the interests, hopes, and desires of others. This movement toward seeking and understanding the disposition of others shows how rhetoric unavoidably makes us think of ourselves in terms of others, so that in appealing to the interests of others we confront our neediness. In this way, the very nature of communication triggers once more the pretense of being someone else but in this case aggravating inauthenticity by its public display. Authenticity therefore questions the legitimacy of persuasive speech but especially public speaking, which shows itself as necessarily corrupting by forcing us to please others. There is therefore something profoundly unrhetorical or even anti-rhetorical about authenticity that has its source in its essentially private character. If true individuality requires a move away from the public to the private, then all public acts are essentially inauthentic. One of the most public acts—political or persuasive public speech—is the most revealing example of the public humiliation that society inflicts on individuals by insisting that they show their weakness and neediness in public displays of begging that all pretend are noble exercises of public service.

We find a comparable challenge by authenticity to rhetoric when we shift our focus from speakers to the audience in public deliberations. In trying to see if the speaker is "authentic," we start with the presupposition that each one of us is unique. Yet this uniqueness makes any judgment of authenticity fraught with difficulty. How do I know you are being "you" if we are all sui generis and by definition special? To meet this challenge, we have to at least initially defer to the authenticity of each other; we have to withhold our inclination to judge and in judging distort or even disfigure the genuine attempts of others to seek their happiness in the wholeness of individualism and authenticity. So our suspicion of inauthenticity, provoked by our insights into the nature of authenticity and the forced public display of rhetoric, has to be in turn forcefully suppressed by that very same insight. As modern auditors of public rhetoric, we are therefore always uneasy, caught between deep suspicion of the speaker, "smelling the rat" of inauthenticity, while at the same time forcing ourselves into a sentimental disposition that hopes to suppress such suspicions, insisting on the individuality and uniqueness of the speaker. This sense of debilitating disequilibrium, vacillating uneasily between doubt and affirmation, makes us more open to the "ugly"—the "natural," the crude, unmanufactured—as somehow more "real" or authentic than the beautiful (which we suspect has probably had a "makeover"). It also encourages us to avoid public speakers and formal occasions of public speaking and rhetoric, seeking solace in the comforting private that releases the tightened strings of our sentiments and allows us to relax and "be ourselves."

The uniqueness inherent in authenticity points to a deeper challenge to rhetoric. If authenticity is essentially about our sentiments, our dis-position, and our feelings, then it is more about *who* we are rather than *what* we say. Such a foundation in an ineluctable "being" seems to make authenticity impervious to reason, justice, and morality, the standards we commonly deploy in judging rhetoric. It issues in a rhetoric that works only on our feelings, one that we cannot engage with in terms that tran-scend the uniqueness of the individual and thereby raise questions of the common advantage or the common good. Such a rhetoric will likely rely on symbols, images, and impressions rather than persuasive speech.[37] But because this possibility potentially subverts the larger ambitions of rhetoric, reducing it at best to self-expression, "performance art," or even amusement, what usually happens is that to preserve rhetoric, it is in effect split into two. Having sundered the question of the character of the speaker from the merits and plausibility of what is being said, a new twofold rhetoric, a rhetoric of authenticity and a rhetoric of persuasion and deliberation, is proffered. The rhetoric of authenticity serves no other purpose than to demonstrate the authenticity of the speaker, whatever this may be in each instance, inevitably vulnerable to the contradictory dynamic we have just observed, seeking to endorse a self-directed, independent, and "real" person who is at the same time a needy individual seeking my attention, consent, and permission. In contrast, the truncated rhetoric of deliberation will appeal to the reason and judgment of the audience and thereby seem to recover the idea of rhetoric as persuasive speech. Yet in doing so it will expose its weakness: it will always be unable to answer the question of *cui bono* or for whose interest the proposal should be adopted precisely because it has chosen to leave unattended the rhetoric of authenticity. Consequently, even when the one part of the new rhetoric proves to be successful, whether it be the rhetoric of authenticity or deliberation, it will draw attention to its missing other half and therefore partial character of its ambitions. Bifurcation of the rhetoric of authenticity and the rhetoric of deliberation proves to be of limited success in defending or recovering a comprehensive art of rhetoric, confirming the formidable challenge that authenticity and therefore identity politics presents to persuasive speech and therefore modern leadership.

BETWEEN FAME AND IDENTITY

The Hobbesian leadership-honor dynamic has allowed us to see with greater clarity the origins of the two distinctive and influential features of contemporary politics—fame and identity politics—that have had far-reaching implications for leadership. Dispersed leadership appeared to have solved the problem of honor by instituting a contractual foundation for politics that presumed a psychology of power and a politics of rational self-interest and calculation. It has, in fact, reintroduced a new politics of honor in the form of two apparently opposed trajectories that gravely challenge the legitimacy and therefore authority of political leaders. Honor as a measure of power yielded and liberated fame, itself a source of power uncoupled from excellence. As a result, fame has made possible the modern celebrity, simulacra of good leaders who vie with them for attention, legitimacy, and authority. At the same time, and dissatisfied with the ignoble foundations of this new approach, there have been attempts to repair the deficiencies of the dispersed leadership approach by restoring dignity to individuals. Yet each such attempt at ennoblement has proven to be insufficient, with subsequent and more ambitious initiatives increasingly appealing to transpolitical and metaphysical principles to defend individual worth and dignity. Contests over identity have therefore reinstituted honor into politics, albeit on grounds that challenge the ability of leaders to engage reasonably with such claims. The limits on persuasion imposed by claims for authenticity are indicative of the new onerous demands mandated by this approach.

What is remarkable about these two opposed conceptions of modern honor is that, rather than negating each other, fame and identity politics coexist, combining in a volatile mix of a modernity that celebrates both a fugitive fame and a heroic authenticity. Indeed, in certain important respects these contradictory impulses reinforce each other. Both approaches, for example, are consistent in their response to excellence, at best neglecting it or seeing it as unique, specific to each individual, thereby depreciating the role of reason and persuasion in politics. Both also question the role of leaders, the first in equalizing and dispersing it, the second in radically restricting leadership on the basis of identity. Finally, both culminate in an anti-politics, the one by avoiding the dangers of political contestation, the other by seeking human worth in increasingly abstract, metaphysical realms. Combined, both present formidable challenges to contemporary leaders and their followers. Rather than conclusively solving the problem of honor, dispersed leadership in fact reintroduced it in more complex and unstable forms, confronting leaders and their followers with a modern politics that is shifting, murky, and febrile. It would seem that the ambition to solve the problem of bad leaders by removing the spur of honor did not appreciate sufficiently the centrality, resilience, and reach of the passion of honor in the human soul.

CHAPTER 9

PATRIOTISM AND NATIONAL PRIDE

"By some unknown sweetness one's native soil lures back everyone and does not allow them to forget it" are the bittersweet reflections of Ovid (2005, I.3.35, 63), exiled far from home, never to return. Home has such a powerful hold over us that to be a homeless stranger seems the cruelest fate. If "home is where the heart is," then all political leaders must necessarily be home lovers or patriots who will know intimately every contour of their place, both physical and imaginary, and must have as their "second nature" the language, history, and traditions of their home. They will naturally be proud of their country and defend it instinctively. Good leadership therefore means preeminently patriotic leadership. Yet what this may entail in practice appears more complicated. For some, our only focus should be patriotism understood as love of country.[1] Others, more critical of patriotism, favor a form of universalism or cosmopolitanism.[2] For others still, there is an attempt to secure a middle ground between these two extremes, but in terms that redefine *patria* as constitution, or freedom, or compassion.[3] Importantly, this entire discussion is overshadowed by the fear of the "blood brother" of patriotism, modern "nationalism."[4] There is, therefore, a deep ambiguity regarding the meaning of patriotism, patriotic leadership, and how it may differ from good leadership.[5]

The meaning of patriotism may seem evident and uncontested in times of present danger, where the safety and security of the country take unambiguous precedence over most other considerations. How American President George W. Bush responded to the 9/11 attacks and what he did to ensure national security became the preeminent measures for judging his leadership. Beyond the immediate exigencies of national security, however, the question of patriotism becomes especially complicated when entangled with notions of national pride (and shame). Consequently, the public perception of leaders' pride in their country, and how they will uphold and defend it, become important measures of their integrity and credibility. Consider, for example, how the politics of patriotism as the politics of honor and shame has been a major challenge for Japanese leaders in their contemporary foreign relations with China.[6] Seeking to prove their patriotic credentials by honoring the heroism of those who sacrificed themselves in the service of Japan, Japanese Prime Ministers Ryutaro Hashimoto, Junichiro Koizumi, and more recently Shinzo Abe, as well as diplomats and legislators, have visited the Shinto Yasukuni Shrine in Tokyo that enshrines and commemorates the spirits of nearly 2.5 million who died in wars involving Japan. As 1,068 of these spirits are convicted war criminals (notably the fourteen Class A criminals who were enshrined in a secret ceremony in 1978), these visits have been decried by Chinese leaders as reneging on Japanese apologies for wartime atrocities, especially regarding the Nanking Massacre.[7] Thus the seemingly unexceptional visits to the shrine by political leaders, either in their private capacity or as prime ministers, are interpreted in Japan as a measure of an individual leader's patriotism, while in the region and internationally they are viewed as a defiant endorsement of past imperialism.[8]

These complex problems concerning patriotism and the politics of honor and shame can also be found in the challenges political leaders confront in dealing with historical injustices, including genocide and colonial dispossession that have the potential to cast their country in a shameful light. Political leaders have had to make difficult choices in addressing historical injustices while accommodating and reconciling them with the demands of national honor. Depending on the nature of the claim and the specific circumstances confronting each leader, the responses have varied from the ambiguous denial of incidents, as in Turkish President Recep Erdoğan's rejection of the Armenian genocide, to partial apologies, as in Australian Prime Minister Kevin Rudd's apology for the removal of children from Aboriginal families, to complete acceptance of responsibility and provision of financial recompense, as in West German Chancellor Konrad Adenauer's response to the Holocaust or Shoah. The politics of patriotic honor and shame have also determined the way these concerns have been addressed, ranging from criminal sanctions to lustrations, Truth and Reconciliation commissions, and constitutional enactments.[9]

Patriotism and pride in one's country link leaders and citizens in a common bond and impose significant obligations and responsibilities on both. Yet for able leaders, such patriotism also provides valuable opportunities in statecraft, revealing the darker aspects of patriotism. The coincidence of the public's powerful desire for national pride and prosperity and individual leaders' love of glory and honor means that leaders will be celebrated not only for protecting their country, but also for glorifying it through aggrandizement. Because international conquests confer benefits on one's own country and citizens while quenching ambitious leaders' thirst for immortal fame, the entanglement of national pride and individual glory proves to be a heady and intoxicating passion that can tempt leaders and citizens to international aggression and conquest. One need only reflect on the glorious reputations bestowed on Alexander the Great and Julius Caesar, who become models for subsequent leaders with mixed talents but insatiable passions, to see the grim aspect of patriotism. In the same way, adroit but unscrupulous leaders may exploit patriotism for domestic personal advancement, as weapons to mobilize the public against those they oppose, especially the moderate and sober, whose prudence can always be mocked as at best contemptible cowardice, at worst treachery. As the leader who liberated Zimbabwe from British colonial rule, President Robert Mugabe exploited these patriotic, anti-colonial sentiments by distinguishing between "patriots" and "traitors," as well as using violence and vote rigging, to keep himself in office for an unprecedented thirty-seven-year reign.[10]

Patriotism and pride in one's country therefore provide leaders with a magnificent opportunity for displaying their noble ambition and sacrifice for the greater good. Equally, however, it is the questionable means for engineering divisions domestically and sating a dangerous passion that celebrates with Triumphal Arches victories gained through international aggression. It was this nexus between leadership, honor, and patriotism and in particular the Janus face of patriotism that prompted each of the three leadership-honor dynamics we have examined to reconceive and redefine patriotism. Classical magnanimity, Machiavellian *gloria*, and Hobbesian dispersed leadership each gave different answers to the promise and dangers of patriotism. Though each approach continues to be influential, the predominance of the dispersed leadership view has tended to dominate our understanding of both leadership and patriotism. In this chapter we focus on this Hobbesian view of patriotism, not only because of its influence, but also because the new conception of the "state" it devised to ameliorate the dangers of patriotism gave rise to novel, unintended forms of love of country, such as nationalism, that have transformed the challenges and opportunities that patriotism presented to leaders.

In the following discussion, we start with the way classical magnanimity reconceived the idea of land and *patria* by moderating its impulse toward restrictive conceptions of citizenship. Socrates's myths can be seen as attempts to introduce and secure the "good" as an important element of the love of one's own that necessarily moves and motivates the patriot leader and citizens. In contrast, the modern approach initiated by Machiavelli ennobled a patriotism that had been abnegated as Babylon in the glorification of the Christian "City of God." His elevation of the republic liberated the possibility of the glory of the founder, ensuring the virtue and liberty of the republican citizens. Faced with these alternatives, Hobbes's dispersed leadership sought to overcome the danger of leaders who would be tempted to exploit their "popularity" and pander to the greed of citizens ambitious for imperial gain by redefining altogether the idea of patria. The new state deflated patriotism by reducing leaders to enforcers of agreements, and subjects to mere parties to a legal contract. Though largely successful, this dispersed leadership solution gave birth to nationalism, an unintended and therefore unexpected amalgam of patria and contract that exacerbated rather than solved the problems of patriotism. The leadership-honor dynamic therefore allows us to see more clearly the source of the new, more volatile notion of nationalism that aggravates imperial ambition in international relations and intransigent xenophobia in domestic foreign affairs, themes we take up in our concluding reflections on Xi Jinping's leadership of China.

CLASSICAL PATRIOTISM

A useful starting point for understanding the nature of patriotism is the classical conception of leadership that sought to defend yet moderate patriotism's reach and influence. "My country, right or wrong" is the patriot's call to duty and sacrifice, but always with the hope or expectation that my country will be in the right. This tension between the good and what is one's own is at the core of classic political philosophy and its understanding of patriotism.[11] In Plato's *Republic*, Socrates shows how our erotic longing for the good and the beautiful has to confront our sense of love of our own, which has its origin in our *thumos* or spiritedness, the powerful source of our love of country. We have seen how Socrates's joke about "philosophical dogs" shows the importance of spiritedness in the soul. It is this account of spiritedness and how it is most concerned with one's body and therefore the city as land that nurtures and sustains the body that explains, according to Socrates, the importance of patriotism and the need for noble lies even in the best city.

Socrates in the *Republic* argues that spiritedness is concerned with guarding or protecting, initially what is uniquely its own, its body, and, by extension or education, what it can regard as its own. In defending the familiar or what it knows is a friend from the enemy, it appears consistent with Polemarchus's definition of justice as helping friends and harming enemies. As such, it is the source of the actions we praise as noble and beautiful, ranging from the protection of family and friends to the defense of city and country. Spiritedness is therefore the preeminently political passion, explaining our wholehearted commitment to those things larger than ourselves, most obviously our country. The beauty of spiritedness is qualified, however, by its darker aspects. Because of the inherent tension between our erotic love of the good and our intransigent will to defend what is our own, there are limits to the openness of spiritedness to reason. Importantly, though, as a mainstay of our conception of justice, spiritedness may often exceed its due measure, especially in its impulse to attribute or imagine intentionality and culpability, which sometimes leads it beyond justified indignation, to intemperate anger, and, in the extreme, blind fury or rage.

These features of spiritedness and their implications for patriotism can be seen in Socrates's famous account of the role of lies in politics. In addition to undergoing extensive selection and training, Socrates admits that the guardians of the best city will have to be told *gennaion pseudos* or noble lies (*Republic* 414e–15c). In introducing these noble lies, Socrates concedes that the best city (and by implication all cities) are necessarily defined by constitutive stories that are not strictly true. But these lies are said to be noble precisely because they moderate and ennoble spiritedness. We can see this in the first lie, that we are born of the earth and are brothers. That we are born of the earth acknowledges the spirited attachment of all citizens and cities to land (as territory, country, soil, earth). Yet the associated claim that we are all brothers ennobles this attachment by asserting an egalitarianism that undermines potential claims of divine or ancient lineage as proof of superior citizenship. Similarly, the second lie, that each citizen has a different metal in his soul, justifies ranking and hierarchy, yet at the same time qualifies it by noting that golden-souled individuals may be born in any family, and therefore the city should be open to their promotion and advancement. The Socratic insight into spiritedness—that it is essential for the sacrifice needed for the city's defense—explains why he thinks noble lies and therefore patriotism are inevitable in politics. There are limits to the extent that a city can be founded solely on reasoning and calculation, or, put differently, spiritedness imposes constraints on the openness of politics to philosophical reflection. Nevertheless, that spiritedness is open to reason allows Socrates to moderate its worst excesses and in doing so shows why classical magnanimity viewed patriotism as politically essential, though morally and philosophically ambiguous and complex.

THE MODERN PATRIOT

The Socratic understanding of spiritedness accounts for why Greek cities were said to be closed and therefore inevitably "waspish" in their disposition. With the notable exception of the Stoics, cosmopolitanism was for classical political philosophers only viable for the philosophical few, if only because attempts to broaden the scope of spiritedness risked another great danger—the problem of talented and seductive leaders like Alcibiades, whose intense longing for glory and honor pointed to grand enterprises, especially imperial conquest. Machiavellian glory, confronted by "imaginary Kingdoms," sought to return to the "this worldly" classical conception of patriotism. As Machiavelli confessed in a letter to his friend Francesco Vettori, "I love my native city more than my soul."[12] Yet Machiavelli's insight that politics is defined by the desire to acquire and is always shaped by the few who want to oppress and the many who long not to be dominated meant that his conception of republicanism was radically different from the classical understanding of the mixed regime. Machiavelli's rehabilitation of glory for leaders, rather than a new conception of the common good, is his major innovation for refounding his new, this-worldly politics. As we have seen, Machiavelli argues in favor of republics over principalities because they preserve the glory of the founder by permitting a variety of leaders with different characters and *virtù* to confront and overcome the variable exigencies of *fortuna*.

Yet, as Machiavelli indicates, that most natural of desires, the desire to acquire, means these humors cannot be confined to the boundaries of a country without undermining the stability of the republic. Machiavelli's republic is not, therefore, the inward-looking classical regime fearful of the dangers of foreign relations. To the contrary, Machiavelli liberates the imperial ambitions of leaders because the ambitions of the few and the stability of the republic mandates the external discharge of humors. An aggressive foreign policy leads to civic health because it lets leaders gain glory without being tempted to turn their ambitions to civil wars, and it provides for the security and property of the many not from redistribution of wealth but through the acquisition of the property of others. Of course Machiavelli is aware of the dangers that confront martial republics. For this reason, he advocates the Roman approach of imperial advancement through partnerships rather than leagues (D II 4.1). He also favors major but brief wars, so leaders can gain their triumph within a year, limiting their ambitions at home (D II 6.2). Importantly, Machiavelli rejects money as a sinew of war—gold cannot find a good soldier, while a good soldier can find gold (D II 10.1). Such a martial republic that secures the liberty of the many while showing due gratitude to the ambitions of the few promises stability and may even be perpetual, according to Machiavelli (D III, 17, 22).[13]

Machiavelli's republicanism returns to the "real" world, and in doing so he transforms the meaning of patriotism. His view that republics, principalities, and sects are "mixed bodies" questions the basis on which we love our country. The naturalness of our acquisitive desire calls into question the uniqueness of our own land and depreciates our commitment to "this" earth; indeed, it seems to regard the whole world as potentially mine. Machiavelli therefore uses patria to fuel martial ambition of the few and love of security and property of the many and in doing so liberates spiritedness from my country defined by boundaries and borders. Foreign policy shapes domestic policy, so that *Roma Caput Mundi* or Imperial Rome, rather than the Eternal City of seven hills, is the new foundation of patria that will inspire and move future leaders and subjects.

STATE AND PATRIA

Hobbes's dispersed leadership took a completely opposed view to the classical and modern approaches regarding patriotism. The radical character of Hobbes's ambition is evident from his attempt to solve conclusively the dangers posed by "glorious gladiators" who are moved by pride and "vaineglory" to wage imperial wars and to oppress their people.[14] His new concept of power and his debunking of honor are important elements of the larger plan that is completed by the creation of a new "state" that denied leaders any support in patriotism for such dangerous self-aggrandizing ambitions.

The radical nature of Hobbes's institutional solution of the state does not become evident until we see how he intends it to replace the forms of government Aristotle's *Politics* famously (and influentially) described as monarchy, aristocracy, and democracy (L Introduction, 81; L 17, 227). Hobbes acknowledges that people will fight over the form of government. For example, love of country can become influential in politics as a source of power, because "Reputation of love of a man's Country, (called Popularity,)" is power, for the same reason reputation of power is power, "because it draweth with it the adhearence of those that need protection" (L 10, 150). Country and the form of government therefore are potentially a source of honor and dangerous pride. Hobbes's "state" is intended to undermine such potential. It does so in three important ways. The first is by reminding us that the state is "Artificiall," of our own making, and therefore designed to serve the specific purpose of securing peace. The state is made for security, and its usefulness is to be judged by this principle. If it cannot fulfil this task, we can unmake it, as it were, and seek another instrument to serve our purpose. Such an instrumental view of the state limits contentions about it. This view is confirmed in the *Leviathan* by an elaborate mechanical metaphor used to represent the state, intended to deny it any authority and dignity it once possessed, whether from divine, natural, or traditional sources (L Introduction, 81). Second, as we have seen, Hobbes rejects the view that there is a qualitative difference between different forms of rule, for example, between monarchy and republicanism. His definition of the state reduces the question of the regime to simply the size of the executive, so that difference between Monarchy, Aristocracy, and Democracy is now the more neutral and prosaic question of how many exercise sovereignty—one, few, or many (L 19, 239). Finally, Hobbes denies Aristotle's claim that the polis is more than a defensive alliance for conducting business but aims for a complete and self-sufficient life (*Politics*, Book 3). The state no longer has a moral dimension for Hobbes precisely because it is concerned not with the good life but with security (L 19, 239–40). In denying the state this moral dimension, Hobbes weakens its affective hold on its subjects and therefore defuses its potency in political disputes.

Hobbesian dispersed leadership therefore attempts to solve the problem of patriotism by stripping sovereignty of all those aspects that may encourage or sustain claims of inherent dignity or worth. Government is literally a fabrication, a legal arrangement of institutions with no overarching moral ambitions. This approach to sovereignty, where politics is reduced to a matter of security and not to the pursuit of virtue, either in its classical or pious sense, means that the state no longer has the potential to provide the locus or source for the struggle over honor and therefore pursuit of "pride" in Hobbesian terms. There is nothing august, noble, or beautiful about the state; it is another "*Automata*," no more than a useful tool to overcome our perilous condition.

NATIONALISM

Hobbes's insight into the dangerousness of the pride of leaders explains why he attempts to undermine patriotism and pride in one's country with his innovation of a contractual, artificial "state." The contemporary influence and reach, both philosophically and politically, of the modern concept of the state would testify to the extraordinary success of this Hobbesian approach to politics. Yet, as we will see below, this success is tempered in two significant respects. The first is that, rather than defusing patriotism, Hobbes's solution initiated and therefore reinstituted a new source of pride in the "state" itself, including the notion of contract and individual rights. The second is that to the extent that this new entity was removed from "one's own," both in the sense that it was not linked to a specific place and because as contract it was universal, it could not sustain a meaningful or potent spirited attachment. Consequently, love of one's own, now ostensibly unmoored from country yet seeking to alight on anything that was not universal or cosmopolitan, readily settled on those things that approximated the country—its language, religion, traditions, history, ethos, and ethnos. Thus, Hobbes's experiment gave birth to an unintended nationalism, a form of patriotism that was now much more volatile and politically unpredictable because it was no longer anchored in the traditional patria or mother-/ fatherland. In this way, Hobbes's new patriotism as "nationalism" issued in a contingent universalism in the form of the modern state, and a radically fluid particularism that was no longer defined and limited by the noble lie of "earth," exacerbating, rather than solving, the political problem of pride. In the discussion below, we outline each of these innovations in patriotism.

DIVINE MODERN STATE

The fabricated or artificial nature of the state seemed to be a powerful reason for denying its intrinsic goodness. Because our handiwork is inferior to us, its maker, and because these products are designed to serve a specific purpose or can be seen as instruments of our own desires, the merits or goodness of our fabrications would inevitably be defined and understood in terms of their usefulness rather than inherent goodness. Though Hobbes attempts to strip the state of any dignity and thereby its status as a source of pride, these two aspects of the state—that it is made and is useful—ironically form the basis for its potential elevation to something admirable, sowing the seeds for its subsequent rehabilitation and ennoblement. That the state is our handiwork may depreciate its dignity, but equally, because we love what is ours, especially those things of our own making, the state's origin as our work will make it admirable. From this perspective, the state is "us" writ large, a comprehensive and magnified articulation of all our hopes and ambitions. But, more than this, in important respects the state is superior to us. Though no more than our handiwork, the state is essential for the enjoyment of our natural rights; more than a useful instrument, it is a foundational device that secures and assures our lives, property, and importantly our commodious living. As such, it is no mere instrument—it is the most important thing we have made. Yet, unlike other instruments, the state is more powerful than each of us. The social contract that made the state has also made me its subject, and therefore in keeping my contract I must now obey this new entity that is overwhelmingly more powerful than I could ever be and is potentially terrifying because it may lawfully kill me. If honor is now the measure of power, then the state is the most honorable thing in this world. It is not accidental that such earthly glory, evident in its power and beneficence, makes this "Artificiall Man" seem like a *"Mortall God."* Thus the state is not only close to the divine, but its very existence indirectly confirms my own dignity as a keeper of contracts and implicitly reveals our god-like grandeur as maker of something that is of "greater stature and strength than the Naturall" (L Introduction, 81; L 17, 227). Therefore the *Leviathan*, a new artificial yet divine creature superior to those created by God, not only ensures an unending commodious life here on earth, but also allows us to share in its immortality, especially in the contemplation of our "laudable actions," where we will delight in imagining now the fame we will anticipate in the future (L 11, 162). Though the state is greater, and in a sense more divine than I can ever be, in acknowledging this very insight, I gain the reflected glory and satisfaction of being its maker and therefore its essential origin or source.

Hobbes did not seek to emphasize these aspects of the Leviathan state. Yet it is these features that were taken up and developed by subsequent thinkers. Consider, for example, Hegel—one of the most influential political thinkers who helped articulate such an elevated conception of the state. Hegel accepts the importance of the social contract state initiated by Hobbes and subsequently refined by Locke and Rousseau. Such a state, which he calls civil society, provides the necessary foundation for individual security and preservation of property. But Hegel is also critical of this conception because, in its instrumental fulfilment of the subjective morality (*Moralität*) and subjective will of its members or the *bourgeois*, it does not sufficiently acknowledge the objective will or universal spirit. The *citoyen*, who according to Hegel is superior to the bourgeois, is only to be found in the modern state where both the subjective and objective will are reconciled in an absolute ethical life (*Sittlichkeit*). It is true that few existing states manifest such a reconciliation, and that the world of religion and art transcends it. Nevertheless, Hegel's state is the final, non-contradictory expression and the completion of the progressive march of God and spirit in the world.[15] In Hegel, the state assumes a god-like stature. It is therefore tempting to regard Hegel as the fulfilment or completion of a line of reasoning that we discerned in Hobbes's initiation of the state. The state as Hegel sees it overcomes a fundamental problem that social contract theorists could not answer, or answered by means of *petitio principii*, namely, why would anyone die for the state? Hegel endows the state with sufficient dignity and moral authority to justify individual sacrifice for the greater good. He therefore claims to have recovered the public spiritedness evident in the ancient polis in the light of modern subjective will.

COLDEST OF COLD MONSTERS

Such apparent deification of the state, combined with the Kantian rehabilitation of Hobbesian rights of nature into "human rights," reinstituted in the state the pride that Hobbes hoped to strip from patriotism. Yet there seemed to be something missing in this new patriotism. It was hard to warm to it. Perhaps it was its premise in contract and calculation—it seemed too instrumentally "rational" to be noble, beautiful, and therefore loveable. Maybe it was because it abstracted too much from all things that made politics so human—it seemed indifferent to the color, texture, and flow of particularity that made traditional patriotism so powerful. The state was too abstract and universal, too cosmopolitan to speak directly to any one people. We can see this in Hegel, who, consistent with Hobbes, regards the state as "neutral" regarding territory, language, and culture of each state. Though Hegel knows there is a specific spirit to each nation, such *Volksgeist* or national character is for him an accidental feature or aspect, not decisive in the formulation of the modern state.

These reservations about the state are strikingly summarized in Nietzsche's telling observation that the state is the "coldest of all cold monsters." In *Thus*

Spoke Zarathustra ("On the New Idol," Part I, 11), Nietzsche provides a detailed analysis and critique of the assertions that the modern state is noble, admirable, and the "ordering finger of God," and argues that they are all lies of what he calls this new monster. Nietzsche's debunking counter that the state is a mere idol confirms the pervasiveness of the view he sought to reject, that the state was somehow divine. Yet his critique also captured the core inadequacy or insufficiency of the experiment that was Hegelian patriotism. The coldness of the modern state did not satisfy the spiritedness that sustained traditional patriotism. Indeed, as we will see, it was this very coldness that issued or resulted in another version of modern patriotism, nationalism.[16] There is of course an extensive scholarship on nationalism, most of which takes a sociological approach to the question.[17] As this scholarship shows, there is a general consensus regarding the modernity of nationalism, though its character and exact origins remain contested. I suggest our examination of the leadership-honor dynamic, and how it has shaped Hobbesian patriotism, provides an important theoretical account for understanding the distinctive features of nationalism.

Nationalism was in one sense a testament to the limited success of the Hobbesian experiment with patriotism. Hobbesian patriotism had learned to shift its focus from the land to more abstract elements, such as the contractual state and rights. Consequently, it could not repair the problem of coldness by simply returning to classical or Machiavellian patriotism. Nationalism was therefore a response to this deficiency in Hobbesian patriotism, a return from the "state" to traditional patriotism but on a new modern basis. This meant retaining the Hobbesian commitment to abstract concepts and principles, with the consequence that nationalism could be founded on a number of general conceptions that were at the same time unique and specific to each country, whether it was culture, language, or race. We can see this in the early advocates of different forms of nationalism who saw in it a necessary improvement on the concept of the state.[18] But unlike classical patriotism, nationalism's new attachments were no longer limited, moderated, or bound by ties to "land" or territory. This meant nationalism, both in its shift of attachment and in its vehemence or ardor, was much more volatile than either classical or Hobbesian patriotism. It is in this sense that nationalism represents both the success and failure of the Hobbesian experiment to moderate spiritedness and honor in politics, as is evident in the contemporary responses to nationalism. Having experienced the power and destructiveness of nationalistic movements in the twentieth century, modern students of nationalism have been unsure in their response, with most attempting to return nationalism to its origins in Hobbesian patriotism.[19]

CONTEMPORARY PATRIOTIC LEADERSHIP

Our examination of patriotic leadership through the lens of the leadership-honor dynamic has revealed the origins of the different and contending notions of patriotism. Though Hobbesian dispersed leadership with its attendant notion of the social contract has come to predominate in contemporary politics, it is clear that the other approaches persist, especially nationalism, which casts its dark shadow over all modern states. To see the complex interrelations between these different notions, and the formidable demands—and opportunities—they present to leaders, we conclude this chapter by examining the leadership of China's Xi Jinping. Xi is a valuable case study not only because of the increasing influence of China in contemporary politics, but also because seismic changes in Chinese politics allow us to see with greater clarity the complex and ambiguous role of patriotism in Chinese domestic politics and foreign affairs.

Xi Jinping was elected to the post of general secretary of the Communist Party of China (CPC) in 2012, and president of the People's Republic of China and chairman of the Central Military Commission in 2013. Since assuming office, Xi has consolidated his power by creating and leading "Central Leading Groups" that bypass existing institutions and through his popular anti-corruption campaigns. In 2017, "Xi Jinping Thought" was incorporated in the Party Constitution, and in 2018 the National People's Congress removed term limits for the president and vice president and reappointed Xi, now in effect president for life. Described as "paramount leader" and given the title of "Core Leader" by the CPC in 2016, Xi has become one of the most powerful leaders in modern Chinese history, raising questions concerning his own ambitions and what he hopes to achieve in China.[20] For some, his consolidation of power recalls Mao's cult of personality and points to his ambitions to be a modern emperor. For others, he is a leader who has concluded that strong leadership and rule by the CPC is essential for the next phase of China's development, and therefore all his actions facilitating such a transition mark him as a true patriot. Patriotism, and how it is both an opportunity and a burden, is therefore an important question for evaluating Xi's and China's intentions and ambitions. It is in this context that we see the different conceptions of patriotism—as classical patria or land, Hobbesian contract, and modern nationalism—being deployed to further Xi's and China's political goals and aspirations.

China as "motherland" or "sacred" territory that must be secured and defended is an important form of patriotism for Xi and the CPC.[21] The CPC regularly claims it was the great defender and liberator of China from the imperial aggression of European powers and later by Imperial Japan.[22] This understanding of China's recent history has resulted in the strategic use of patriotism and shame in "Patriotic Education Campaigns" that have emphasized China's "one hundred years of humiliation" at the hands of both Europeans and the Japanese, the insistent demands for apologies for such actions, and the aspirations to recover China's rightful place on the world stage.[23] China's hosting of the 2008 Olympics, the 2009 National Military Parade, and the 2010 Shanghai Expo were intended to celebrate its great cultural and technological achievements and to show a resurgent China on the world stage. For Xi, China as territory has justified his significant investment in the military. He has relied on patriotism to claim islands in the South China Sea and mount an assertive claim over the so-called nine-dash territory.[24] Land is also an implicit foundation of his major One Belt One Road initiative, ostensibly an extensive international network of land and sea routes reminiscent of the ancient Silk Roads to facilitate cooperation and trade, yet notable because all routes emanate from and terminate in territorial China.[25] This emphasis on land has also made Xi vulnerable to accusations regarding its treatment of Tibet and the Xinjang in western China as well as leading to international tensions with respect to the status of Taiwan and Hong Kong as Chinese territory.[26] Significantly, territory has also exposed Xi to concerns regarding the treatment of the land, especially environmental degradation and the citizens' access to clean water, air, and food, a disturbing aspect of the otherwise extraordinary economic development and prosperity.

Chinese patriotism as defense and acquisition of land or territory coexists, however, with another powerful view of China. China as a "state" is indebted to the Hobbesian concept of patriotism, though modified by Hegelian and subsequent Marxist principles, as is evident from its Constitution. This defines China as a "socialist state under the people's democratic dictatorship led by the working class and based on the alliance of workers and peasants" (Article 1). China as a socialist state has been the bulwark and justification for the CPC. But the legacy of Mao's rule, especially the Great Leap Forward and the Cultural Revolution, as well as Deng's economic reforms starting in 1978 have profoundly challenged the legitimacy of the socialist state. The "three belief crisis"—crisis of faith in socialism, crisis of belief in Marxism, and crisis of trust in the party—has been a problem not only for the CPC but for Xi personally, who as the son of the Communist revolutionary Xi Zongxun is considered a "princeling."[27] Xi has therefore faced the hard choice of being challenged by those on the "New Left," who decry the injustices and oligarchic exploitation inaugurated by the Deng era and long to return to what they consider the golden era of Maoist fairness and equality, and "Charter 08" liberals who lament the destruction and desolation of the Mao years and want to complete Deng's revolution by introducing multiparty democracy, separation of powers, judicial review, and liberal rights. Faced with such formidable yet opposed and irreconcilable forces, Xi has decided to negotiate an uncertain course between them. He has therefore invested everything in the legitimacy of the Party by defending Mao's legacy and the CPC as the great defender of Chinese socialism,[28] while retaining the role of modern markets and private property as essential for the future prosperity of China.[29] It is difficult, however, to discern the extent to which Xi means to defend the legitimacy of socialism because he endorses it ideologically and the extent to which it serves his personal advantage. Xi's popular anti-corruption campaigns, his insistence that the party cadre must act morally, are clearly intended to present socialism in a new light. Yet they were also deployed by him to attack his enemies and consolidate his power. Similarly, Xi Jinping Thought may represent his attempt to reinvigorate socialism with Chinese characteristics, but it has also allowed him to add his name to those of Mao, Deng, and Jiang, effectively securing his authority. The use of socialism in this way is fraught with theoretical and practical difficulties. Theoretically, there is the enduring puzzle of what socialism with "Chinese characteristics" means and how to reconcile the role of the Party with the sovereignty of the people and rule of law enshrined in the Constitution. Practically, the difficulties include the need to censor minor or trivial matters, such as the disparagement of Xi as "Pooh Bear," or major matters, notably the 1989 Tiananmen Uprising and regular protests by citizens, not to mention instances of endemic corruption due to family connections and Party affiliation. Though Xi has wagered most of his political capital on the vision of China as a socialist constitutional state, it is perhaps the formidable nature of these challenges that has tempted him to experiment with a different version of Chinese patriotism: nationalism.[30]

The phrase "China Dream" was first used by Xi during a visit to the National Museum of China on November 29, 2012, where Xi and his Standing Committee colleagues were attending a "national revival" exhibition.[31] Since then, the phrase has become Xi's distinctive, quasi-official aspiration for "great rejuvenation of the Chinese nation," which means "achieving a rich and powerful country, the revitalization of the nation, and the people's happiness."[32] Reminiscent of the "American Dream," the concept has tended to emphasize not individual improvement and opportunity but instead has been linked to the rejection of the so-called *tao guang yang hui* doctrine—to "coldly observe, secure our positions, cope calmly, conceal our capabilities and bide our time, keep a low profile, never take the lead and make a contribution"—in favor of a more assertive revival of the Chinese nation or people.[33] As such, the China Dream seems to vault over the notions of territory and constitution to appeal directly to the people's hearts. The dream of recovering China's once proud dominance in the world, repairing injustices and slights to acknowledge the thousands of years of Chinese contribution to the arts and sciences, and pushing back against Western imperialism to assert a Chinese identity and ethos is the heady nationalist vision now implicit in these formulations. But like all these images and appeals, close examination dispels their charm and force. China Dream remains powerful as long as the question of what China *is* remains unresolved. Is China constituted by its terrain, famously depicted in its unique paintings? Is it the Han people, even though the preamble to the Constitution rejects "Han chauvinism"? Perhaps China is fundamentally a culture, informed by Confucianism, Legalism, Daoism, and Buddhism along with the *pǔtōnghuà* or "Standard Mandarin" that the numerous CPC-funded Confucius Institutes celebrate and export around the world. Equally unclear is what the Dream represents: Is it "a moderately prosperous society" that implicitly denies communist aspirations? Is it a search for Chinese respect and dignity? Perhaps it is the renaissance of China as an imperial "middle kingdom"? Whatever the core, Xi's recourse to the "China Dream" is in an important sense his acknowledgment that patria as land and as socialist state may be insufficient in contemporary politics. It therefore represents his attempt to use modern nationalism to secure his place and advance his larger agenda that cannot always be achieved by relying solely on his own "personality," on security and prosperity, or on socialist ideology. "China Dream" therefore shows the complexity of the politics of patriotism; how it confronts both leaders and citizens with a powerful vision that unites, while at the same time making possible contests as to what one's country is and why we should sacrifice for it. As the case of Xi and China demonstrates, pride in one's country is both an ennobling and a dangerous passion for both leaders and their followers.

PART 4

CONCLUSION

CHAPTER 10

NOBLE AMBITIONS, DANGEROUS PASSIONS

The fabulous stories of the Arabian Nights, with kings and viziers, djinns and demons, flying carpets, and talking animals have captured the world's imagination for centuries.[1] Less well known, however, is the larger context of these stories and what they were intended to achieve. In the prologue to *The Thousand and One Nights*, we are told of King Shahrayar, who is so enraged with the infidelity of his wife and slave girls that he resolves never to endure such treachery and indignity again, vowing to spend each night with the daughter of a merchant or a commoner and have her put to death next morning. It is said that he continued to do this until "all the girls perished, their mothers mourned, and there arose a clamor among the fathers and mothers, who called the plague upon his head, complained to the Creator of the heavens, and called for help on Him who hears and answers prayers" (Haddawy 1990, 14). Confronted with this situation, Shahrazad, daughter of the vizier to the king, proposed to her father, "I would like you to marry me to the King Shahrayar so that I may either succeed in saving the people or perish and die like the rest" (15).

Shahrazad was a remarkable woman who had

> read the books of literature, philosophy, and medicine. She knew poetry by heart, had studied historical reports, and was acquainted with the sayings of men and maxims of sages and kings. She was intelligent, knowledgeable, wise and refined. She had read and learned. (14–15)

163

Shahrazad's exemplary character and extraordinary achievements, and the likelihood of her fate, naturally made the vizier try hard to persuade his daughter against this plan. Yet, to his increasing distress, Shahrazad persisted in her request until the vizier approached the king, who was astonished with his proposal but readily accepted.[2] That night when King Shahrayar took Shahrazad to bed she started crying, asking if she could say goodbye to her sister Dinarzad before daybreak. Dinarzad was sent for and spent the night under the bed, and as the night wore on, and after the king was satisfied, she asked, as previously instructed, "Sister, if you are not sleepy, tell us one of your lovely little tales to while away the night, before I bid you good-bye at daybreak, for I don't know what will happen to you tomorrow." When the king gave his permission, Shahrazad began telling her first story, an account of a merchant and a demon. But at dawn, just as the demon in the story raises his sword to kill the merchant to avenge his son's death, Shahrazad fell silent. Burning with curiosity to hear the rest of the story, the king decided to spare Shahrazad another night. And so, each night at the request of the king, Shahrazad would continue to tell one of her extraordinary stories, and each dawn the king would vow not to kill her until he could hear the rest of the story in the evening. In this way, Shahrazad told stories for two hundred and seventy-one nights.

The Thousand and One Nights shows how kings and political leaders more generally are moved by the longing for distinction and how this passion can have dangerous political consequences for both leaders and their subjects. King Shahrayar is so sensitive to the indignity of being cheated that he is willing to punish not only those who shame him, but in anticipation anyone who comes close to him, resulting in cruelty and injustice to innocent individuals and ultimately undermining the legitimacy of his rule. As we can see from the prologue, Shahrazad takes an extraordinary risk in deciding to spend the night with the king. She does so for her own sake (her father is vizier, so her family's prospects are bound up with the king's) and for the welfare of people in the kingdom. Yet what is perhaps more remarkable is her confidence that the king's curiosity or erotic longing in hearing stories would override his anger, allowing her the opportunity to tell tales that reveal in various forms how leaders seek honor and the consequences of succumbing to its charms and dangers. Each of these accounts therefore represents the wise Shahrazad's instructions in good leadership, moderating and ennobling the king's love of honor by showing how he can solicit and secure greater honor by eschewing fear and terror in favor of exemplary deeds of public service and benefaction.[3] We can only presume that Shahrazad must have judged that the king was open to this form of education.[4] And of course with the final story we too are tantalized, unsure of how successful Shahrazad has been with her education, though there is a tradition that suggests she went on to become the king's wife, bearing his children and in effect assuming the responsibility of the king's consort and wise counselor for life.

The color and drama of *The Thousand and One Nights* provides a charming education in leadership, showing how leadership and honor are mutually constitutive. It also instructs on the ideal form of this relationship, revealing a Socratic understanding of the ennobling and potential dangerous character of honor, with a crucial role for education in ensuring statesmanship. This Socratic approach makes us see more clearly the radical nature of the alternatives we have discerned regarding the subtle and dynamic relationship between leadership and honor. Both Machiavellian glory and Hobbesian dispersed leadership approaches accept the need for education, yet each proposes a fundamentally different lesson for leaders. Machiavellian glory endorses the classical premise regarding the primacy of honor for leaders, but rather than moderating the longing for glory, it seeks to liberate it, discerning in its untrammeled flow the only mediating passion between those who seek distinction above all, and those who want to be left alone in safety and security. By contrast, the dispersed leadership of Hobbes is ironically much more ambitious, educating us to calculate what is in our interest, warning us away from pride as a feverish ailment of the few that can be purged for the welfare of all.

In this book I have argued that leadership and honor are mutually constitutive and that this leadership-honor dynamic influentially defines major aspects of contemporary politics. In the close scrutiny and explication of three seminal conceptions of this dynamic, I have shown how each offers a radical critique and alternative to the others, and in doing so intimates the promise of not only good leadership but also the best political ordering. In detailing the arguments of each approach, I have presented their theoretical provenance and attempted to depict with precision where these theoretical contests meet, confront, and engage. These theoretical reflections in the second part of the book have in turn formed the basis for reflecting on major contemporary political challenges in part 3, allowing us to interrogate the merits of various ambitious claims of each approach, and, importantly to see if these perspectives yield new useful insights into formidable and enduring problems. Consequently, our discussion has ranged from the examination of the contemporary views on transformative and transactional leaders; to the ambitions of individual founders; the relationship between leaders and their advisors; the broader questions concerning fame and identity that inform and shape the relations between leaders and followers; to overarching questions about how national pride in the form of patriotism and nationalism both fortifies and constrains leaders both domestically and in foreign affairs. In each case, our leadership-honor dynamic lens has yielded new insights into contemporary political problems. Our examination of transformative and transactional leadership has traced the distinction to classical magnanimity. The study of Singapore's Lee Kuan Yew has shown that his "idealistic" leadership is indebted to both Machiavellian glory and classical magnanimity. The importance of honor for leaders has also disclosed their vulnerability to flattery by those closest to them and thereby challenged the possibility of a common good and the feasibility of the philosopher king. The influence of dispersed leadership has shown the power of modern anti-politics and thereby the divergent responses of fame and identity politics that present modern leaders with complex challenges in attempting to appeal to and persuade their followers. Finally, love of country, as patria, the state and as modern nationalism, shows the formidable influence of pride, honor, and shame in its largest signification, arming leaders with new resources for persuading their followers while also imposing stringent and often unyielding limits on their authority, as we can see in the case of China's Xi Jinping.

In addition to such specific insights, these accounts taken together reveal a complex picture, where the classical, Machiavellian, and dispersed leadership approaches continue to shape our understanding of political thought and practice, vying for authority and influence. This observation has to be tempered, however, by the contemporary predominance of the dispersed leadership approach, whereby honor is either neglected, reduced to calculable interest or, if acknowledged, is seen as politically pathological. This prevalence would seem to endorse the theoretical truth and political merits of the dispersed leadership approach, but upon closer inspection reveals that such dominance has come at cost. Dispersed leadership has succeeded in forgetting honor, and in doing so has obscured the complex relationship between leadership and honor and contributed to our incapacity to recognize its political salience. It has disregarded or neglected, for example, the powerful force of love of honor for both leaders and followers, and how such a passion can be a spur to noble ambition and sacrifice for both founding and defending nations. In addition to obscuring or even effacing the pertinence of honor in politics, the success of dispersed leadership has also issued in unintended and unwelcome consequences. The politics of fame and its counter, politics of identity, favor a modern anti-politics, just as nationalism is the dangerous and unforeseen outcome of attempts to mitigate the unscrupulous use of patriotism by ambitious leaders. These limitations suggest that the ostensible success of dispersed leadership in extirpating dangerous honor conceals in important ways honor's continuing political vitality, reasserting itself in contemporary politics in more complex and potent forms, justifying our posing the question of honor to confront and engage profound, enduring, and often intractable political questions. In these concluding remarks, it may be useful to indicate three important areas—innovation, moral leadership, and democratic resilience—where the question of honor, and the leadership-honor dynamic we have explored in the book, may provide such new conceptual purchase and practical insights.

The nature of political innovation is an enduring and significant question. The Ship of Theseus, a thirty-oar boat that Athens' founder Theseus used to save the youth of Athens from the Minotaur, was recognized as such even though after several centuries of repair few of its original timbers remained the same (Plutarch, *Theseus* 23, 1). One need not endorse Heraclitus's famous claim that one can never step twice into the same river to acknowledge the ubiquity and subtlety of change. Certainly individuals play an important role in instigating or resisting political change. Yet there are larger forces at play, too, as Pericles indicates in his famous funeral oration where his encomium of Athenian democracy celebrates Athens' daring and innovation, contrasting it with Spartan intransigent conservativism and immobility.[5] The leadership-honor dynamic provides useful new insights into the character of political innovation by showing how honor is an important passion that both drives change and defends tradition. As we have seen, the desire for glory is a potent motivating force for innovation that can lead to progress and reform while risking mere fame and notoriety. At the same time, resistance to change and innovation can also be traced to honor, as doing the right thing to avoid shame and thereby sustaining the noble and heroic defense of tradition. These two faces of honor therefore reveal the influential passions at the heart of change and innovation. The leadership-honor dynamic thereby recasts the debates on the meaning of progressive and conservative and does so comprehensively, looking both at individual inclinations of leaders and followers while comprehending the larger institutional, cultural, religious, and historical contexts that, in defining both the admirable and shameful, shape the ambit and pace of permissible change.

The leadership-honor dynamic also provides a new approach to understanding moral leadership. There is an enduring fascination with the hope and promise of a "strong" leader who is real or authentic, who defends the many from the predations of "elites," and acts resolutely before seemingly obdurate or endemic problems, whether it be unemployment, corruption, or international security. Such a desire for a statesman who is also a moral leader is understandable in representative parliamentary democracies where most politicians seem venal or self-serving at best, corrupt at worst. But how can one distinguish these strong leaders from "strongmen," who appear above the law and moral constraints and whose main ambition is self-aggrandizement? The contemporary understanding of leadership, to the extent that it is dominated by the dispersed leadership approach, does not arm us with the necessary language or theoretical architecture for making these distinctions precisely because it regards all individuals as power seekers. Yet as the various formulations to capture such strongmen leaders—as "populist," "dictators," or "authoritarians"—suggest, there is a nuance and complexity here that warrant closer examination. Such an exploration is certainly not aided by the variety of terms such as "hybrid," "semi-authoritarian," "dictatorship," and "totalitarian" to capture those regimes that are not simply democratic. A recovery of honor as both a dangerous and ennobling passion that moves leaders would therefore provide a new and valuable insight into the character of modern tyrants and the nature of modern tyranny. It would, for example, distinguish the old-fashioned kleptocrat from the pious zealot and the ardent ideologue.[6] In doing so, it would afford a more subtle approach to dealing with such leaders and their regimes beyond the now dominant and competing "realism" of appeasement and accommodation and the "idealism" of military interventions to promote democracy and protect vulnerable citizens.

Finally, the rise of "smart" authoritarian leaders around the world has coincided with a crisis of confidence within modern democracies.[7] Disenchantment with representative politics and political parties and especially career politicians now seen as mercenary and self-interested has given rise to populist leaders and parties that are directly challenging the core premises of liberal freedom and toleration, the integrity of elections, the credibility of the free press, the independence of the courts, and the role of elected representatives.[8] This fascination with and longing for an authentic or genuine leader who understands us and our plight, who will solve all our problems and save us from mendacious opportunists and entrenched "elites," is the ever-present challenge to democratic politics. The rise of populists parallels a general neglect of those leaders who dedicate their lives to public service to pursue the common good. Modern democracies, fearful of the dangerously ambitious few, appear to leave little scope to acknowledge and honor those good leaders who are essential for democratic rule. They therefore present obstacles to all those who want to dedicate themselves to public welfare while encouraging the "machine men" who see politics as a career rather than a vocation.[9] Understanding the leadership-honor dynamic and the importance of honor for democratic leaders is therefore an essential starting point for ensuring the civic health of modern democracies that need good leaders but tend to neglect them. It especially reminds us of the need to accommodate the best or exceptional leaders whose vision and ambition aspire to grand causes, enterprises, and prizes of distinction, and whose neglect in modern democracies may tempt them to seek the satisfaction of glory not by defending but enlarging and distorting offices or even overturning the laws and the constitution.[10] Doing so also highlights the equally important responsibility to recognize and acknowledge the noble sacrifice of ordinary citizens who will defend democracy by standing up for its core principles.[11]

Leaders, according to Aristotle, seek honor because it is the greatest of external goods we assign to the gods, the prize conferred on the noblest people and sought by people of worth (*Nicomachean Ethics*, 1123b 15). In seeking honor, leaders therefore aspire to the highest nobility, a form of divine transcendence. Yet in pursuing such noble ambitions, they expose mundane politics to the most dangerous political passion. How leadership and honor are mutually constituted and defined, and the danger and promise they hold for divine and quotidian politics, is the profound question of honor we have posed and sought to answer in this book.

NOTES

CHAPTER 1

1. See generally Kane and Patapan (2012, 151–68).

2. This became one of five Solas by the Protestant movement: *sola gratia* (by grace alone), *solo Christo* (on the basis of Christ alone), *sola fide* (through the means of faith alone), *soli Deo gloria* (to the ultimate glory of God alone), *sola Scriptura* (as taught with the final and decisive authority of Scripture alone).

3. For a general overview of these different approaches, see Rost (1993); Schedlitzki and Edwards (2014), and in particular Elgie's (2015) useful distinction between the positivistic, constructivist, and scientific realist ontological and episte-mological approaches.

4. See Becker (1976, 5); Lazear (2000, 99–146). On the importance of history and economics, see Gruber (1983); Seligman (1902).

5. Compare, for example, Thomas Carlyle's (1840) *On Heroes, Hero Worship and the Heroic in History* with Herbert Spencer's (1873) critique of "great man" approach in his *The Study of Sociology* and more generally Bentley (1969). Significant though more difficult to discern is the influence of *Führerprinzip* on contemporary debates of "strongman" leadership.

6. The *Oxford Handbook on Leadership* (2013) has no references to "honor," five to recognition (66, 106, 109, 132, 215), two passing reference to prestige (251, 329), four to esteem (in the context of self-esteem or self-motivation) (72, 73, 86, 138), one to glory (as "self-glory": 446). The *Oxford Handbook on Political Leadership* (2014) has four passing references, mostly as quotes, to honor (16, 38, 183, 504), five to recognition, three of which refer to selection of leaders (122, 334, 583, 589, 674), three to prestige, all quotes (29, 149, 441), three to esteem (as self-esteem, equal esteem, and narcissism) (78, 136, 336), and an extensive discussion of glory, but in the context of the pathology of narcissism (33–34, 336–37, 343).

7. See Greenstein (2009, 4–5) on the prestige of office, Elgie (1995) on ambition. On personality types, see Harold Lasswell (1930), *Psychopathology and Politics*; Barber (1972); and the recent five-factor model (FFM) (Elgie 2015, 121–25).

8. See Ospina and Sorenson (2007) and Winkler (2010) on the premises and defining characteristics of these new approaches.

9. See Bligh (2011) for an overview, Kelley (1992) and Kellerman (2008, 2012) for a typology of followers.

10. Encompassing a range of approaches, including shared leadership, ethical and authentic leadership, social identity, and relational and social construction theories of leadership.

11. Drawing on post-structuralism, feminist, and critical management scholarship (Collinson 2011).

12. Rost (1993) defines the new approach as a "post-industrial" paradigm, based on a noncoercive relationship between leaders and followers.

13. Haslam, Reicher, and Platow (2010).

14. See especially the discussion of "Leaders as entrepreneurs of identity" (chapter 6) and "Leaders as embedders of identity" (chapter 7).

15. These include studies of the different notions of honor in various nations and communities, such as Mediterranean honor (Peristiany 1966), Bedouin honor (Stewart 1994), Southern honor (Wyatt-Brown 1982), Latin America honor (Johnson and Lipsett-Rivera 1998), and Asian "face" (Hu 1944; Benedict 2005; Hwang 1987). On honor codes, see Appiah (2010); French (2003).

16. See, for example, Tocqueville (2000, 596), who provides a subtle and perceptive assessment of democratic honor when he notes in *Democracy in America* that though honor is found in democracies and aristocracies, it "presents another face" in modern democracies: "Not only are its prescriptions different; we are going to see that they are less numerous and less clear and that one follows its laws more loosely."

17. For a history of honor, see Bowman (2006), who argues we live in a "post-honor" society; Braudy (1997), who provides a historical account of the modern lack of discrimination regarding fame; and more generally Stewart (1994) on the collapse of honor. Albert O. Hirschman, in *The Passions and the Interests: Political Arguments for Capitalism Before Its Triumph* (1977), examines the decline of honor in early modernity, while Johnson (2012) assesses the Enlightenment's response to honor by examining the works of Locke and Rousseau.

18. Peter Olsthoorn's (2015) *Honor in Political and Moral Philosophy* examines the role of honor in making us do the right things; Robert L. Oprisko's (2012) *Honor: A Phenomenology* demonstrates how the practice of honor structures all aspects of society; while Alexander Welsh (2008) in *What Is Honor? Question of Moral Imperatives* reminds us that some of the most subtle and thoughtful meditations on honor are to be found in works of the muses.

19. In *The Federalist Papers* (No. 72), Hamilton opposes term limits for the presidency, giving as one of his main reasons the character of the passions that moved good leaders, noting how "love of fame" would "prompt a man to plan and undertake extensive and arduous enterprises for the public benefit."

20. Adair (1974) shows how the American founders' understanding of fame was shaped not only by the influential models they read in Plutarch's *Lives of the Noble Grecians and Romans*, but also by two contending views, which placed at the apex of greatness the *conditores imperiorum* or founder of the state and commonwealth, such as Julius Caesar, or those philosophers-scientists-inventors, such as Bacon, Newton, and Locke, whose benefits are "gifts to mankind" (13–17). Adair notes the various historical rankings, comparing Machiavelli's ranking, which has founders of religions at the top (*Discorsi*, Chapter 10), with Bacon's two versions, one in the *Essays* listing the *conditores imperiorum* and the other in the *Advancement of Learning*, where a sixth superior rank was given to "philosophers" (15–17).

21. In doing so he denies that he is trying "to restore a comprehensive honor culture" as per Bowman, is critical of Krause on the grounds that she "decapitates the phenomenon" by "recommending a new type of honor that disavows any connection with perfection of soul," and rejects Baudy's approach that decries modern fame, yet in his historicism rejects the possibility of learning anything useful from the past (10–13).

22. See Newell (2009) on greatness and leadership; Menaldo (2013) on transformative leadership in international relations.

CHAPTER 2

1. See King (1987), who shows Achilles's influence on Greek poets and philosophers (Pindar, Sophocles and Euripides, and Plato), on Roman poets and statesman (Cicero and Virgil), and on subsequent Medieval and Renaissance thought.

2. Cicero, in *Tusculan Disputations*, (V, IV, 1–3), states, "Socrates on the other hand was the first to call philosophy down from the heavens and set her in the cities of men and bring her also into their homes and compel her to ask questions about life and morality and things good and evil." See generally Berland (1986). Socrates did not write (he seems to justify his reluctance to write by noting the limitations of the written form in Plato's *Phaedrus* 274b–77a). Accordingly, we have to rely on other sources and accounts of who he is and what he said. In this book, I focus on the "Platonic" Socrates because of the extensive nature of the material and its historical influence. On the problem of authorial intent of Plato, Aristophanes, and Xenophon in their Socratic works, see Zuckert (2009). References to Platonic dialogues are to the following translations: *Phaedrus* (Plato 1998b); *Republic* (Plato 1991); *Laws* (Plato 1980) *Symposium* (Plato 1993); *Gorgias* (Plato 1998a).

3. On the nature of the quarrel, see Barfield (2011).

4. For references to Achilles, see *Apology* 28b–31c; *Crito* (44a–b), *Phaedo* (63e–d; 84a–b); and especially *Republic* (386c–387a; 388b–b; 389d–c; 390e; 391a–c), where Socrates criticizes Achilles's view of death, his insolence, greed, and arrogance. Socrates proposes to banish Homer (Rep 398a–b; 606e–607a), and in the Myth of Er Achilles is not reincarnated.

5. See, for example, the Platonic dialogues *Sophist, Gorgias, Protagoras* on sophists and rhetoricians, and *Parmenides* and *Theaetetus* on other philosophers. The entire Platonic corpus can be seen as an intellectual biography of Socrates, starting, for example, with his early years (*Parmenides*), his debates with philosophers in maturity (e.g. *Gorgias, Protagoras*), his trial (*Apology*), and execution (*Phaedo*).

6. Our discussion is necessarily indicative or tentative because each Socratic conversation provides an important though partial insight into the nature of the human soul. Consequently, a comprehensive understanding of Socratic psychology would require a deep engagement and understanding of all the Platonic dialogues, noting in particular how the character of each interlocutor shapes the questions asked and directs the course of the discussion.

7. On the meanings of *thumos* or *thumoeidetic* in classical Greek thought, see Ludwig (2002, 170–220). For a detailed account of the nature of Platonic *thumos*, see Pangle (1976); Pangle's "Interpretive Essay" on the *Laws* in Plato (1980, especially 452–57); and Pangle (2009). On the theme of *thumos* in the *Republic*, see Bloom's "Interpretive Essay" in Plato (1991) and Craig (1994). On the theme of *thumos* more generally, see Newell (2000); Ludwig (2002); Koziak (2000); Tarnopolsky (2010).

8. For a discussion of the contemporary views regarding the "boundaries of the self" and the difference between "oneness" as unity or identity, see Ivanhoe (2017, 1–34).

9. See Zeno's praise of the young Socrates in Plato's *Parmenides* (128c; Plato 1939): "You are as quick as a Spartan hound to pick up the scent and follow the trail of the argument."

10. On the tripartite soul, see in general Craig (1996, 81–103); Irwin (1977, 191–95); Kamtekar (2017); Penner (1971); Robinson (1971); Stalley (1975); Wilson (1995); Woods (1987).

11. On a detailed comparison of Leontius and Oedipus, see Newell (2000, 153–56).

12. See Averroes's (1969, 222–23) discussion of Plato, where he notes that one who minds his own business will be considered a fool and a madman, deficient and small-minded. The citizens praise and call mighty those who rule and do not mind their own business.

13. On this distinction and its implications for politics, see Bloom (1991); Craig (1996, 77ff). The source of the distinction, as we will see below, lies in the greater erotic nature of the victory lover (see Patapan 2018).

14. This is the charge made against Socrates. See, for example, Thrasymachus's claim that Socrates is an honor lover who uses dialectics as a martial tool for victory (*Republic* 335b ff). On the eristic as opposed to dialectical arts, see Plato's *Gorgias* and *Protagoras*. Craig (1996, 104) favoring a Nietzschean understanding of philosophy as a spirited act, a form of will to power and will to knowledge, is forced to distinguish between a base and noble spiritedness.

15. The *Republic*, in its concern with spiritedness, seems to have few kind words for eros. Cephalus calls it "a sort of frenzied and savage master" (328c). It is

true that the philosopher is described as erotic, desiring wisdom (475b–c), "lovers of the sight of truth" (475e), and "always in love with that learning which discloses to them something of the being that *is* always and does not wander about, driven by generation and decay"(485b–e). Yet the tyrant is also said to be erotic, oppressed by love's tyranny (574e), though it would seem that it is sexual desire that is the lawless desire in this case. What this suggests is that to gain a more complete understanding of eros we need to look at those dialogues where it is a prominent theme.

16. For detailed discussion of the *Symposium*, see Strauss (2001); Rosen (1968); Nichols (2009); Lutz (1998); Bury (1969). For a general discussion of eros in Platonic political philosophy, see Ludwig (2000); Nussbaum (1986); Geier (2002); Newell (2000); Price (1989).

17. On Socrates as a natural scientist, see Aristophanes's *Clouds*, Plato's *Apology of Socrates*, and *Parmenides*. In the *Phaedo*, Socrates explains how his initial fascination with Empedocles was replaced by Anaxagoras's "Mind," but only to return to material causes. Thus, Plato's Socrates discovers eros or neediness as well as mind in the soul, and thereby has as his Delphic mission (see *Apology of Socrates*) the attempt to see if his discovery of ignorance is a wisdom that is shared by anyone else.

18. See generally Plato's *Phaedrus* and *Phaedo* and Ahrensdorf (2000) regarding the longing for immortality as an important element of honor.

19. The ladder simile is proposed by the Neoplatonist Plotinus (*Ennead* 1.3.2) and subsequently deployed by Christian theologians such as Gregory of Nyssa, Origin, Bonaventura, and Augustine: see Lesher (2007, 59–76); Patapan (2006).

20. Taken up in the question of the "sublime": see Edmund Burke's *A Philosophical Enquiry into the Origin of Our Ideas of the Sublime and Beautiful* (1757), Kant's *Critique of Judgment* (1790), and William Wordsworth's "Ode: Intimations of Immortality from Recollections of Early Childhood" (1807).

21. Otherwise mundane and unremarkable though admittedly unusual for Socrates, who always goes barefoot (*Phaedrus* 229a; *Symposium* 219e). On Socrates's noble actions, see in this context Alcibiades's account of Socrates at war, where he saves Alcibiades but declines the honor. His retreat at Delium evinces, according to Alcibiades, a courage and boldness that save him and his colleagues (*Symposium* 221b).

22. Not only does his eroticism make him late, but it puts Apollodorus in an awkward predicament, arriving at a party uninvited. Alcibiades confirms Socrates's tendency to think, uninterrupted, with his story of Socrates standing for an entire day, trying to solve a problem (*Symposium* 219e). He similarly withdraws into himself even on his day of execution (*Phaedo* 95e).

23. In the *Phaedo* (67e), in the context of his imminent death by execution, Socrates wonders about the immortality of the soul after the death of the body, suggesting that the only true immortality available to us may be the self-forgetting that takes place when we think or contemplate, so that philosophy can appropriately be called the "practice of dying and being dead." Socrates's extended periods of meditations show both how much he may not need others, and how long one can "die" in philosophical contemplation. This form of immortality, or a separa-

tion from our particular selves, is clearly different from the conventional hopes for personal immortality. See in this context the discussion by Schaefer (1990, 289–311).

24. On the Greek *to kalon* or the noble and the Latin *honestas*, see Welsh (2008, 40–49).

25. The prophecy was that whoever untied the knot of cornel wood on a wagon dedicated by Midas, son of Gordius, would be the next ruler of Asia (see Plutarch, *Lives*; Alexander 18.4).

26. See Borowitz (2005). His punishment was that it was forbidden for anyone to mention his name in speech or in writing. For a modern version of the *damnatio memoriae* law, see, for example, the decision by the New Zealand Prime Minister Jacinda Ardern not to name the 2019 Christchurch mosque killer: "We in New Zealand will give him nothing—not even his name" (https://news.sky.com/story/ill-never-mention-mosque-killers-name-vows-new-zealand-pm-jacinda-ardern-11669842).

27. Though Plato includes his brothers and even relatives in his dialogue, he is absent throughout. For his justification, see his famous statement in the *Second Letter* (314c) that "no writing of Plato exists or ever will exist, but those now said to be his are those of a Socrates become beautiful and new." Arguably Plato is replaced in the *Republic* by his two brothers, suggesting that a philosopher needs to be a combination of both Glaucon and Adeimantus.

28. According to Xenophon's *Memorobilia* (3.6), Glaucon was attempting to become an orator and striving for political leadership even though he was younger than twenty years old. None of his friends or relations could check him, except for Socrates, who took an interest in him for the sake of Plato and his uncle Charmides.

29. As Socrates admits to Glaucon, this third proposal of the philosopher-king (in addition to communism of property and wives) will be especially ridiculed by the people: see Nichols (1984); Steinberger (1989); Duncan and Steinberger (1990).

30. Other lovers include Charmides and Euthydemus, according to Alcibiades (*Symposium* 222c).

31. See, for example, *Symposium*, *Protagoras*, *Gorgias* (482d; 519b) and *Euthydemus* (275a–b). Two dialogues are devoted to him: *Alcibiades* I and II. Socrates's *daimonion* or inner voice stops him from accepting some students, such as Theages, while favoring others. But who does Socrates love and why? Does the poor, ugly, and politically insignificant Socrates love Alcibiades because of what he can get from him? This is the accusation Hobbes levels against Socrates: see Patapan and Sikkenga (2008).

32. On the charge of corruption, see *Apology* 19a ff. On the problem of Alcibiades and his imperial ambition, see Plato's *Alcibiades* I and II; Forde (1989) and Faulkner (2007, 58–126).

33. Plato seems to concur: in the *Symposium*, the unplanned entry of the uninvited drunken Alcibiades means that the party is immediately disrupted, with Alcibiades soon changing the drinking rules and making himself the center of

attention. For a detailed discussion of Thucydides's view of Alcibiades, see generally Forde (1989).

34. See Xenophon's *Cyropaedia*, 1.4.24. "Alcibiades," according to Forde (1989, 114), "contains within himself the most unusual, even paradoxical, combinations of political qualities. His vision of justice is without vindictiveness, his ambition without revenge, his spiritedness without anger. Alcibiades combines the fiercest love of victory with an exceptional levity of style, and a keen sense of irony toward the political world with an indomitable thirst for political engagement."

35. See Forde (1989, 92, 108–10, 186, 189) as well as Palmer (1992).

36. We can see this in *Alcibiades II*, where even in the midst of deep problems, when Alcibiades turns to the gods, Socrates manages to moderate Alcibiades's passions. On the scholarship, see the discussion in Faulkner (2007).

37. The force and constancy of spiritedness will be one of the most important elements that will shape their conversation. The reason for this lies in the peculiar Socratic way of inquiring, the dialectical approach of putting speeches side by side, the bringing together and separating of opinion that results in the famous Socratic *elenchus* or refutation (*Phaedo* 101b–e), where *endoxa* or strongly held common opinions provide the basis for our judgment of what is *kalon*, or fine, noble, or beautiful, and therefore what is *aischron* or shameful. On shame and its role in Platonic political thought, see generally Tarnopolsky (2010).

38. As we can see from *Cleitophon* and *Meno*, Socrates's erotic art is incapable of instructing everyone. Indeed, it would seem Socrates can only benefit individuals he can converse with in person. The reason for this is that Socrates does not claim to teach anything—he does not possess mysteries or novel doctrines that will reconstitute the soul. All he can achieve, as a midwife or "pimp" of philosophy, is *metastrephein* or to turn the soul around (*Theaetetus* 151b; *Republic* 518b–d), by leading it through speeches (*Phaedrus* 261a).

39. On the magnanimous and the philosopher as the two major peaks of human excellence in the *Ethics*, see Tessitore (1996). On the character of classical and modern leadership, see Arnhart (1983).

40. On the core ambiguity of honor—that honor could not be sought for itself, which is love of mere fame, see Pangle (1999).

41. On subsequent influence, see, for example, Turner (1981).

42. See Menaldo (2013), who relies on Aristotle and Machiavelli to understand the moral dimension of political ambition and the role of statesmanship.

CHAPTER 3

1. See, for example, "I am the Lord; that is my name; my glory I give to no other, nor my praise to carved idols" (Isaiah 42: 8); "To the King of ages, immortal, invisible, the only God, be honor and glory forever and ever. Amen" (1 Timothy 1:

17); "The whole earth is full of his glory!" (Isaiah 6: 3); and "The heavens declare the glory of God, and the sky above proclaims his handiwork" (Psalm 19: 1–14); "everyone who is called by my name, whom I created for my glory, whom I formed and made" (Isaiah 43: 7).

2. "In the sweat of thy face shalt thou eat bread, till thou return unto the ground; for out of it wast thou taken: for dust thou art, and unto dust shalt thou return" (Genesis, 3: 19).

3. "Thus says the Lord: 'Let not the wise man boast in his wisdom, let not the mighty man boast in his might, let not the rich man boast in his riches' " (Jeremiah 9: 23). Similarly, "Blessed are the poor in spirit, for theirs is the kingdom of heaven" (Matt. 5: 3).

4. On the difference between orthodoxy and orthopraxy, see Fortin (1996).

5. On "Christian" leadership, see generally Herring (2006). On how theological controversies defined "church leadership," see Galvão-Sobrinho (2013).

6. On the nature of prophets, see Wagner (2016). On how they were influenced by the hierarchy of the Church, see Ash Jr. (1976), Kyrtatas (1988). On the origins and development of monasticism, see Caner (2002); Smither (2016).

7. See generally Davidson (1993).

8. See generally Calvin (1989); for a historical account, see De Mey (2009). For a more recent discussion of the *Munus Triplex*, see the Second Vatican Council's *Lumen Gentium*.

9. As Machiavelli observes in the *Discourses on Livy*, he "can do no other than marvel and grieve" when he sees the honor given to antiquity by recovering "a fragment of ancient statute" or great works imitated by artists, while in contrast, the works of "kings, captains, citizens, legislators and others" are "rather admired than imitated" (D, Preface, 5). References to the *Discourses on Livy* are by book, chapter, page (Machiavelli 1996); to the *Prince*, by chapter and pages (Machiavelli 1985).

10. References to the *Discourses on Livy* are by book, chapter, page (Machiavelli 1996); to the *Prince*, by chapter and pages (Machiavelli 1985).

11. On the importance of glory and honor for Machiavelli, see generally Strauss (1959); Price (1977); Eldar (1986); Santi (1979); Varotti (1998); Kahn (1993); Zmora (2007).

12. See Cornell and Malcolmson (2009, 67), who examine Machiavelli's works more generally to explore the link between Machiavellian leadership and the requirements of prudence.

13. Thus, he says, "Whoever considers present and ancient things easily knows that in all cities and in all peoples there are the same desires and the same humors, and there always have been" (D I.39, 83). Machiavelli thus rejects Christian eschatology (that the world changed with the coming of Christ) and even suggests, following Aristotle rather than Plato, that the world is eternal (D II.5, 138–39).

14. This explains why we are discontented with what we have and therefore desire innovation, complaining in evil times and becoming restless in good times (D I. 37, 78; D I.53, 105; Patapan 2003).

15. It is the *grandi* who have *ambizione*, a passion "so powerful in human breasts that it is never satisfied, however high men rise" (see especially, Price 1982, 401, fn 128 for numerous specific examples). On whether the few or all have ambition, see Price (1982, 407–8), who rejects Fleisher (1973), and Santi (1979), who claims that all men have ambition: "It should be concluded, then, that Machiavelli thought that in the comparatively few men who were moved by it, ambizione was a passion so strong that it was rarely if ever satisfied. But the vast majority of men do not desire office or power, and there is no reason to think that Machiavelli considered their desires to be insatiable" (Price 1982, 407–8). See also D II, 27; D I, 46; D III 4.

16. Contrasting *umori* are the "source (*cagione*) of all the evils (*mali*) that afflict cities or states" FH III, 1: Price (1982, 399).

17. See, for example, Moses (P 4), Agathocles (P 8), Francesco della Rovere (FH VII, 22), who all had low stations.

18. These humors in turn drew on the four elements of earth, wind, water, and fire. For a detailed overview of the medieval and renaissance conceptions of humors, see Parel (1990); Fischer (1997; 2000). See Mansfield (1998, 304); and Fischer (1997, 801), who notes that Machiavelli replaces *anima* or the intellective soul, with *animo*, the spirit, as the motivating principle of man.

19. See the helpful discussion in Fischer (1997, 801).

20. For a detailed discussion of Machiavelli's use of the term, especially in the context of Roman *ambitio* and its synonyms such as *cupididatas* and *libido dominandi*, see Price (1982).

21. For a detailed overview, see Price (1982). "The ambition of men and the desire they have to perpetuate the name of their ancestors as well as their own: nor did they remember that many who have not had the opportunity to acquire fame through some praiseworthy deed have contrived to acquire it with despicable things" (*Florentine Histories*, Preface, p. 7; Zmora 2007, 452). Or they will do so through writing, as Aristotle, Plato, and many others have, suggesting that previous thinkers were chiefly concerned with their glory (see *A Discourse on Remodeling the Government of Florence*, Chief Works, I, p. 114).

22. A tendency evident in the scholarship: see for example McCormick (2011).

23. An early formulation of what Mancur Olson (1971) termed a collective action problem.

24. Which also leads to their intemperate anger, cruelty, and ingratitude. See, for example, the peoples' inclination to burn the Decemvirs alive (I, 44) and their treatment of Scipio (I, 28; 29).

25. See generally his *Tercets on Ambition* and Patapan (2003).

26. On Machiavelli's use of "brain" (*cervello*) for mind, see Fischer's (2000) reference to Medieval physiology.

27. There are only two references to magnanimous (*magnanimo*) in Machiavelli's major political works (Patapan 2018, 465). In *The Prince* (P 7, 32), Machiavelli notes how his model, Cesare Borgia, used force and fraud and made himself loved

and feared by the people and was "severe and pleasant, magnanimous and liberal."
Magnanimity, it would seem, is an instrumental virtue, but one of the many ways
a new prince can maintain a principality. This new Machiavellian understanding
of magnanimity is clarified and confirmed in the *Discourses* (III, 34, 289), where
Machiavelli notes how princes can maintain reputation: "For nothing makes them
so much esteemed as to give rare examples (*sé rari esempli*) of themselves with some
rare act or saying conforming to the common good, which shows the lord either
magnanimous, or liberal, or just, and is such as to become like a proverb among his
subjects." Machiavelli here indicates that magnanimity is not a comprehensive virtue
of character but a politically useful reputation that can be acquired or engineered
by "rare" but memorable actions.

28. See the reference to *mondana gloria* (D II, 2) and his statement that "God
does not want to do everything, so as not to take from us our free will and a part
of that glory that belongs to us" (P 26, 103), and more generally Price (1977, 592).

29. As Strauss (1958, 286) puts it, the desire for perpetual and immortal
glory "is the link between badness and goodness, since while it is selfish in itself,
it cannot be satisfied except by the greatest possible service to others." Or as Santi
(1979, 126) states, it harmonizes the private good with the common weal. In Eldar's
(1986, 422) formulation, it is a "mediated acquisition."

30. Of course, as Zmora (2007) notes, this is not true immortality. But it is
perhaps the only one available on earth. In any case, even if one's founding fades or
dissipates, as Machiavelli says it will, one's name will still be recalled as a founder.
Glory provides a distance from life and property and allows them to be sacrificed
for the common good, yet also for personal gain of one's own glory. Or as Strauss
(1958, 286) puts it, "The desire for immortal glory . . . liberates men . . . from
the fear of death."

31. But religion is a two-edged sword and may not be capable of simple
manipulation by leaders. It may lead to deference of rulers and willingness to accept
one's lot, but in doing so it will also limit the actions of the leader. On contrasting
views regarding Machiavelli's use of religion, compare Najemy (1999); Fontana
(1999); Coby (1999); Sullivan (1996); Zmora (2007); Strauss (1958); Beiner (2012).

32. Both humanity and harshness give rise to *gloria*, depending on the circumstances, such as the corruption of the regime (see, for example, Scipio, Torquatus,
and Corvinsu Cunctator). It is therefore better not to rely just on love or fear but
on a combination of both (D III 21; P 17; Patapan 2006).

33. The example of the immoral Agathocles is interesting because it shows a
leader who did not understand the potential that glory confers both in present security
and in future immortality: see Price (1977); Kahn (1993, 2013); McCormick (2015).

34. See Strauss (1958, 272), Price (1977, 618 fn 198).

35. "Thus it is the safety of a republic or a kingdom to have not one prince
who governs prudently while he lives, but one individual who orders it so that is
also maintained when he dies" (D I.11.58; Varotti 1998, 421–23).

36. The ideal for Machiavelli is a free and independent republic that does not engage in war or does not seek to expand (acquire territory and maintain independence, that is, for offensive and defensive reasons: D I 29). But this is not possible because: 1) it would need to be on a strong site, formidable to arouse fears, and its constitution forbids expansion, a rare or unusual case; 2) even if it existed, stability is not possible, due to flux, and therefore being forced to expand without the means will undermine it (D I 6; indolence or *ozio* means it becomes weak or *effeminata* or divided internally: Price 1982, 422). Therefore, it is necessary to assume it will be forced to expand, and make sure it keeps territories it holds. This will mean using the Roman technique of acquiring empire and glory and not seeking a quiet life (Price 1982, 425; D II, 13).

37. Principalities and republics engage in wars for two main reasons: necessity due to hunger or wars for new territory, thereby killing or expelling its inhabitants (D II, 8). There are two reasons for waging wars on republics: to subjugate them; or because one fears being attacked by them (D I, 6). Laudable and detestable methods both succeed, but there is much greater scope for the detestable in international affairs. Cyrus was honored because he had no vices (D III, 20), but he used fraud in international matters (D II.13). Moral concerns do not arise as readily with empire because 1) the desire to found a state is natural; 2) expansion of state is a matter of common advantage so that no one will complain unless you fail (D II 19). Machiavelli thus promotes *bene commune, comune utilita, publica utilita* (but not common good). Moreover, Machiavelli does not appear to have a conception of "universal" community, perhaps because it may encourage the glory seeker to a) start unnecessary wars; b) take unnecessary risks; c) give rise to costly rivalry between the ambitious.

38. Lord (2003), for example, sees Machiavelli's *The Prince* as a modern manual for political practice. The significance and usefulness of these approaches is confirmed by Deluga (2001), who shows that Machiavellianism may account for the actions of presidents, and that it is more complex than the question of corruption, involving choices between desirable alternative outcomes.

39. There are of course many other important streams of thought that have been influenced by Machiavelli's conception of glory and leadership. Consider, for example, his conception of ambition and how it has influenced modern constitutionalism, especially regarding the role of the modern executive. For a historical overview of executive power and the various attempts to tame the Machiavellian prince, see Mansfield (1993).

40. On charismatic leadership generally, see Turner (2003); Riesebrodt (1999); Bensman and Givant (1975).

41. On the influence of others, such as Rudolf Sohn and Robert R. Marett, on Weber, see Riesebrodt (1999).

42. He claims, for example, in *Twilight of the Idols* (2005, 225), that Thucydides and Machiavelli's *Principe* "are most closely related to me," and in *Beyond Good and Evil* (Part II, section 28), he praises the "long, difficult, hard dangerous

thoughts and the *tempo* of the gallop and the very best, most capricious humor" of *The Prince*. For further references and discussion of the influence of Machiavelli on Nietzsche, see von Vacano (2007).

43. On the new table of values to be written by the overman, see *Thus Spoke Zarathustra* (Prologue; Book I). On the nature of leadership adopted by the "last man," see *Thus Spoke Zarathustra* (Prologue; Book I): "Who still wants to rule? Who obey? Both require too much exertion. No shepherd and one herd! Everybody wants the same, everybody is the same: whoever feels differently goes into the madhouse." On the "herd" more generally, see *Beyond Good and Evil* (2002, 86–90).

44. For the influence of Nietzsche on Weber, see the overviews by Stauth (1992); Warren (1992). For a thoughtful account of Nietzsche's influence on Weber in terms of suffering and its implications for politics, see Shaw (2014).

45. The charismatic leader "does not derive his claims from the will of his followers, in the manner of an election; rather, it is their *duty* to recognize his charisma" (Weber 1978a, 1113; Shaw 2014, 371).

46. On the "pathos of distance," see *Beyond Good and Evil* (section 257).

47. Weber (1978b, 128).

48. For an overview of the scholarship, see Korom (2015); Best and Higley (2010); Putnam (1976); Nevitte and Gibbins (1990); Higley and Burton (2006).

49. On the earlier use by Diderot to refer to refined or outstanding goods, see Korom (2015).

50. One approach is to deny a ruling elite model, replacing it with what Robert Dahl in *Who Governs* (1961) calls a polyarchy. Another is to show how elitism and democracy could be reconciled through leadership accountability, as in Lasswell and Kaplan's *Power and Society: A Framework for Political Inquiry* (1950), or the view of representative democracy as free competition between elites for the people's vote, as in Schumpeter's *Capitalism, Socialism and Democracy* (1942). On "democratic elitism," see Borchert (2009).

CHAPTER 4

1. Consider, for example, Hobbes's *Behemoth*, a counterpart to his *Leviathan*, and his *A Dialogue between a Philosopher and a Student of the Common Laws of England*, where the interlocutors are not even named.

2. Reference to Hobbes's *Leviathan* is as follows: *Leviathan* (L, chapter, and page number) (Hobbes 1968).

3. Hobbes writes as a form of public service, in the spirit of Godolphin, and "without partiality, without application, and without other designe" than "to advance the Civill Power" (L, A Review and Conclusion, 728).

4. At the very end of his most well-known work, *Leviathan*, Hobbes states that having completed his "Discourse of Civill and Ecclesiasticall Government,

occassioned by the disorders of the present time," he will "return to my interrupted Speculation of Bodies Naturall; (if God give me health to finish it,) I hope the Novelty will as much please, as in the Doctrine of this Artificial Body it useth to offend" (L, A Review and Conclusion, 728–29).

5. "For every man, if he be in his wits, will in all things yield that man an absolute obediance, by virtue of whose sentence he believes himself to be either saved or damned" (L 30, 385).

6. Hobbes's consistent reference to his teaching as a "Novel Doctrine" shows that his attempt to refound politics on a rational basis is really a replacement of Scholastic Doctrine with what appears to be his new scientific piety, with peace as its credo and power as its theology (L, A Review and Conclusion, 726). Therefore, his "Principles of Reason" are another contending dogma, and *Leviathan* is the new Bible of the Hobbesian world, even containing its own Ten Commandments (L 30, 380–83).

7. For an extensive discussion of the role of honor in Hobbes, see, for example, the seminal discussion by Strauss (1953); Slomp (2000); Hampton (1989); Sacksteder (1989); Altman (1989).

8. Without pride, the diffident (and perhaps the competitive to a great degree) could lead a life as peaceful and productive as those of bees or ants (L 17, 225). Note that Hobbes's list of six elements that distinguish social animals (bees and ants) and humans (L 17, 225–27) emphasizes the problem of honor.

9. As Hobbes notes, "the nature of Power, is in this point, like to Fame, increasing as it proceeds" (L 10, 150). See generally Patapan and Sikkenga (2006); Patapan (2018).

10. See, for example, his amusing account of the origins of "Coates of Armes" and titles of honor (L 10, 157–58).

11. His passing remark on divine providence at the start of the chapter, that "the secret working of God, which men call Good Luck," is indicative of his judgment generally (L 10, 150).

12. See the discussion regarding the "Objection from the Incapacity of the vulgar" (L, 30, 378–79).

13. Bentham extends this Hobbesian argument to its limits when he suggests in his *Panopticon* that institutions may not need to rely on anyone for their proper functioning.

14. See, however, Vanden Houten (2002) on Hobbes's complex treatment of this question.

15. Note, however, how he seemingly retracts this position—equality must be the new consensus, even if not true: "or if Nature have made men unequall; yet because men that think themselves equall, will not enter into conditions of Peace, but upon Equall termes, such equalitie must be admitted." The breach of this precept is called "Pride" (L 15, 211). For his more profound critique of prudence, see his distinction between "Prudence," based on experience, and "Science," which

relies on "Reason" and "*Reckoning* (that is, Adding and Substracting (sic)) of the Consequences of generall names agreed upon" (L 3, 97; L 5, 111–15).

16. See, for example, the discussions of the rights of the sovereigns by institution (L 18); of the liberty of subjects (L 21); of the public ministers of sovereign power (L 23); and especially of the office of the sovereign representative (L 30). On counsel to sovereigns, see Mara (1988).

17. See in this context Hobbes's distinction between the *justice* of laws, and their *goodness*. All laws made by authorized sovereigns are thereby, by definition, just. But not all just laws are good laws—as Hobbes says, "A good Law is that, which is *Needfull*, for the *Good of the People*, and withall *Perspicuous*" (L 30, 388). Though not bound by natural laws strictly understood because there are none to enforce them, it is in the sovereign's interest to yield to natural laws, or right reason. Consequently, it is possible to judge the reasonableness of a sovereign's actions, even if we cannot question or challenge its justice.

18. Hobbes, of course, knew of these dangers. As he notes, "Yet in all times, Kings, and Persons of Soveraigne authority, because of their Independency, are in continuall jealousies, and in the state and posture of Gladiators" (L 13, 187). On whether Hobbes's "new" political science, with its promise of an "everlasting" commonwealth, is undermined by his understanding of international politics, see Patapan (2009).

19. The fundamental law of nature, "That every man, ought to endeavour Peace, as farre as he has hope of obtaining it; and when he cannot obtain it, that he may seek, and use, all helps, and advantages of Warre" (L 13, 190; original italics), yields, according to Hobbes, nineteen other laws. As we have seen, one of the most important of these is the Second Law of Nature, a willingness, if others are also willing, to lay down one's right to all things.

20. On the meaning of "self-interest," see Mansfield (1995).

21. On rational choice, see Green and Shapiro (1994).

22. On prestige in international relations, see Nye (2004); Schelling (1960); Mercer (1996). For the "economy of esteem," see Brennan and Pettit (2005). On political marketing, see Lees-Marshment et al. (2014).

23. These problems of individual agency reemerge in unexpected places, for example, the originalism debates regarding the proper approach to the interpretation of the constitution, where the intentions of founders assume prominence, and in the role of judges in exercising judicial review and overruling democratic enactments, thereby raising questions regarding the legitimacy of their individual discretion and judgment.

24. Consider the recent scholarship on "epistemic democracy": Estlund (2008); Goodin and Spiekermann (2018).

25. See the general discussion in Kane and Patapan (2014).

26. See, for example, Kellerman (2008; 2012).

CHAPTER 5

1. On "strong" and "toxic" leaders, see Brown (2014); Lipman-Blumen (2006).

2. On the political, economic, and social circumstances that required both moral leadership and attention to followers, see Wilson (2013, 52–53); Trottier, van Wart, and Wang (2008, 323).

3. Part of the problem here has been the applicability of the dichotomy to organizational settings (Pawar 2003), leading to its reformulation in business settings to leaders and managers: see Gronn (1995, 18); Zaleznik (1992). Others have noted that many studies listing the attributes of transformational leaders have occurred at the narrow corporate dyadic level rather than at the group or social level, focusing on the leader rather than the more dispersed leader-follower networks: see Mitra (2013, 398); Yukl (2010, 287).

4. For Wilson (2013, 52–53), Burns's dichotomy rescued leadership studies from its conceptual malaise because of the failure of trait-based approaches.

5. Allix (2000, 7); Mitra (2013, 398); Yukl (2010, 287); Fu et al. (2010: 222, 224–25).

6. Fu et al. (2010) argue that the dichotomy lacks clarity, depth, and coherence, with little attention paid to cultural, structural, and contextual factors, with assumptions of universal applicability and with little detail provided about the underlying processes.

7. See Collinson (2014, 38); Hollander 1993 cited in Pawar (2003, 399); Gronn (1995, 18); Fu et al. (2010, 222–23).

8. Bass (1985, 21) questions whether all transformational leaders are moral. The subsequent scholarship in "ethical" leadership shows the ambiguities in the claims: see, for example, Turner et al. (2002); Brown and Treviño (2006); Price (2003); Deluga (2001).

9. Burns is aware of the larger tradition, as we can see from his passing references to, for example, Plato's concept of the ship of state (23); Machiavelli and Erasmus on advice to princes (125); Hegel and Nietzsche in the context of the "great man" theory (51); and Weber's charismatic leader (243).

10. On the ranking of desires in Thomas, see *Summa Theologiae* Q 94, Art 2, which lists three natural inclinations, the third being the natural inclination to know the truth about God and to live in society.

11. Those who hold and wield power have a variety of motives, according to Burns, where "some may pursue not power but status, recognition, prestige, and glory, or they may seek power as an intermediate value instrumental to realizing these loftier goals" (14).

12. Burns is especially concerned with appeals to "base" instincts and the manipulators such as Joseph McCarthy (458, 462).

13. It is therefore ironic that the subtitle to *Roosevelt: The Lion and the Fox* (1956) is an allusion to Machiavelli's advice in *The Prince* to use the lion and fox, that is, both power and guile.

14. See generally Rhode (2006); Ciulla, Price, and Murphy (2006); Kane (2001).

CHAPTER 6

1. This chapter draws extensively on Patapan (2006). I am grateful to Brill Academic Publishers for permission to use this material.

2. See https://www.bbc.com/news/world-asia-32046137.

3. As Barr (2000, 100) notes, Lee's paternal grandfather, Lee Hoon Leong, who had left Guandong province for Singapore in 1863, regarded the Englishman as the "model of perfection" and decided his first-born grandson would grow up to be "equal of any Englishmen."

4. During the Japanese occupation, Lee ran a successful black-market operation. He also learned to read Chinese and Japanese and worked for the Japanese propaganda department transcribing Allied wire reports.

5. See generally Bellows (1970, 67–100); George (1973, 59–73).

6. I refer throughout to Lee's speeches collected in Han et al. 1998. See Lee Kuan Yew, speech to school principals, Victoria Theatre, August 29, 1966, in Han et al. (1998, 394).

7. Lee Kuan Yew, speech at a seminar on communism and democracy, April 28, 1971, in Han et al. (1998, 315).

8. Lee Kuan Yew, speech at a seminar on communism and democracy, April 28, 1971, in Han et al. (1998, 315).

9. See Barr (2000, 97–136), for an extensive discussion of Lee's conception of meritocracy. According to Barr and Skrbis (2008, 44), "Cambridge was the point at which his personal experience and philosophy of elitism articulated into an ideological position." In this context, see also Lee (1998, 115–130).

10. Lee Kuan Yew, speech in Parliament on a White Paper on ministerial salaries, November 1, 1994, in Han et al. (1998, 337).

11. Lee cited in Han et al. (1998, 135).

12. Lee cited in Han et al. (1998, 135).

13. Lee Kuan Yew, speech to public servants at the Political Study Centre, June 14, 1962, in Han et al. (1998, 362).

14. Lee cited in Han et al. (1998, 136).

15. Lee cited in Han et al. (1998, 229).

16. Lee cited in Han et al. (1998, 126). For an assessment of this episode, see Tan (2009).

17. Lee cited in Han et al. (1998, 229).

18. Lee cited in Han et al. (1998, 229).

19. Lee Kuan Yew, interview following address to the Royal Society of International Affairs in London, May 1962, in Han et al. (1998, 367).

20. Lee cited in Han et al. (1998, 98).

21. Lee, speech in Parliament, cited in Han et al. (1998, 338).

22. Lee cited in Han et al. (1998, 98).

23. Lee cited in Han et al. (1998, 101).

24. Lee cited in Han et al. (1998, 99).

25. Lee cited in Han et al. (1998, 101).

26. Lee, speech in Parliament, cited in Han et al. (1998, 89).

27. Confucian meritocracy has recently become an important area of scholarship: see Chan (2013); Kim (2014). On the importance of meritocracy in Singapore and the wider region, see Barr and Skrbis (2008), Hood and Peters (2003).

28. Cited in McCarthy (2006, 80). For a general overview, see Englehart (2000), Barr (2000, 160–62).

29. See De Bary (1991); McCarthy (2006, 88).

30. Tan (2012) argues that pragmatism has provided an important link between economic growth and an authoritarian, meritocratic, and technocratic government in Singapore. Lee (1998, 104–5) was aware of the postwar debates in the UK regarding socialism and liberalism and notes in particular Harold Laski's influence on socialist thought in 1946. But what seemed to impress him more was the fairness of the system rather than the nature of the specific debates. Thus, the early years of the PAP showed a commitment to socialism, but, as Barr (2000) argues, Lee never intended to build a welfare state, and his socialism was a means to an end rather than an end in itself, evolving to such an extent that he could claim in the 1990s that he was an economic liberal.

31. Lee Kuan Yew, speech at Hong Lim PAP Branch 15th anniversary celebration dinner, July 14, 1972, in Han et al. (1998, 180–81).

32. On the debate generally, see McCarthy (2006); Englehart (2000); de Bary (2000); Barr (2002).

33. On the nature of these debates, see Cumings (1999); Weiss (2000).

34. See, for example, Kim (1994); Lee (1995).

35. Perhaps what he has in mind is the specific context of the 1950s–1960s Cold War and later Hot War in East Asia, giving rise to a new generation of leaders in the region. For a general overview, see Bertrand (2013); Christie (2000).

36. According to Lee (1998, 242), he had been trying since 1968 to get a successor and by 1976 was getting anxious. He set a target of 1988, when he turned sixty-five, but was asked to stay on until 1990, the 25th anniversary of Singapore's independence.

37. Lee, speech to school principals, in Han et al. (1998, 93).

38. Lee, speech to school principals, in Han et al. (1998, 93).

39. Lee, speech in Parliament, in Han et al. (1998, 336).

40. To pursue the question of what Lee understands by idealistic leadership, we assume that Lee did indeed sacrifice substantial wealth (even though Singaporean politicians are the highest paid in the world).

41. Lee in Han et al. (1998, 31).

42. Lee in Han et al. (1998, 256).

43. Lee in Han et al. (1998, 133).

44. For an overview of decolonization in Asia, see Tarling (1999). For the development of Singapore as a city-state within a largely Malay environment, see Régnier (1991); Chua (1985).

45. Consider, for example, the Kim dynasty in North Korea, the Aquinos in the Philippines, the Gandhis in India. On comparable dynastic tendencies in the West, see, for example, the Kennedys, Bushes, and Clintons in the United States.

46. See generally Yap et al. (2009, 517–19).

47. Yap et al. (2009, 506).

48. Lee refers to influence peddling in the British Parliament as well as the money paid to former leaders, e.g., Thatcher, for their books; Lee, speech in Parliament, in Han et al. (1998, 331–42). For the legitimacy problems raised by such payments, see Wong and Xunming (2010). For a general discussion of corruption in the region, see Quah (2003); Lee and Oh (2007).

49. Lee, speech in Parliament, in Han et al. (1998, 331).

50. Lee Kuan Yew, speech to undergraduates at the National University of Singapore and Nanyang Technological Institute, August 22, 1988, in Han et al. (1998, 406–10).

51. Barr (2000, 154).

52. Lee in Han et al. (1998, 407).

53. Cited in Barr (2000, 155).

54. Lee in Han et al. (1998, 179); Zakaria (1994, 109–26).

55. Lee in Han et al. (1998, 174).

56. In a 1967 speech to the Foreign Correspondents' Association, he distinguishes between East Asia and Cambodia, Thailand, Burma, and Ceylon, in terms of the type of Buddhism. Unlike the Mahayana Buddhists, he argues, these countries are Hinayana Buddhists, influenced by compassion; Lee in Han et al. (1998, 177).

57. Lee in Han et al. (1998, 174).

58. Lee in Han et al. (1998, 183).

59. Lee in Han et al. (1998, 181).

60. Lee Kuan Yew, speech to Southeast Asia Business Committee meeting, school principals, Hotel Singapura, May 12, 1968, in Han et al. (1998, 398–402).

61. On "performance legitimacy" in contemporary political science, see Kane et al. (2011).

CHAPTER 7

1. Kissinger secretly taped his incoming and outgoing phone conversations and had his secretary transcribe them. After destroying the tapes, Kissinger took the transcripts with him when he left office in January 1977, claiming they were "private papers." In 2001, the National Security Archive initiated legal proceedings to force the government to recover the transcripts and declassify most of them. The Kissinger tapes can be found in the Digital National Security Archives: https://www.proquest.com/products-services/dnsa.html; see also https://nsarchive2.gwu.edu/NSAEBB/NSAEBB263/index.htm.

2. From February 1971, Nixon secretly taped conversations and telephone calls in several locations, including the Oval Office, his office in the Old Executive Office Building, the Cabinet Room, and Camp David. For an overview, see the Nixon Presidential Library and Museum, https://www.nixonlibrary.gov/virtuallibrary/tapeexcerpts; Brinkley and Nichter (2015).

3. See generally Parker and Parker (2017).

4. In his biography of Kissinger, Isaacson (2005, 150) observes that, "Nixon's thirst for flattery and Kissinger's penchant for providing it helped to seal a complex relationship, but it did not make Kissinger a social chum like Bebe Robozo or Robert Abplanalp." Similarly, Hersh (1984, x) notes that "Nixon had a consuming need for flattery and Kissinger a consuming need to provide it."

5. Cited in Dallek (2007, 318). Dallek goes on to observe that the comment was "essentially a repeat of what Kissinger often said to buck up and ingratiate himself with Nixon. 'Mr. President,' Kissinger told him, 'without you this country would be dead'" (2007, 318).

6. Conversation 001–010; April 7, 1971; 9:31–9:39; mp3 (5.5m): http://nixontapes.org/hak.html.

7. For a general overview of flattery, see Regier (2007); Eylon and Heyd (2008).

8. For a detailed examination of flattery in classical political philosophy, see Nerdahl (2011); Konstan (1996).

9. A political advisor, according to Shaw and Eichbaum (2017, 313), is a "temporary public servant employed to provide advice to a member of the political executive, and who is exempt from the impartiality requirements that apply to the permanent public service." For useful overviews of advisors, also described as political staffers, exempt staff, or program managers, see Craft (2015); Shaw and Eichbaum (2015). For historical accounts and international trends, see Andweg (1999); Blick (2004); Eichbaum and Shaw (2010); Dahlstrom, Peters and Pierre (2011); Yong and Hazell (2014).

10. For an early philosophical examination of the responsibility of advisors, see Thompson (1983). On expert political judgment, see Tetlock (2005). For accountability, see Tiernan (2007).

11. On "whispering," see Gains and Stoker (2011, 49). Maley (2000) distinguishes in the Australian context five distinctive policy roles: agenda setting; linking ideas, interests, and opportunities; mobilizing; bargaining; and "delivering." See also Burke (2005) on the "honest broker" model; Gains and Stoker (2011) on special advisors as "key entrepreneurial actors"; and Connaughton (2015), who lists four "types" of advisors: expert, partisan, coordinator, and minder.

12. See, for example, Esselment, Lees-Marshment, and Marland (2014).

13. On the "second wave" and its attempt to draw on wider public policy concepts to understand advisors, see the special issue on ministerial advisors in *Public Administration* (June 2017), and especially Shaw and Eichbaum (2017, 312), who use the "Public Service Bargain (PSB)" to clarify the "parameters of the agreements struck by ministers and political advisers and the lexicon used to describe them."

14. For a detailed and thoughtful overview of flattery for Hobbes, noting its important role for Hobbes's critique of democratic and aristocratic regimes, see Kapust (2011).

15. See the discussion in Kapust (2011, 684–85) regarding Hobbes's evaluation of the role of demagogues in Athens, and especially his view that in public deliberations, fear "which for the most part adviseth well, though it execute not so) seldom or never sheweth itself or is admitted."

16. See generally *Gorgias* 463b ff; *Phaedrus* 240b–d; *Republic* 6.494d–495a; Eylon and Heyd (2008, 692–93).

17. See Nerdahl's (2011) discussion of Plutarch's *Life of Dion* and the importance of philosophy to counter the dangers of tyranny.

18. On the conception of *Parrhesia* in Greek thought, see Landauer (2012). On its positive aspect in modern democracies, see Foucault (2001).

19. On *The Prince* as a work in the tradition of the mirror of princes, see Gilbert (1968).

20. The writings by advisors is mixed, with some using Machiavelli's famous statements in *The Prince* to frame discussion. See, for example, Powell (2010); Morris (1999), while others are more theoretical: Lord (2003); Jay (1994); McAlpine (2000); Meltsner (1990).

21. There is an extensive scholarship on *The Prince* (for an indicative overview, see Machiavelli 1992). The theme of advisors remains less examined, except perhaps in the context of rhetoric: see Belliotti (2009); Benner (2009); Benner (2013); Dietz (1986); Kain (1995); Viroli (1998); Wheelan (2004); Wiethoff (1974, 1991).

22. Antonio Giordana da Venafro (1459–1530) was professor of law, Studio di Siena. In the *Discourses* (III, 6), Machiavelli calls Pandolfo "tyrant of Siena" (cf P 20, 85), making us wonder if a good advisor may even efface the reputation of being a tyrant.

23. Machiavelli alludes to Hesiod, *Works and Days* (lines 295ff), but Hesiod, who is ostensibly counseling his brother Perses, refers to *noesis* rather than "brains": "That man is altogether best who considers all things himself and marks what will

be better afterwards and at the end; and he, again, is good who listens to a good adviser; but whoever neither thinks for himself nor keeps in mind what another tells him, he is an unprofitable man." On Machiavelli's truncated notion of prudence, see Garver (1987).

24. This discussion suggests that the modern initiatives such as New Public Management (NPM) as well as use of Key Performance Indicators, short-term contracts, and golden handshakes in performance management of senior civil servants are premised on the inadequacy, if not absence, of a notion of a common view regarding public service or duty. See generally Aucoin (2012). For the Australian debate, see Podger (2007); Shergold (2007). On NPM in the UK, see Richards and Smith (2016). On the European and American debates, see Peters and Pierre (2004).

25. The Machiavelli scholarship does not seem to recognize and therefore explain this contradiction.

26. See generally Aucoin (2012); Podger (2007); Shergold (2007); Richards and Smith (2016); Peters and Pierre (2004).

27. On groupthink, see Janis (1982); Kowert (2002).

28. Initiated by Habermas's theory of "communicative action" and Rawls's concept of public reason, the "deliberative turn" in democratic theory has become increasingly influential though challenged by a range of scholars. For an early overview, see Dryzek (2002); for a recent evaluation, see Chappell (2012).

29. See Hood and Lodge (2006); Hood (2001); Lodge (2010); Shaw and Eichbaum (2017, 317–18); and the discussion of the reward structures and reward bargains for political advisors in Shaw and Eichbaum (2017, 316–17).

30. See Hood and Lodge (2001) on trustee bargains; Mulgan (2000); Denhardt and Denhardt (2000) on the public good.

31. See Keynes's (1936, 383–84) well-known and amusing account of his own influence: "The ideas of economists and political philosophers, both when they are right and when they are wrong, are more powerful than is commonly understood. Indeed the world is ruled by little else. Practical men, who believe themselves to be quite exempt from any intellectual influence, are usually the slaves of some defunct economist."

CHAPTER 8

1. For a detailed account of the power and pointlessness of dueling, see Alexander Pushkin's *Eugene Onegin*, made even more poignant given the death of the author by dueling. On the dueling see Appiah (2010, 1–52).

2. See in this context the myth of Narcissus, which is often used to show the pathology of fame. Yet to the extent that fame looks out rather than in, it appears to disrupt the infinite reflex and self-absorption of Narcissus. Moreover, Narcissus

may not be directly relevant to the extent that a different account has him as too proud to love anyone, a version which suggests an implicit standard of excellence.

3. See also his discussion of *tyrannophobia* (L 29).

4. What remains unresolved is whether this view is merely a useful or cautionary prejudice, in the spirit of Hume's "just political maxim," that "every man must be supposed a knave." On the contemporary problem of anti-politics, see Flinders (2012).

5. On Tocqueville's attempt to revive a version of honor for preserving democratic freedom, see Krause (2002, 67–96).

6. Disciplines such as education, which presume to teach excellence, reveal the dynamic tensions between the two principles: see Phillips (1997).

7. On the "economy of prestige," see English (2008).

8. For a general overview of celebrity, see Marshall (1997); Redmond and Holmes (2007). For a psychology of fame and celebrity, see Giles (2000). For the political implications of celebrity, see Street (2004); 't Hart and Tindall (2009).

9. On the "culture industry," see Adorno (1991).

10. See https://www.theglobeandmail.com/arts/film/these-hollywood-stars-hailed-hugo-chavez-as-a-hero-and-friend/article9336154/. On Villa de Cine, see https://www.bbc.com/news/av/world-latin-america-17755757/how-chavez-hopes-to-break-the-dictatorship-of-hollywood.

11. Identity politics, according to Bernstein and Taylor (2013, 1), "refers to activism engaged in by status-based social movements organized around such categories as in contrast to class-based movements." Hill and Wilson (2003, 2–3) distinguish between "identity politics" and "politics of identity." For introductory overviews, see Alcoff (2006); Bernstein (2005); Calhoun (1994); Kenny (2004).

12. See Appiah (2005); Gutmann (2003); Kymlicka (1995); Taylor (1994); Tully (1995), who attempt to accommodate identity with the requirements of human rights, freedom, and democratic citizenship.

13. For liberals, identity politics undermines individualism, institutes contending group identities, and challenges the possibility of reasonable public debate and compromise. In fracturing political consensus, it threatens national unity. See Gutmann (2003), who argues that identity groups are not the ultimate source of democratic value; for an egalitarian critique, see Barry (2001); see Parker (2005) for an overview of critical arguments. For those on the left, identity politics challenges the politics of redistribution that sees class as the politically salient source of identity and difference: Fraser and Honneth (2003); Hobsbawm (1996); Bickford (1997); Kauffman (2001).

14. See, for example, claims based on race (Lee 2008; Marable 1993; Crenshaw 1991); gender (Ryan 1997; Weir 2008); culture (Amin 2014; Hale 1997); sexuality (Slagle 1995; Bernstein 2002).

15. For a recent overview of the scholarship and a comprehensive argument regarding the origins of individualism, see Siedentop (2014, 334–36). Siedentop's

secularization argument traces the origins of modern individualism to the uniqueness of the Christian soul. Yet in tracing the origins of individualism to the thirteenth century and emphasizing religion, he pays insufficient attention to the detailed debates regarding individualism within modernity.

16. References throughout to the *Groundwork for the Metaphysics of Morals* are by section and page to Kant (1993). On the significant differences, see Ginsberg (1974, 115–19).

17. A hypothetical imperative "says only that an action is good for some purpose," a categorical imperative "declares an action to be of itself objectively necessary without reference to any purpose, i.e., without any other end." It is therefore not concerned with an action or its result, but in the "mental disposition": Kant, *Groundwork* (415, 25; 416, 26). As a law of morality, the categorical imperative "is an a priori synthetic practical proposition" (420, 29).

18. There is a debate on the number of formulations, and how they are related to each other: see Allison (2012, 124–36).

19. Kant makes a comparable argument based on the "kingdom of ends" (434, 40).

20. See the antinomies of reason in Kant (1996). Thus freedom, god, and immortality abide in the noumenal world.

21. See generally Rosen (1974); Williams (1997); Pippin (1989).

22. Hegel's engagement with Kant takes place on a number of levels. Hegel charged Kant's moral theory with formalism, abstract universalism, on the impotence of the "ought," and the dangers of pure conviction: see Smith (1973); Habermas (1989); Geiger (2007).

23. Or, as Westphal (1991, 157–60) puts it, "Kant's dichotomy between categorical and hypothetical imperatives is probably not exhaustive. If this dichotomy is not exhaustive, then Kant cannot defend motivational internalism simply by rejecting consequentialism and its hypothetical imperatives."

24. See generally Smith (1973, 448 ff); Ameriks (1985); Pippin (1989).

25. Hegel (1977, B IV, 175, 110).

26. Hegel (1977, 177). As Williams (1997, 35) puts it, "spirit constituting process of recognition involves four elements: autonomy, union, self-overcoming, and *Freigabe*."

27. See, for example, Grant (1997) on Rousseau and integrity; Trilling (1972).

28. On the difference between *individium* and *dividium*, see Golomb (2012).

29. For a history of the concept, see Trilling (1972); Berman (2009); Guignon (2004); Golomb (2012).

30. See Kierkegaard (1983); Nietzsche (1995; 1989); Heidegger (1996); Sartre (1989); and generally Carman (2006); Ferrara (1998).

31. Existentialist authors can show the substance of authenticity in practice only by referring to literary figures. Consider, for example, Kierkegaard and Abraham; Nietzsche and Zarathustra; Sartre and Mathieu.

32. "L'enfer, c'est les autres" in Sartre's play *No Exit*.

33. See, for example, Eisenberg and Kymlicka (2011).

34. Though the scholarship seems beset with this problem too, without the same excuse. For example, though starting with Kantian "autonomy" in the *Theory of Communicative Action*, Habermas in *Philosophical Discourse of Modernity* sought to incorporate authenticity into autonomy: see Ferrara (1997, 9); Habermas (1984; 1989). See also Taylor's (1994) use of authenticity and recognition to justify group rights for Québécoise. Autonomy, for example, has taken on a diversity of meanings beyond its Kantian formulation. Recognition has cast aside its Hegelian moorings to confront the problem of "diversity." And authenticity has left existentialism to capture the contemporary longing for the "real."

35. On the limitations of the language of politics of identity, see Brubaker and Cooper (2000).

36. See Aristotle's *Rhetoric*, especially the discussion of *ethos* (1356a1–13) and *pathos* (1356a14–16; Bk II, Chs 2–11). See, also Hardt (1993) on rhetoric, authenticity, and its implications for critical theory; and Birks (2011) on the importance of the emotional authenticity of "ordinary people."

37. See Street (2004) regarding the "visual" nature of modern rhetoric.

CHAPTER 9

1. For a history of patriotism, see Dietz (1989); Viroli (1995). For advocates of patriotism, see MacIntyre (2002); Schaar (1981); Rorty (1998); Berns (2007); Miller (1995).

2. Johnston (2007, 13, 15), for example, claims that patriotism has a "Manichean logic" and can be shown to "depend on and produce the cult of endless enmity." Nussbaum (1996) favors "becoming a citizen of the world" and is therefore a strong advocate of cosmopolitanism (but note that she subsequently modifies her views in Nussbaum 2008).

3. For constitutional patriotism, see Habermas (1996); Ingram (1996); Müller (2007); Dietz (1989). For republican patriotism, see Viroli (1995). For "moderate" patriotism, see Baron (2002); Appiah (1997); Walzer (1974); Tan (2004).

4. See Schaar (1981). For the extensive scholarship on nationalism, see the discussion below.

5. For an earlier exploration of the main themes of this chapter, see Patapan (2014).

6. Contemporary international relations theory significantly influenced by Hobbesian realism disputed the importance of honor in foreign relations: see Markey (1999), who argues that both modern realism and neorealism reject or neglect prestige as an end in itself. For a critical engagement with Markey, see Joshi (2008), who attempts to use an alternative theory of "negative honor" or "shame

aversion" to conceptualize honor. On honor in international relations more generally, see Lebow (2006). Prestige defined instrumentally as "reputation for power" is a subject of realist thinkers such as Morgenthau (1985) and Herz (1950). But the neorealism of Waltz (1979), with its materialist ontology and systemic framework, rejects prestige altogether. On a discussion of instrumental prestige and deterrence theory, see Schelling (1960); Mercer (1995); Copeland et al. (1997). For a brief discussion of different national conceptions of prestige, see Nicolson (1937). For an extended discussion of deterrence theory that draws upon social psychology to undermine the claims of reputation as an end, arguing "we should never go to war because of our reputation," see Mercer (2006). For the importance of symbols in international relations, see O'Neill (1999).

7. The Nanking Massacre (December 1937–January 1938) was the mass killing and rape of Chinese citizens and capitulated soldiers by soldiers of the Japanese Imperial Army after its seizure of Nanjing, China, on December 13, 1937, during the Sino-Japanese War. The number of Chinese killed in the massacre has been subject of much debate, with most estimates ranging from 100,000 to more than 300,000.

8. On the importance of shame and pride in international relations between Japan and China, see McGregor (2017, 144–68; 169–89).

9. There is an extensive scholarship on transitional justice: see, for example, Girelli (2017); Murphy (2017); Williams et al. (2012).

10. On the ZANU-PF use of "Patriotic History" in which the political battle is always between "patriots" and "traitors," see Tendi (2010).

11. See, for example, Aristotle's discussion in the *Politics* (Book 3) of whether the good person is different from the good citizen.

12. Machiavelli to Vettori, April 16, 1527, in Atkinson and Sices (1996, 416).

13. Though he acknowledges that threats to republics may be unexpected (such as the Agrarian Law reforms: D III, 17.1) and that in due course there may be a need to return to origins or the beginnings to refound republic (D III 22.3).

14. See generally Patapan (2009). As Hobbes notes, "yet in all times, Kings, and Persons of Soveraigne authority, because of their Independency, are in continuall jealousies, and in the state and posture of Gladiators" (L 13, 187). Moreover, his account of the continuous skirmishes by the "infinite number of little Lords" in Germany (L 10, 158) suggests that glory (with its attendant "insatiable appetite, or Bulimia, of enlarging Dominion": L 29, 375).

15. See generally Hegel's *Philosophy of Right* (1821) and generally his *Phenomenology of Spirit* (1807).

16. See in this context Gellner (1983, 138), who views nationalism as a "very distinctive species of patriotism," and Schaar (1981, 245), who argues: "when liberalism had proceeded so far in its work of breaking the bonds among men that new ones were needed to provide at least the minimum of warmth and some measure of connectedness and direction."

17. For a general overview of the scholarship, see Hutchinson and Smith (1994); McKim and McMahan (1997); Smith (1998); Spencer and Wollman (2005); Özkirimli (2010). On political theory works on nationalism, see Beiner (1999); Canovan (1996).

18. Consider, for example, Rousseau's advocacy of an "esprit de corps," Herder's "Volk," Hegel's "phenomenology of spirit" and "civilization," and Fichte's emphasis on language.

19. This explains the various attempts to constitutionalize nationalism (Habermas 1996) or make it "republican" (Viroli 1995) or even "liberal" (Tamir 1993).

20. See generally Li (2016); Lampton (2014); Brown (2016).

21. On the notion of motherland and sacred territory, see the Preamble, Constitution of the People's Republic of China (as per March 14, 2004, amendments): http://www.npc.gov.cn/englishnpc/Constitution/2007-11/15/content_1372962.htm.

22. The history is more complicated, with the Japanese contributing to the defeat of Russian and other European forces, and the Kuomintang or Nationalist Party instrumental in fighting the Japanese until its defeat by CPC.

23. On the role of the "Patriotic Education Campaign," see Wang (2008). As Wang (2008, 789) notes, national humiliation was not used by leaders during Mao's time, where class struggle and "victor narrative" was emphasized and China's failures were attributed to internal corruption and the incompetence of feudal and capitalist rulers, the Qing Court, and the nationalist Kuomintang: "In the 1990s, with the decline of Communist ideology as a source of legitimacy, the CCP leaders realized that history education on national humiliation was an effective device for the regime to legitimize its rule. National humiliation discourse thus was revived in the service of patriotic education."

24. Recent instances include its anger over Japan's nationalizations of the Senkaku Islands (also known as Diaoyu Islands by the PRC), the land reclamation on Fiery Cross Reef in the Spratly Islands in the South China Sea, and China's defeat in 2016 before the International Tribunal for the Law of the Sea in The Hague, Netherlands, in an action by the Philippines regarding the Scarborough Shoal, where the tribunal concluded that there was no legal basis for China to claim historic rights to resources within the sea areas falling within the "nine-dash line."

25. On "One Belt, One Road," see, for example, Ferdinand (2016).

26. Consider, for example the Preamble to the Chinese Constitution (2014) that states, "Taiwan is part of the sacred territory of the People's Republic of China. It is the inviolable duty of all Chinese people, including our compatriots in Taiwan, to accomplish the great task of reunifying the motherland."

27. On the crisis of legitimacy, see Chen (1995). Xi's father, Xi Zongxun (1913–2002), was a Chinese Communist revolutionary and political official in PRC. He was part of the first generation of Chinese leadership and was imprisoned and purged a number of times by Mao.

28. Rejecting Deng's view that Mao was 70 percent right and 30 percent wrong, with the major mistakes in his final years. At the same time, Xi rejected the excesses and dangers of the Cultural Revolution, imprisoning for corruption another notable charismatic princeling, Bo Xilai, who attempted to revive "Sing Red, Strike Black" and other mass mobilization techniques.

29. While rejecting human rights and "Western" democracy. This has resulted in stringent limits on freedom of speech, a concerted attack on human rights lawyers, and repudiation of Western capitalism.

30. For an overview of Chinese nationalism and its implications for foreign policy, see Duan (2017).

31. https://www.economist.com/leaders/2013/05/04/xi-jinping-and-the-chinese-dream. See also Ferdinand (2016) and Callahan (2015, 1001), who argues that China Dream has a "socialist/civilizational" dynamic that draws on Mao and *Book of Rites* to defend a statist tradition opposed to "liberalism, the West and the United States."

32. Xi Jinping in Zhonggong zhongyang wenxian yanjiushi, ed., Xi Jinping guanyu shixian Zhonghua minzuweida fuxing de Zhongguo meng: Lunshu gaobian [Xi Jinping on Realizing the China Dream of the Great Rejuvenation of the Chinese Nation: Discussion Edition] (Beijing: Zhongyang wenxian chubanshe, December 2013), 3, 5.

33. See Guangkai (2010) on Chinese diplomatic strategy.

CHAPTER 10

1. On the origins of the stories and how they were adapted and altered, see Haddawy (1990); Mahdi (1995); Irwin (2009).

2. King Shahrayar is said to be from the Persian Sasanid dynasty (CE 226–641). He initially marries the daughter of princes, an army officer, and then a merchant before deciding to choose from commoners. Interestingly, he never approaches his vizier and his daughters (Haddawy 1990, 14).

3. For other interpretations of the work, see Mahdi (1995, 126–80), "Three Interpretations."

4. The king's receptivity to philosophy and knowledge is evident from his first practical response to the treachery and the subsequent rage he felt, which was in a sense an exploration of the phenomenon and how to ameliorate it. Only after his experience with the Story of the Demon, which shows that not even a demon is immune from infidelity, is he convinced that there is no solution and he must resort to the cruel method he adopts (Irwin 2009, 159–77).

5. See Thucydides, *Peloponnesian Wars*, 2.37; and Harris (1992), who examines the speech for the insights it yields into the institutional aspect of Athenian democracy.

6. See Arendt (1951; 1963); Geddes, Wright, and Frantz (2014); Newell (2016). Compare, for example, the ambitions of China's Xi Jinping and Russia's Vladimir Putin with the kleptocracy of Mbasogo of Equatorial Guinea, Zuma of South Africa. On African kleptocracy, see generally Carter (2018).

7. On "smart authoritarianism," see Morgenbesser (2017). On the crisis of democracy, see Freedom House (2018). Regimes that were thought to be in transition to democracy now appear to be favoring authoritarianism. On the rise of so called "hybrid" regimes, consider Hungary, Poland, Serbia, Russia, Turkey, and Ukraine in Central and Eastern Europe; Venezuela, Brazil, Bolivia, Nicaragua, and Ecuador in Latin America; Zambia and Burundi in Africa; and Bangladesh, Thailand, and the Philippines in Asia-Pacific. See generally Levitsky and Ziblatt (2018); Mounk (2018); Mechkova, Lührmann, and Lindberg (2017).

8. Across Europe, the average share of the vote won by populist parties has more than doubled since the 1960s, their share of seats has tripled, they form the largest opposition party in Germany and the Netherlands, and they hold government office in countries such as Austria, Norway, and Switzerland: see Norris and Inglehart (2018).

9. For the influential distinction, see Weber (1978b).

10. See Lincoln's famous speech "The Perpetuation of our Political Institutions" (1943), where he notes, "towering genius disdains a beaten path"; Kane and Patapan (2012, 151–68).

11. See generally Krause (2002).

REFERENCES

Adair, Douglass. 1974. "Fame and the Founding Fathers." In *Fame and the Founding Fathers: Essays by Douglass Adair*, edited by Trevor Colbourn, 3–26. New York: W. W. Norton & Company.

Adler, Alfred. 1924. *The Practice and Theory of Individual Psychology*. London: Routledge and Kegan Paul.

Adorno, Theodor. [1972]. 1991. *The Culture Industry: Selected Essays on Mass Culture*. London: Routledge.

Ahrensdorf, Peter J. 2000. "The Fear of Death and the Longing for Immortality: Hobbes and Thucydides on Human Nature and the Problem of Anarchy." *American Political Science Review*, September, 94 (3): 579–93.

Alcoff, Linda. 2006. "The Political Critique." In *Visible Identities: Race, Gender, and the Self*, by Linda Alcoff, 20–46. Oxford: Oxford University Press.

Allison, Henry E. 2012. *Essays on Kant*, by Henry E. Allison, 124–36. Oxford: Oxford University Press.

Allix, Nicholas M. 2000. "Transformational Leadership: Democratic or Despotic?" *Educational Management & Administration* 28 (1): 7–20.

Altman, Andrew. 1989. "Glory, Respect, and Violent Conflict." In *The Causes of Quarrel—Essays on Peace, War and Thomas Hobbes*, edited by Peter Caws, 114–27. Boston: Beacon Press.

Ameriks, Karl. 1985. "Hegel's Critique of Kant's Theoretical Philosophy." *Philosophy and Phenomenological Research* 46 (1): 1–35.

Amin, Sara N. 2014. "The Impact of Identity Politics in Challenging National Narratives: A Case Study among Canadian Muslims." *Studies in Ethnicity and Nationalism* 14 (3): 418–35.

Appiah, Kwame Anthony. 1997. "Cosmopolitan Patriots." *Critical Inquiry*, Spring, 23 (3): 617–39.

Appiah, Kwame Anthony. 2005. *The Ethics of Identity*. Princeton: Princeton University Press.

Appiah, Kwame Anthony. 2010. *The Honor Code: How Moral Revolutions Happen*. New York: Norton and Company.

Aquinas, St Thomas. [1256–1272]. 1947–1948. *Summa Theologica*. Translated by Fathers of the English Dominican Province. London: Burns & Oates.

Arendt, Hannah. 1951. *The Origins of Totalitarianism*. New York: Harcourt.

Arendt, Hannah. 1963. *Eichmann in Jerusalem: A Report on the Banality of Evil*. New York: Viking Press.

Aristophanes. 1984. "Clouds." In *Four Texts on Socrates*, translated by Thomas G. West and Grace Starry West, introduction by Thomas G. West, 115–76. Ithaca: Cornell University Press.

Aristotle. 1962. *Nicomachean Ethics*. Translated by Terence Irwin. Indianapolis: Hackett Publishing Company.

Aristotle. 1984. *The Politics*. Translated by Carnes Lord. Chicago: University of Chicago Press.

Arnhard, Larry. 1983. " 'Statesmanship as Magnanimity: Classical, Christian and Modern.' " *Polity* 16: 263–83.

Ash Jr., James L. 1976. "The Decline of Ecstatic Prophecy in the Early Church." *Theological Studies* 37 (2): 227–52.

Atkinson, James B., and David Sices, eds. 1996. *Machiavelli and His Friends: Their Personal Correspondence*. Translated by James B. Atkinson and David Sices. DeKalb: Northern Illinois University Press.

Aucoin, Peter. 2012. "New Political Governance in Westminster Systems: Impartial Public Administration and Management Performance at Risk." *Governance* 25 (2): 177–99.

Averroes. [1177]. 1969. *Averroes' Commentary on Plato's Republic*. Edited by Erwin Isak Jakob. Cambridge: Cambridge University Press.

Barber, James David. 1972. *The Presidential Character: Predicting Performance in the White House*. Englewood Cliffs, NJ: Prentice Hall.

Barfield, Raymond. 2011. *The Ancient Quarrel Between Philosophy and Poetry*. Cambridge: Cambridge University Press.

Baron, Marcia. 2002. "Patriotism and Liberal Morality." In *Patriotism*, edited by Igor Primoratz, 59–86. Amherst: Humanity Books.

Barr, Michael D. 2000. "Lee Kuan Yew's Fabian Phase." *Australian Journal of Politics & History*, March, 46 (1): 110–26.

Barr, Michael D. 2002. *Cultural Politics and Asian Values: The Tepid War*. London: Routledge.

Barr, Michael D., and Zlatko Skrbiš. 2008. *Constructing Singapore: Elitism, Ethnicity and the Nation-Building Project*. Copenhagen: NIAS Press.

Barry, Brian 2001. *Culture and Equality: An Egalitarian Critique of Multiculturalism*. Cambridge: Harvard University Press.

Bass, Bernard. 1985. *Leadership and Performance Beyond Expectations*. Glencoe: Free Press.

Becker, Gary S. 1976. *The Economic Approach to Human Behavior*. Chicago: University of Chicago Press.

Beiner, Ronald. 2012. *Civil Religion: A Dialogue in the History of Political Philosophy*. Cambridge: Cambridge University Press.

Beiner, Ronald, ed. 1999. *Theorizing Nationalism*. Albany: State University of New York Press.

Belliotti, Raymond A. 2009. "Methods, Motivations and Purposes: The Prince." In *Niccolò Machiavelli: The Laughing Lion and the Strutting Fox*, by Raymond A Belliotti, 63–98. Lanham: Lexington Books.

Bellows, Thomas. 1970. *The People's Action Party of Singapore: Emergence of a Dominant Party System*. New Haven: Southeast Asia Studies, Yale University.

Benedict, Ruth. 2005. *Chrysanthemum and the Sword*. Boston: Houghton Mifflin.

Benner, Erica. 2009. "Legislators and Princes." In *Machiavelli's Ethics*, by Erica Benner, 407–50. Princeton: Princeton University Press.

Benner, Erica. 2013. "Why Princes Need the Truth." In *Machiavelli's Prince: A New Reading*, by Erica Benner, 273–82. Oxford: Oxford University Press.

Bensman, Joseph, and Michael Givant. 1975. "Charisma and Modernity: The Use and Abuse of a Concept." *Social Research* 42 (4): 570–614.

Bentley, Eric. 1969. *The Cult of the Superman*. Gloucester, MA: Peter Smith.

Berger, Peter. 1984. "On the Obsolescence of the Concept of Honour." In *Liberalism and its Critics*, edited by Michael Sandel, 149–58. Oxford: Basil Blackwell.

Berland, K. J. H. 1986. "Bringing Philosophy Down from the Heavens: Socrates and the New Science." *Journal of the History of Ideas* 47 (2): 299–308.

Berman, Marshall. [1970]. 2009. *The Politics of Authenticity: Radical Individualism and the Emergence of Modern Society*. London: Verso.

Berns, Walter. 2007. "Patriotism and Multiculturalism." In *The Many Faces of Patriotism*, edited by Philip Abbott, 3–14. Lanham: Rowman & Littlefield.

Bernstein, Mary. 2005. "Identity Politics." *Annual Review of Sociology* 31: 47–74.

Bernstein, Mary. 2002. "Identities and Politics: Toward a Historical Understanding of the Lesbian and Gay Movement." *Social Science History* 26 (3): 531–81.

Bernstein, Mary, and Verta Taylor. 2013. "Identity Politics." In *The Wiley-Blackwell Encyclopedia of Social and Political Movements*, edited by David A. Snow, Donatella della Porta, Bert Klandermans, and Doug McAdam, 1–4. Hoboken: Wiley-Blackwell.

Bertrand, J. 2013. *Political Change in Southeast Asia*. New York: Cambridge University Press.

Best, Heinrich, and John Higley. 2010. *Democratic Elitism: New Theoretical and Comparative Perspectives*. Brill: Leiden.

Bickford, Susan. 1997. "Anti-Anti-Identity Politics: Feminism, Democracy, and the Complexities of Citizenship." *Hypatia* 12 (4): 111–31.

Birks, Jen. 2011. "The Politics of Protest in Newspaper Campaigns: Dissent, Populism and the Rhetoric of Authenticity." *British Politics*, June, 6 (2): 128–54.

Blick, Andrew. 2004. *People Who Live in the Dark: The History of the Special Advisor in British Politics*. London: Politicos.

Bligh, Michelle C. 2011. "Followership and Follower-Centred Approaches." In *The SAGE Handbook of Leadership*, edited by Alan Bryman, David L. Collinson, Keith Grint, Brad Jackson, and Mary Uhl-Bien, chapter 31, 425–36. London: Sage.

Bloom, Alan. 1991. "Interpretive Essay." In Plato's *Republic*, translated by Alan Bloom. New York: Basic Books.

Borchert, Jens. 2009. "They Ain't Making Elites Like They Used To: The Never Ending Trouble with Democratic Elitism." *Comparative Sociology* 8 (3): 345–63.

Borowitz, Albert. 2005. *Terrorism for Self-Glorification: The Herostratos Syndrome*. Kent: Kent State University Press.

Bourdieu, Pierre. [1989]. 1996. *The State Nobility: Elite Schools in the Field of Power*. Translated by Lauretta C. Clough. Cambridge: Polity Press.

Bowman, James. 2006. *Honor: A History*. New York: Encounter Books.

Braudy, Leo. 1997. *The Frenzy of Renown: Fame and Its History*. New York: Vintage Books.

Brennan, Geoffrey, and Philip Pettit. 2005. "The Feasibility Issue." In *The Oxford Handbook of Contemporary Philosophy*, edited by Frank Jackson and Michael Smith, chapter 10, 258–79. Oxford: Oxford University Press.

Brinkley, Douglas, and Luke A. Nichter. 2015. *The Nixon Tapes: 1973*. Boston: Houghton Mifflin Harcourt.

Brown, Archie. 2014. *The Myth of the Strong Leader: Political Leadership in the Modern Age*. New York: Vintage Books.

Brown, Kerry 2016. *CEO, China: The Rise of Xi Jinping*. London: I. B. Tauris.

Brown, Michael E., and Linda K. Treviño. 2006. "Ethical Leadership: A Review and Future Directions." *The Leadership Quarterly* 17 (6): 595–616.

Brubaker, Rogers, and Frederick Cooper. 2000. "Beyond Identity." *Theory and Society* 29 (1): 1–47.

Burke, John P. 2005. "The Contemporary Presidency: Condoleezza Rice as NSC Advisor: A Case Study of the Honest Broker Role." *Presidential Studies Quarterly* 35 (3): 554–75.

Burke, Edmund. [1757]. 2008. *A Philosophical Enquiry into the Origin of our Ideas of the Sublime and Beautiful*. New York: Dover Publications.

Burns, James MacGregor. 1956. *Roosevelt: The Lion and the Fox*. New York: Harcourt, Brace & Jovanovich.

Burns, James MacGregor. 1978. *Leadership*. New York: Harper & Row.

Bury, Robert G. 1969. *The Symposium of Plato*. Edited, with introduction, critical notes, and commentary. 2nd ed. Cambridge: Heiffer and Sons.

Calhoun, Craig. 1994. "Social Theory and the Politics of Identity." In *Social Theory and the Politics of Identity*, edited by Craig Calhoun, 9–36. Cambridge: Blackwell.

Callahan, William A. 2015. "History, Tradition and the China Dream: Socialist Modernization in the World of Great Harmony." *Journal of Contemporary China* 24 (96): 983–1001.

Calvin, Jean. 1989. "The Work of Christ." In *Calvin's Institutes: A New Compendium*, edited by Hugh T. Kerr, 75–80. Louisville: Westminster and John Knox Press.

Caner, Daniel. 2002. "Introduction." In *Wandering, Begging Monks: Spiritual Authority and the Promotion of Monasticism in Late Antiquity*, by Daniel Caner, 1–18. Berkeley: University of California Press.

Canovan, Margaret. 1996. *Nationhood and Political Theory*. Cheltenham: Edward Elgar.

Carlyle, Thomas. 1840. *On Heroes, Hero Worship and the Heroic in History*. London: Chapman and Hall.

Carman, Taylor. 2006. "The Concept of Authenticity." In *A Companion to Phenomenology and Existentialism*, edited by Hubert L. Dreyfus and Mark A. Wrathall, 229–39. Malden: Blackwell Publishers.

Carroll, Lewis. 1976. *Alice's Adventures in Wonderland*. London: Academy Editions.

Carter, Brett L. 2018. "Autocrats Versus Activists in Africa." *Journal of Democracy* 29 (1): 54–68.

Caws, Peter, ed. 1989. *The Causes of Quarrel—Essays on Peace, War and Thomas Hobbes*. Beacon Press: Boston.

Chan, Joseph. 2013. *Confucian Perfectionism: A Political Philosophy for Modern Times*. Princeton: Princeton University Press.

Chappell, Zsuzsanna. 2012. *Deliberative Democracy: A Critical Introduction*. Basingstoke: Palgrave Macmillan.

Chen, Jie. 1995. "The Impact of Reform on the Party and Ideology in China." *Journal of Contemporary China* 4 (9): 22–34.

Christie, Clive J. 2000. *Ideology and Revolution in Southeast Asia 1900–80: Political Ideas of the Anti-Colonial Era*. New York: Routledge.

Chua Beng-Huat, 1985. "Pragmatism of the People's Action Party Government in Singapore: A Critical Era." *Southeast Asian Journal of Social Science* 13 (2): 29–46.

Cicero. 2005. *De Officiis*. Cambridge: Harvard University Press.

Ciulla, Joanne B., Terry L. Price, and Susan E. Murphy, eds. 2006. *The Quest for Moral Leaders: Essays on Leadership Ethics*. Cheltenham: Edward Elgar.

Coby, Patrick J. 1999. *Machiavelli's Romans: Liberty and Greatness in the Discourses on Livy*. Lanham: Lexington Books.

Collinson, David. 2011. "Critical Leadership Studies." In *The SAGE Handbook of Leadership*, edited by Alan Bryman, David L. Collinson, Keith Grint, Brad Jackson, and Mary Uhl-Bien, chapter 13, 181–94. London: Sage.

Collinson, David. 2014. "Dichotomies, Dialectics and Dilemmas: New Directions for Critical Leadership Studies?" *Leadership* 10 (1): 36–55.

Connaughton, Bernardette. 2015. "Navigating the Borderlines of Politics and Administration: Reflections on the Role of Ministerial Advisers." *International Journal of Public Administration* 38 (1): 37–45.

Copeland, Dale C., Paul K. Huth, and Jonathan Mercer. 1997. "What's in a Name? Debating Jonathan Mercer's Reputation and International Politics." *Security Studies* 7 (1): 32–113.

Cornell, Christine, and Patrick Malcolmson. 2009. "Prudence and Glory: Machiavelli on Political Leadership." In *The Ashgate Research Companion to Political Leadership*, edited by Mikhail A. Molchanov, W. Andy Knight, and Joseph Masciulli, 65–85. Farnham: Ashgate.

Craft, Jonathan. 2015. "Conceptualizing the Policy Work of Partisan Advisers." *Policy Science* 48 (2): 135–58.

Craig, Leon. 1996. *The War Lover*. Toronto: University of Toronto Press.

Crenshaw, Kimberle. 1991. "Mapping the Margins: Intersectionality, Identity Politics, and Violence against Women of Color." *Stanford Law Review* 43 (6): 1241–99.

Cumings, Bruce. 1999. "Webs with no Spiders, and Spiders with no Webs: The Genealogy of the Developmental State." In *The Developmental State*, edited by Meredith Woo-Cumings, 61–92. Ithaca: Cornell University Press.

Dahl, Robert. 1961. *Who Governs: Democracy and Power in an American City*. New Haven: Yale University Press.

Dahlstrom, Carl, B. Guy Peters, and Jon Pierre, eds. 2011. *Steering from the Centre: Strengthening Political Control in Western Democracies*. Toronto: University of Toronto Press.

Dallek, Robert. 2007. *Nixon and Kissinger: Partners in Power*. New York: HarperCollins.

Davidson, N. S. 1993. "Temporal Power and the Vicar of Christ: The Papal State from 1450 to 1650." *Renaissance and Modern Studies* 36 (1): 1–14.

De Bary, W. Theodore. 1991. *The Trouble with Confucianism*. Cambridge, MA: Harvard University Press.

De Bary, W. Theodore. 2000. *Asian Values and Human Rights*. Cambridge, MA: Harvard University Press.

De Mey, Peter. 2009. "The Bishop's Participation in the Threefold Munera: Comparing the Appeal to the Pattern of the Tria Munera at Vatican II and in the Ecumenical Dialogues." *Jurist* 69 (1): 31–58.

Deluga, Ronald J. 2001. "American Presidential Machiavellianism Implications for Charismatic Leadership and Rated Performance." *The Leadership Quarterly* 12 (3): 339–63.

Denhardt, Robert B., and Janet V. Denhardt. 2000. "The New Public Service: Serving Rather than Steering." *Public Administration Review* 60 (6): 549–59.

Dietz, Mary G. 1986. "Trapping *The Prince*: Machiavelli and the Politics of Deception." *The American Political Science Review* 80 (3): 777–99.

Dietz, Mary G. 1989. "Patriotism." In *Political Innovation and Conceptual Change*, edited by Terence Ball, James Farr, and Russell L. Hanson, 177–93. Cambridge: Cambridge University Press.

Dryzek, John S. 2002. *Deliberative Democracy and Beyond: Liberals, Critics, Contestations*. Oxford: Oxford University Press.

Duan, Xiaolin. 2017. "Unanswered Questions: Why We May Be Wrong about Chinese Nationalism and Its Foreign Policy Implications." *Journal of Contemporary China* 26 (108): 886–900.

Duncan, Christopher M., and Peter J. Steinberger. 1990. "Plato's Paradox? Guardians and Philosopher-Kings." *American Political Science Review* 84 (4): 1317–22.

Eldar, Dan. 1986. "Glory and the Boundaries of Public Morality in Machiavelli's Thought." *History of Political Thought* 7 (3): 419–38.

Eichbaum, Chris, and Richard Shaw, eds. 2010. *Partisan Appointees and Public Servants: An International Analysis of the Role of the Political Adviser.* London: Edward Elgar.

Eisenberg, Avigail, and Will Kymlicka. 2011. "Bringing Institutions Back In: How Public Institutions Assess Identity." In *Identity Politics in the Public Realm: Bringing Institutions Back In,* edited by Avigail Eisenberg and Will Kymlicka, 1–30. Vancouver: UBC Press.

Elgie, Robert. 1995. *Political Leadership in Liberal Democracies.* Basingstoke: Palgrave Macmillan.

Elgie, Robert. 2015. *Studying Political Leadership: Foundations and Contending Accounts.* Hampshire: Palgrave Macmillan.

Englehart, Neil. 2000. "Rights and Culture in the Asian Values Argument: The Rise and Fall of Confucian Ethics in Singapore." *Human Rights Quarterly* 22 (2): 548–68.

English, James F. 2008. *The Economy of Prestige: Prizes, Awards, and the Circulation of Cultural Value.* Cambridge, MA: Harvard University Press.

Erasmus. [1514]. 1997. *The Education of a Christian Prince.* Edited by Lisa Jardine, translated by Neil M. Cheshire and Michael J. Heath. Cambridge: Cambridge University Press.

Esselment, Anna L., Jennifer Lees-Marshment, and Alex Marland. 2014. "The Nature of Political Advising to Prime Ministers in Australia, Canada, New Zealand and the UK." *Commonwealth & Comparative Politics* 52 (3): 358–75.

Estlund, David. 2008. *Democratic Authority: A Philosophical Framework.* Princeton: Princeton University Press.

Eylon, Yuval, and David Heyd. 2008. "Flattery." *Philosophy and Phenomenological Research* 77 (3): 685–704.

Faulkner, Robert. 2007. *The Case for Greatness: Honourable Ambition and its Critics.* New Haven: Yale University Press.

Ferdinand, Peter. 2016. "Westward Ho—The China Dream and 'One Belt, One Road': Chinese Foreign Policy under Xi Jinping." *International Affairs* 92 (4): 941–57.

Ferrara, Alessandro. 1997. "Authenticity as a Normative Category." *Philosophy & Social Criticism,* May, 23 (3): 77–92.

Ferrara, Alessandro. 1998. *Reflective Authenticity.* London: Routledge.

Fischer, Markus. 1997. "Machiavelli's Political Psychology." *The Review of Politics* 59 (4): 789–829.

Fischer, Markus. 2000. *Well-ordered Licence: On the Unity of Machiavelli's Thought.* Lanham: Lexington Books.

Fleisher, Martin. 1973. "Machiavelli and the Nature of Political Thought." *Political Theory* 1 (1): 79–91.

Flinders, Matthew. 2012. *Defending Politics*. Oxford: Oxford University Press.

Fontana, Benedetto. 1999. "Love of Country and Love of God: The Political Uses of Religion in Machiavelli." *Journal of History of Ideas* 60 (4): 639–58.

Forde, Steven. 1989. *The Ambition to Rule: Alcibiades and the Politics of Imperialism in Thucydides*. Ithaca: Cornell University Press.

Fortin, Ernest L. 1996. *The Birth of Philosophic Christianity*. Edited by J. Brian Benestad. Lanham: Rowman and Littlefield.

Foucault, Michael. 2001. *Fearless Speech*. Boston: MIT Press.

Fraser, Nancy, and Axel Honneth. 2003. *Redistribution or Recognition? A Political-Philosophical Exchange*. London: Verso.

Freedom House. 2018. "Freedom in the World, 2018: Democracy in Crisis." https://freedomhouse.org/report/freedom-world/freedom-world-2018.

French, Shannon. 2003. *The Code of the Warrior: Exploring Warrior Values Past and Present*. Lanham: Rowman and Littlefield.

Fu, Ping, Anne S. Tsui, Jun Liu, and Lan Li. 2010. "Pursuit of Whose Happiness? Executive Leaders' Transformational Behaviors and Personal Values." *Administrative Science Quarterly* 55 (2): 222–54.

Gains, Francesca, and Gerry Stoker. 2011. "Special Advisers and the Transmission of Ideas from the Policy Primeval Soup." *Policy & Politics* 39 (4): 485–98.

Galvão-Sobrinho, Carlos R. 2013. *Doctrine and Power: Theological Controversy and Christian Leadership in the Later Roman Empire*. Berkeley: University of California Press.

Garver, Eugene. 1987. *Machiavelli and the History of Prudence*. Wisconsin: University of Wisconsin Press.

Geddes, Barbara, Joseph Wright, and Erica Frantz. 2014. "Autocratic Breakdown and Regime Transitions: A New Data Set." *Perspectives on Politics* 12 (2): 313–31.

Geier, Alfred. 2002. *Plato's Erotic Thought: The Tree of the Unknown*. Rochester: University of Rochester Press.

Geiger, Ido. 2007. *The Founding Act of Modern Ethical Life: Hegel's Critique of Kant's Moral and Political Philosophy*. Stanford: Stanford University Press.

Gellner, Ernest. 1983. *Nations and Nationalism*. Oxford: Oxford University Press.

George, Thayil J. S. 1973. *Lee Kuan Yew's Singapore*. London: Andre Deutsch.

Gilbert, Allan. 1968. *Machiavelli's Prince and its Forerunners: The Prince as a Typical Book de regimeine principum*. New York: Barnes & Noble.

Giles, David. 2000. *Illusions of Immortality: A Psychology of Fame and Celebrity*. Houndmills: Macmillan Press.

Ginsberg, Robert. 1974. "Kant and Hobbes on the Social Contract." *The Southwestern Journal of Philosophy* 5 (1): 115–19.

Girelli, Giada. 2017. *Understanding Transitional Justice: A Struggle for Peace, Reconciliation*. Cham: Springer.

Golomb, Jacob. 2012. *In Search of Authenticity.* Abingdon: Routledge.

Goodin, Robert, and Kai Spiekermann. 2018. *An Epistemic Theory of Democracy.* Oxford: Oxford University Press.

Grant, Ruth. 1997. *Hypocrisy and Integrity: Machiavelli, Rousseau, and the Ethics of Politics* Chicago: Chicago University Press.

Green, Donald P., and Ian Shapiro. 1994. *Pathologies of Rational Choice Theory.* New Haven: Yale University Press.

Greenstein, Fred. I. 2009. *The Presidential Difference: Leadership Style from FDR to Barack Obama.* 3rd ed. Princeton: Princeton University Press.

Gronn, Peter. 1995. "Greatness Re-Visited: The Current Obsession with Transformational Leadership." *Leading and Managing* 1 (1): 14–27.

Gruber, Howard E. 1983. "History and Creative Work: From the Most Ordinary to the Most Exalted." *Journal of the History of the Behavioral Sciences*, January, 19 (1): 4–14.

Guangkai, Xiong. 2010. "China's Diplomatic Strategy: Implication and Translation of 'tao guang yang hui.'" Chinese People's Institute of Foreign Affairs, *Foreign Affairs Journal*, no. 98, Winter.

Guignon, Charles B. 2004. *On Being Authentic.* London: Routledge.

Gutmann, Amy. 2003. "The Good, the Bad and the Ugly of Identity Politics." In *Identity in Democracy*, by Amy Gutmann, 1–37. Princeton: Princeton University Press.

Habermas, Jürgen. 1984. *The Theory of Communicative Action.* Boston: Beacon Press.

Habermas, Jürgen. 1989. *The Structural Transformation of the Public Sphere: An Inquiry into a Category of Bourgeois Society.* Cambridge: MIT Press.

Habermas, Jürgen. 1996. "Citizenship and National Identity." Essay Incorporated as Appendix II in *Between Facts and Norms: Contributions to a Discourse Theory of Law and Democracy*, by Jürgen Habermas, 491–516. Cambridge: MIT Press.

Haddawy, Husain. 1990. *Arabian Nights: The Thousand and One Nights.* New York: W. W. Norton & Co.

Hale, Charles R. 1997. "Cultural Politics of Identity in Latin America." *Annual Review of Anthropology* 26 (1): 567–90.

Hamilton, Alexander, James Madison, and John Jay. 1988. *The Federalist Papers.* Toronto: Bantam Books.

Hampton, Jean. 1989. "Hobbesian Reflections on Glory as a Cause of Conflict." In *The Causes of Quarrel—Essays on Peace, War and Thomas Hobbes*, edited by Peter Caws, 78–96. Boston: Beacon Press.

Han Fook Kwang, Warren Fernandez, and Sumiko Tan. 1998. *Lee Kuan Yew: The Man and His Ideas.* Singapore: The Straits Times Press.

Hardt, Hanno. 1993. "Authenticity, Communication, and Critical Theory." *Critical Studies in Mass Communication* 10 (1): 49–69.

Harris, Edward M. 1992. "Pericles' Praise of Athenian Democracy Thucydides 2.37.1." *Harvard Studies in Classical Philology* 94: 157–67.

Haslam, S. Alexander, Stephen D. Reicher, and Michael J. Platow. 2010. *The New Psychology of Leadership: Identity, Influence and Power*. New York: Psychology Press.

Hegel, G. W. F. [1807]. 1977. *Phenomenology of Spirit*. Translated by A. V. Miller. Oxford: Oxford University Press.

Hegel, G. W. F. [1821]. 2012. *Hegel's Philosophy of Right*. Translated by S. W. Dyde. New York: Dover Publications.

Heidegger, Martin. [1927]. 1996. *Being and Time*. Translated by Joan Stambaugh. Albany: State University of New York Press.

Herodotus. 1987. *The History*. Translated by David Grene. Chicago: University of Chicago Press.

Herring, George. 2006. "Introduction: Making All Things New." In *Introduction to the History of Christianity*, by George Herring, 1–46. New York: New York University Press.

Hersh, Seymour. 1984. *The Price of Power: Kissinger in the Nixon White House*. New York: Simon & Schuster.

Herz, John. 1950. "Idealist Internationalism and the Security Dilemma." *World Politics* 2 (2): 157–80.

Hesiod. 1959. *The Works and Days; Theogony; The Shield of Herakles*. Translated by Richard Lattimore. Ann Arbor: University of Michigan Press.

Higley, John, and Michael Burton. 2006. *Elite Foundations of Liberal Democracy*. Lanham: Rowman and Littlefield.

Hill, Jonathan, and Thomas Wilson. 2003. "Identity Politics and the Politics of Identities." *Identities* 10 (1): 1–8.

Hirschman, Albert O. [1977]. 2013. *The Passions and the Interests: Political Arguments for Capitalism before Its Triumph*. Princeton: Princeton University Press.

Hobbes, Thomas. 1968. *Leviathan*. Edited by C. B. Macpherson. New York: Penguin Books.

Hobbes, Thomas. 1978. "*De Cive*." In *Man and Citizen*, edited and translated by Bernard Gert, 87–386. Gloucester: Peter Smith.

Hobsbawm, Eric. 1996. "Identity Politics and the Left." *New Left Review* 217: 38–47.

Holloway, Carson, ed. 2008. *Magnanimity and Statesmanship*. Lexington Books: Lanham.

Hood, Christopher. 2001. "Public Service Bargains and Public Service Reform." In *Politicians, Bureaucrats and Administrative Reform*, edited by B. Guy Peters and Jon Pierre, 13–23. London: Routledge.

Hood, Christopher, and Martin Lodge. 2006. *The Politics of Public Service Bargains: Reward, Competency, Loyalty—and Blame*. Oxford: Oxford University Press.

Hood, Christopher, and B. Guy Peters, eds. 2003. *Reward for High Public Office: Asian and Pacific Rim States*. New York: Routledge.

Hu, Hsien Chin. 1944. "The Chinese Concepts of 'Face.'" *American Anthropologist* 46 (1): 45–64.

Hutchinson, John, and Anthony D. Smith, eds. 1994. *Nationalism*. Oxford: Oxford University Press.

Hwang, Kwang-kuo. 1987. "Face and Favor: The Chinese Power Game." *The American Journal of Sociology* 92 (4): 944–74.

Ingram, Attracta. 1996. "Constitutional Patriotism." *Philosophy Social Criticism* 22 (6): 1–18.

Irwin, Robert. 2009. *The Arabian Knights: A Companion*. Tauris Park: London.

Irwin, Terence. 1977. *Plato's Moral Theory: The Early and Middle Dialogues*. Oxford: Clarendon Press.

Isaacson, Walter. 2005. *Kissinger: A Biography*. New York: Simon & Schuster.

Ivanhoe, Philip J. 2017. *Oneness: East Asian Conceptions of Virtue, Happiness, and How We Are All Connected*. Oxford: Oxford University Press.

James, William. [1890]. 1950. *Principles of Psychology*. New York: Dover Publications.

Janis, Irving L. 1982. *Groupthink*. Boston: Cengage Learning.

Jay, Anthony. 1994. *Management and Machiavelli*. London: Prentice Hall Press.

Johnson, M. Laurie. 2012. *Locke and Rousseau: Two Enlightenment Responses to Honour*. Lanham: Lexington Books.

Johnson, Lyman L., and Sonya Lipsett-Riveras. 1998. *The Faces of Honor: Sex, Shame, and Violence in Colonial Latin America*. Albuquerque: University of New Mexico Press.

Johnston, Steven. 2007. *The Truth about Patriotism*. Durham: Duke University Press.

Joshi, Shashank. 2008. "Honor in International Relations." Paper No. 2008-0146, Weatherhead Center for International Affairs, Harvard University.

Kahn, Victoria. 1993. "*Virtù* and the Example of Agathocles in Machiavelli's *Prince*." In *Machiavelli and the Discourse of Literature*, edited by Albert R. Ascoli and Victoria Kahn, 195–217. Ithaca: Cornell University Press.

Kahn, Victoria. 2013. "Revisiting Agathocles." *The Review of Politics* 75 (4): 557–72.

Kain, Philip J. 1995. "Niccolò Machiavelli: Adviser of Princes." *Canadian Journal of Philosophy* 25 (1): 33–55.

Kamtekar, Rachana. 2017. *Plato's Moral Psychology*. Oxford: Oxford University Press.

Kane, John. 2001. *The Politics of Moral Capital*. Cambridge: Cambridge University Press.

Kane, John, and Haig Patapan. 2006. "In Search of Prudence: The Hidden Problem of Managerial Reform." *Public Administration Review* 66 (5): 711–24.

Kane, John, and Haig Patapan. 2012. *The Democratic Leader: How Democracy Defines, Empowers and Limits Its Leaders*. Oxford: Oxford University Press.

Kane, John, and Haig Patapan. 2014. *Good Democratic Leadership: On Prudence and Judgment in Modern Democracies*. Oxford: Oxford University Press.

Kane, John, Hui-Chieh Loy, and Haig Patapan, eds. 2011. *Political Legitimacy in Asia: New Leadership Challenges*. New York: Palgrave Macmillan.

Kant, Immanuel. [1785]. 1993. *Groundwork for the Metaphysics of Morals*. Translated by James W. Ellington. Indianapolis/Cambridge: Hackett Publishing.

Kant, Immanuel. [1781]. 1996. *Critique of Pure Reason.* Translated by Werner S. Pluhar. Indianapolis: Hackett Publishing.

Kant, Immanuel. [1790]. 2007. *Critique of Judgment.* Translated by James Creed Meredith; revised, edited, and introduced by Nicolas Walker. Oxford: Oxford University Press.

Kapust, Daniel J. 2011. "The Problem of Flattery and Hobbes's Institutional Defense of Monarchy." *The Journal of Politics* 73 (3): 680–91.

Kauffman, L. A. 2001. "The Anti-Politics of Identity." In *Identity Politics in the Women's Movement,* edited by Barbara Ryan, 23–34. New York: New York University Press.

Kellerman, Barbara. 2008. *Followership: How Followers Are Creating Change and Changing Leaders.* Boston: Harvard Business School Press.

Kellerman, Barbara. 2012. *The End of Leadership.* New York: HarperCollins.

Kelley, Robert E. 1992. *The Power of Followership.* New York: Doubleday Business.

Kenny, Michael. 2004. *The Politics of Identity: Liberal Political Theory and the Dilemmas of Difference.* Cambridge: Polity Press.

Keynes, Maynard. 1936. *The General Theory of Employment, Interest and Money.* London: Palgrave Macmillan.

Kierkegaard, Søren. 1983. *Fear and Trembling.* Translated by Howard V. Hong and Edna H. Hong. Princeton: Princeton University Press.

Kim, Sungmoon. 2014. *Confucian Democracy in East Asia.* Cambridge: Cambridge University Press.

Kim Dae-jung, 1994. "Is Culture Destiny? The Myth of Asia's Anti-Democratic Values." *Foreign Affairs* 73 (6): 189–94.

King, Katherine Callen. 1987. *Achilles: Paradigms of the War Hero from Homer through the Middle Ages.* Berkeley: University of California Press.

Kissinger, Henry. 1979. *The White House Years.* Sydney: Hodder and Stoughton.

Konstan, David. 1996. "Friendship, Frankness and Flattery." In *Friendship, Flattery, and Frankness of Speech,* edited by John T. Fitzgerald, 7–19. New York: Brill.

Korom, P. 2015. "Elites: History of the Concept." In *International Encyclopedia of the Social & Behavioral Sciences,* 2nd ed., edited by J. D. Wright, 390–95. Amsterdam: Elsevier.

Kowert, Paul A. 2002. *Groupthink or Deadlock: When Do Leaders Learn from Their Advisors?* Albany: State University of New York Press.

Koziak, Barbara. 2000. *Retrieving Political Emotion: Thumos, Aristotle, and Gender.* University Park, PA: Pennsylvania State University Press.

Krause, Sharon R. 2002. *Liberalism with Honor.* Cambridge, MA: Harvard University Press.

Kymlicka, Will. 1995. *Multicultural Citizenship.* Oxford: Oxford University Press.

Kyrtatas, Dimitris. 1988. "Prophets and Priests in Early Christianity: Production and Transmission of Religious Knowledge from Jesus to John Chrysostom." *International Sociology* 3 (4): 365–83.

Lampton. David M. 2014. *Following the Leader: Ruling China, from Deng Xiaoping to Xi Jinping*. Berkeley: University of California Press.

Landauer, Matthew. 2012. "Parrhesia and the Demos Tyrannos." *History of Political Thought* 33 (2): 185–208.

Lane, Melissa. 2012. "The Origins of the Statesman—Demagogue Distinction in and after Ancient Athens." *Journal of the History of Ideas* 73 (2): 179–200.

Lang, Mabel L. 1972. "Cleon as the Anti-Pericles." *Classical Philology* 67 (3): 159–69.

Lasswell, Harold. 1930. *Psychopathology and Politics*. Chicago: University of Chicago Press.

Lasswell, Harold, and Abraham Kaplan. 1950. *Power and Society: A Framework for Political Inquiry*. New Haven: Yale University Press.

Lazear, Edward P. 2000. "Economic Imperialism." *The Quarterly Journal of Economics* 115 (1): 99–146.

Lebow, R. 2006. "Fear, Interest and Honour: Outlines of a Theory of International Relations." *International Affairs* 82 (3): 431–48.

Lee Kuan Yew. 1998. *The Singapore Story: Memoirs of Lee Kuan Yew*. Singapore: Prentice Hall.

Lee Seung-Hyun, and Kyeungrae Kenny Oh. 2007. "Corruption in Asia: Pervasiveness and Arbitrariness." *Asia Pacific Journal of Management* 24 (1): 97–114.

Lee, Taeku. 2008. "Race, Immigration, and the Identity-to-Politics Link." *Annual Review of Political Science* 11: 457–78.

Lee Teng-hui, 1995. "Chinese Culture and Political Renewal." *Journal of Democracy* 6 (4): 3–8.

Lees-Marshment, Jennifer, Brian Conley, and Kenneth Cosgrove, eds. 2014. *Political Marketing in the US*. New York: Routledge.

Lesher, James. 2007. "Later Views of the Socrates of Plato's *Symposium*." In *Socrates in the Nineteenth and Twentieth Century*, edited by Michael Trapp, 59–76. Farnham: Ashgate/Centre for Hellenic Studies.

Levitsky, Steven, and Daniel Ziblatt. 2018. *How Democracies Die*. New York: Crown.

Li, Cheng. 2016. *Chinese Politics in the Xi Jinping Era: Reassessing Collective Leadership*. Washington DC: Brookings Institution Press

Lincoln, Abraham. [1943]. 1997. "The Perpetuation of our Political Institutions." In *From Many, One: Readings in American Political and Social Thought*, edited by Richard C. Sinopol, 77–84. Washington, DC: Georgetown University Press.

Lipman-Blumen, Jean. 2006. *The Allure of Toxic Leaders: Why We Follow Destructive Bosses and Corrupt Politicians—and How We Can Survive Them*. Oxford: Oxford University Press.

Lodge, Martin. 2010. "Public Service Bargains in British Central Government: Multiplication, Diversification and Reassertion?" In *Tradition and Public Administration*, edited by Martin Painter and B. Guy Peters, 99–113. Hampshire: Palgrave Macmillan.

Lord, Carnes. 2003. *The Modern Prince: What the Leaders Need to Know Now.* New Haven: Yale University Press.

Ludwig, Paul W. 2002. *Eros and Polis: Desire and Community in Greek Political Theory.* Cambridge: Cambridge University Press.

Lutz, Mark J. 1998. *Socrates' Education to Virtue: Learning the Love of the Noble.* Albany: State University of New York Press.

Machiavelli, Niccolò. 1974. *Il Principe [The Prince].* Edited and with an introduction by Luigi Firpo and Federico Chabod. Torino: Giulio Einaudi.

Machiavelli, Niccolò. 1992. *The Prince.* Edited and translated by R. M. Adams. New York: Norton.

Machiavelli, Niccolò. 1985. *The Prince.* Translated by Harvey C. Mansfield Jr. Chicago: University of Chicago Press.

Machiavelli, Niccolò. 1996. *Discourses on Livy,* Translated by H. C. Mansfield Jr. and N. Tarcov. Chicago: University of Chicago Press.

MacIntyre, Alasdair. 2002. "Is Patriotism a Virtue?" In *Patriotism,* edited by Igor Primoratz, 43–58. Amherst: Humanity Books.

Mahdi, Muhsin. 1995. *The Thousand and One Nights.* Leiden: E. J. Brill.

Maley, Maria. 2000. "Conceptualising Advisers' Policy Work: The Distinctive Policy Roles of Ministerial Advisers in the Keating Government, 1991–96." *Australian Journal of Political Science* 35 (3): 449–70.

Mansfield, Harvey C. 1993. *Taming the Prince.* Baltimore: The Johns Hopkins University Press.

Mansfield, Harvey C. 1995. "Self-Interest Rightly Understood." *Political Theory* 23 (1): 48–66.

Mansfield, Harvey C. 1998. *Machiavelli's Virtue.* Chicago: University of Chicago Press.

Mara, Gerald M. 1988. "Hobbes's Counsel to Sovereigns." *The Journal of Politics* 50 (2): 390–411.

Marable, Manning. 1993. "Beyond Racial Identity Politics: Towards a Liberation Theory for Multicultural Democracy." *Race & Class* 35 (1): 113–30.

Markey, D. 1999. "Prestige and the Origins of War: Returning to Realism's Roots." *Security Studies* 8 (4): 126–73.

Márquez, Xavier. 2012. *A Stranger's Knowledge.* Las Vegas: Parmenides Publishing

Marshall, P. David. 1997. *Celebrity and Power: Fame in Contemporary Culture.* London: University of Minnesota Press.

Marx, Karl. [1867]. 2009. *Das Kapital—A Critique of Political Economy.* Introduction by Serge L. Levitsky. Washington, DC: Regnery Publications.

Maslow, Abraham. 1943. *A Theory of Human Motivation.* Midwest Journal Press.

McAlpine, Alistair. 2000. *The Servant.* London: Faber and Faber.

McCarthy, Stephen. 2006. *The Political Theory of Tyranny in Singapore and Burma: Aristotle and the Rhetoric of Benevolent Despotism.* Abingdon: Routledge.

McCormick, John P. 2011. *Machiavellian Democracy*. Cambridge: Cambridge University Press.

McCormick, John P. 2015. "Machiavelli's Inglorious Tyrants: On Agathocles, Scipio and Unmerited Glory." *History of Political Thought* 36 (1): 29–52.

McGregor, Richard. 2017. *Asia's Reckoning: The Struggle for Global Dominance*. New York: Viking Press.

McKim, Robert, and McMahan, Jeff, eds. 1997. *The Morality of Nationalism*. New York: Oxford University Press.

McNamara, Peter, ed. 1999. *The Noblest Minds: Fame, Honor, and the American Founding*. Lanham: Rowman and Littlefield.

McNay, Lois. 2008. *Against Recognition*. Cambridge: Polity Press.

Mechkova, Valeriya, Anna Lührmann, and Staffan I. Lindberg. 2017. "How Much Democratic Backsliding?" *Journal of Democracy* 28 (4): 162–69.

Meltsner, Arnold J. 1990. *Rule for Rulers*. Philadelphia: Temple University Press.

Menaldo, Mark A. 2013. *Leadership and Transformative Ambition in International Relations*. Cheltenham: Edward Elgar.

Mercer, Jonathan. 1996. *Reputation and International Politics*. Ithaca: Cornell University Press.

Mercer, Jonathan. 2006. "Human Nature and the First Image: Emotion in International Politics." *Journal of International Relations and Development* 9 (3): 288–303.

Michels, Robert. [1911]. 1962. *Political Parties*. Introduced by Seymour Martin Lipset, translated by Eden and Cedar Paul. New York: The Free Press.

Miller, David. 1995. *On Nationality*. Oxford: Oxford University Press.

Miller, Gary J. 1997. "The Impact of Economics on Contemporary Political Science." *Journal of Economic Literature* 35 (3): 1173–1204.

Mills, C. Wright. 1956. *The Power Elite*. Oxford: Oxford University Press.

Mitra, Rahul. 2013. "From Transformational Leadership to Leadership Trans-Formations: A Critical Dialogic Perspective." *Communication Theory* 23 (4): 395–416.

Morgenbesser, Lee. 2017. *Behind the Facade: Elections under Authoritarianism in Southeast Asia*. New York: State University of New York Press.

Morgenthau, Hans, J. 1946. *Scientific Man vs. Power Politics*. Chicago: University of Chicago Press.

Morgenthau, Hans, J. 1948. *Politics amongst Nations—The Struggle for Power and Peace*. New York: McGraw Hill.

Morris, Dick. 1999. *The New Prince*. Kent: Renaissance Books.

Morrow, Glenn. 1960. *Plato's Cretan City: A Historical Interpretation of the Laws*. Princeton: Princeton University Press.

Mosca, Gaetano. 1939. *The Ruling Class*. Edited by Arthur Livingston, translated by Hannah D. Kahn. New York: McGraw Hill.

Mounk, Yasha. 2018. *The People vs. Democracy: Why Democracy Is in Danger & How to Save It*. Cambridge, MA: Harvard University Press.

Mulgan, Richard. 2000. "Public Servants and the Public Interest." *Canberra Bulletin of Public Administration* 97: 1–4.

Müller, Jan-Werner. 2007. *Constitutional Patriotism*. Princeton: Princeton University Press.

Murphy, Colleen. 2017. *The Conceptual Foundations of Transitional Justice*. Cambridge: Cambridge University Press.

Najemy, John M. 1999. "Papirius and the Chickens, or Machiavelli on the Necessity of Interpreting Religions." *Journal of the History of Ideas* 60 (4): 659–81.

Nerdahl, Michael. 2011. "Flattery and Platonic Philosophy." *Classical World* 104 (3): 295–309.

Nevitte, N., and R. Gibbins, 1990. *New Elites in Old States: Ideologies in the Anglo-American Democracies*. Toronto: Oxford University Press.

Newell, Waller. 2000. *Ruling Passion: The Erotics of Statecraft in Platonic Political Philosophy*. Lanham: Rowman and Littlefield.

Newell, Waller. 2009. *The Soul of a Leader: Character, Conviction, and Ten Lessons in Political Greatness*. New York: Harper-Collins.

Newell, Waller. 2016. *Tyrants: A History of Power, Injustice, and Terror*. Cambridge: Cambridge University Press.

Nichols, Mary P. 1984. "The Republic's Two Alternatives: Philosopher-Kings and Socrates." *Political Theory* 12 (2): 252–74.

Nichols, Mary P. 2009. *Socrates on Friendship and Community: Reflections on Plato's Symposium, Phaedrus, and Lysis*. Cambridge: Cambridge University Press.

Nicolson, Harold. 1937. *The Meaning of Prestige*. The Rede Lecture 1937. Cambridge: Cambridge University Press.

Nietzsche, Friedrich. [1883–1885]. 1995. *Thus Spoke Zarathustra: A Book for All and None*. Translated by Walter Kaufmann. New York: Modern Library.

Nietzsche, Friedrich. [1887]. 1989. *Genealogy of Morals and Ecce Homo*. Translated by Walter Kaufman and R. J. Hollingdale. New York: Vintage Books.

Nietzsche, Friedrich. 2002. *Beyond Good and Evil: Prelude to a Philosophy of the Future*. Edited by Rolf-Peter Hortsmann and Judith Norman. Cambridge: Cambridge University Press.

Nietzsche, Friedrich. 2005. "Twilight of the Idols." In *Nietzsche: The Anti-Christ, Ecce Homo, Twilight of the Idols: And Other Writings*, edited by Aaron Ridley and Judith Norman, translated by Judith Norman, 153–230. Cambridge: Cambridge University Press.

Norris, Pippa, and Ronald Inglehart. 2018. *Cultural Backlash: Trump, Brexit and the Rise of Authoritarian Populism*. New York: Cambridge University Press.

Nussbaum, Martha C. 1986. *The Fragility of Goodness*. Cambridge: Cambridge University Press.

Nussbaum, Martha C. 1996. *For Love of Country? Debating the Limits of Patriotism*. Edited by Joshua Cohen. Boston: Beacon Press.

Nussbaum, Martha C. 2008. *Liberty of Conscience: In Defense of America's Tradition of Religious Equality.* New York: Basic Books.

Nye, Joseph. 2004. *Soft Power: The Means to Success in World Politics.* Washington: Public Affairs (Perseus Books).

Olson, Mancur. 1971. *Logic of Collective Action.* Cambridge, MA: Harvard University Press.

Olsthoorn, Peter. 2015. *Honor in Political and Moral Philosophy.* Albany: State University of New York.

O'Neill, Barry. 1999. *Honor, Symbols, and War.* Ann Arbor: University of Michigan Press.

Oprisko, Robert L. 2012. *Honor: A Phenomenology.* New York: Routledge.

Ospina, Sonia, and Georgia L. J. Sorenson. 2007. "A Constructionist Lens on Leadership—Charting New Territory." In *The Quest for a General Theory of Leadership,* edited by George R. Goethals and Georgia L. J. Sorenson, chapter 8, 188–204. Northampton, MA: Edward Elgar.

Ovid. 2005. *Epistulae Ex Ponto.* Edited by J. F. Gaertner. Oxford: Oxford University Press.

Özkirimli, Umut. 2005. *Contemporary Debates on Nationalism: A Critical Engagement.* London: Palgrave Macmillan.

Özkirimli, Umut. 2010. *Theories of Nationalism: A Critical Introduction.* 2nd ed. New York: Palgrave Macmillan.

Palmer, Michael. 1992. *Love of Glory and the Common Good: Aspects of the Political Thought of Thucydides.* Lanham: Rowman and Littlefield.

Pangle, Thomas L. 1976. "The Political Psychology of Religion in Plato's Laws." *American Political Science Review* 70 (4): 1059–77.

Pangle, Thomas L. 1980. "Interpretive Essay." In *The Laws of Plato,* edited by Thomas L. Pangle, 375–510. Chicago: University of Chicago Press.

Pangle, Thomas L. 1999. "The Classical and Modern Liberal Understandings of Honor." In *The Noblest Minds: Fame, Honor, and the American Founding,* edited by Peter McNamara, 207–20. Lanham: Rowman and Littlefield.

Pangle, Lorraine Smith. 2009. "Moral and Criminal Responsibility in Plato's *Laws*." *American Political Science Review* 103 (3): 456–73.

Parel, Anthony. 1990. "Machiavelli's Use of Umori in *The Prince*." *Quaderni Italianistica* 11 (1): 91–101.

Pareto, Vilfredo. 1935. *A Treatise on General Sociology.* Translated by Andrew Bongiorno and James Harvey Rogers. Toronto: General Publishing Company.

Parker, Deborah, and Mark Parker. 2017. *Sucking Up: A Brief Consideration of Sycophancy.* Charlottesville: University of Virginia Press.

Parker, Richard D. 2005. "Five Theses on Identity Politics." *Harvard Journal of Law and Public Policy* 29 (1): 53–59.

Patapan, Haig. 2003. "Machiavelli's New Theogony." *Review of Politics* 65 (2): 185–207.

Patapan, Haig. 2006. *Machiavelli in Love: The Modern Politics of Love and Fear.* Lanham: Lexington Books.

Patapan, Haig. 2009. "The Glorious Sovereign: Thomas Hobbes' Understanding of Leadership and International Relations." In *British International Thinkers from Hobbes to Namier*, edited by Ian Hall and Lisa Hill, 11–32. New York: Palgrave Macmillan.

Patapan, Haig, and Jeff Sikkenga. 2008. "Love and the Leviathan: Thomas Hobbes' Critique of Platonic Eros." *Political Theory: An International Journal of Political Philosophy*, December 36 (6): 803–26.

Patapan, Haig. 2014. "Patriotic Leadership in Democracy." In *Good Democratic Leadership: On Prudence and Judgment in Modern Democracies*, edited with John Kane, 212–30. Oxford: Oxford University Press.

Patapan, Haig. 2016. "Magnanimous Leadership: Edmund Barton and the Australian Founding." *Leadership and the Humanities* 4 (1): 1–20.

Patapan, Haig. 2018. "Politics of Modern Honor." *Contemporary Political Theory* 17 (4): 459–77.

Pawar, Badrinarayan S. 2003. "Central Conceptual Issues in Transformational Leadership Research." *Leadership & Organization Development Journal* 24 (7): 397–406.

Penner, Terence M. 1971. "Thought and Desire in Plato." In *Plato*. Vol. II, edited by Gregory Vlastos, 96–118. New York: Doubleday.

Peristiany, John George, ed. 1966. *Honour and Shame: The Values of Mediterranean Society*. Chicago: University of Chicago Press.

Peters, B. Guy, and Jon Pierre, eds. 2004. *The Politicization of the Civil Service in Comparative Perspective: A Quest for Control*. London: Routledge.

Phillips, Melanie. 1997. *All Must Have Prizes*. Boston: Little, Brown.

Pippin, Robert B. 1989. *Hegel's Idealism: The Satisfactions of Self-Consciousness*. Cambridge: Cambridge University Press.

Plato. 1939. "Parmenides *Way of Truth* and Plato's *Parmenides*." In *Parmenides*, translated with introduction and a running commentary by Francis Macdonald Cornford. London: Routledge and Kegan Paul.

Plato. 1961. *Letters*. In *Collected Dialogues of Plato, including the Letters*, edited by Edith Hamilton and Huntington Cairns. Princeton, NJ: Princeton University Press.

Plato. 1984. "Apology of Socrates." In *Four Texts on Socrates*, translated by Thomas G. West and Grace Starry West, introduction by Thomas G. West, 63–98. Ithaca: Cornell University Press.

Plato. 1984. "Crito." In *Four Texts on Socrates*, translated by Thomas G. West and Grace Starry West, introduction by Thomas G. West, 99–114. Ithaca: Cornell University Press.

Plato. 1991. *The Republic*. 2nd ed. Translated with interpretive essay by Allan Bloom. New York: Basic Books.

Plato. 1984. *Plato's Statesman*. Translated by Seth Benardete in *The Being of the Beautiful*. Chicago: University of Chicago Press.

Plato. 1993. *Symposium*. Translated by Seth Benardete. Chicago: University of Chicago Press.

Plato. 1998a. *Gorgias*. Translated with introductory notes and interpretive essay by James H. Nichols Jr. Cornell: Cornell University Press.

Plato. 1998b. *Phaedrus*. Translated with introductory notes and interpretive essay by James H. Nichols Jr. Cornell: Cornell University Press.

Podger, Andrew. 2007. "What Really Happens: Department Secretary Appointments, Contracts and Performance Pay in the Australian Public Service." *Australian Journal of Public Administration* 66 (2): 131–47.

Powell, Jonathan. 2010. *The New Machiavelli*. London: Bodley House.

Price, A. W. 1989. *Love and Friendship in Plato and Aristotle*. Oxford: Oxford University Press.

Price, Russell. 1977. "The Theme of Gloria in Machiavelli." *Renaissance Quarterly* 30 (4): 588–631.

Price, Russell. 1982. "Ambizione in Machiavelli's Thought." *History of Political Thought* 3 (3): 383–445.

Price, Terry L. 2003. "The Ethics of Authentic Transformational Leadership." *The Leadership Quarterly* 14 (1): 67–81.

Primoratz, Igor, ed. 2002. *Patriotism*. Amherst: Humanity Books.

Pushkin, Aleksandr. [1833]. 1964. *Eugene Onegin*. Translated by Vladimir Nabokov. Princeton: Princeton University Press.

Putnam, R. D. 1976. *The Comparative Study of Political Elites*. Englewood Cliffs: Prentice Hall.

Pye, Lucian W., with Mary W. Pye. 1985. *Asian Power and Politics: The Cultural Dimensions of Authority*. Cambridge, MA: The Belknap Press of Harvard University Press.

Quah, Jon S. T. 2003. *Curbing Corruption in Asia*. Singapore: Eastern Universities Press.

Rawls, John. 1971. *A Theory of Justice*. Cambridge, MA: Belknap Press of Harvard University Press.

Redmond, Sean, and Su Holmes, eds. 2007. *Stardom and Celebrity: A Reader*. London: Sage.

Regier, Willis G. 2007. *In Praise of Flattery*. Lincoln: University of Nebraska Press.

Régnier, Philippe. 1991. *Singapore: City-State in South-East Asia*. Honolulu: University of Hawai'i Press.

Rhode, Deborah L., ed. 2006. *Moral Leadership: The Theory and Practice of Power, Judgment and Policy*. San Francisco: Wiley and Sons.

Richards, David, and Martin J. Smith. 2016. "The Westminster Model and the 'Indivisibility of the Political and Administrative Elite': A Convenient Myth Whose Time Is Up?" *Governance* 29 (4): 499–516.

Riesebrodt, Martin. 1999. "Charisma in Max Weber's Sociology of Religion." *Religion* 29 (1): 1–14.

Robinson, Richard. 1971. "Plato's Separation of Reason from Desire." *Phronesis* 16: 38–48.

Rorty, Richard. 1998. *Achieving Our Country: Leftist Thought in Twentieth-Century America*. Cambridge, MA: Harvard University Press.

Rosen, Michael. 2012. *Dignity*. Cambridge, MA: Harvard University Press.

Rosen, Stanley. 1968. *Plato's Symposium*. New Haven: Yale University Press.

Rosen, Stanley. 1974. *G.W.F. Hegel*. New Haven: Yale University Press.

Ross, David. 1954. *Kant's Ethical Theory*. Oxford: Clarendon Press.

Rost, Joseph. 1993. *Leadership for the Twenty First Century*. Westport: Praeger Press.

Rousseau, Jean-Jacques. 1964. *First and Second Discourses*. Edited by Roger D. Masters, translated by Judith R. Masters. Bedford: St. Martin's Press.

Rousseau, Jean-Jacques. 1978. *On the Social Contract*. Edited by Roger D. Masters, translated by Judith R. Masters. New York: St. Martin's Press.

Rumsey, Michael G., ed. 2013. *Oxford Handbook on Leadership*. Oxford: Oxford University Press.

Ryan, Barbara. 1997. "How Much Can I Divide Thee, Let Me Count the Ways: Identity Politics in the Women's Movement." *Humanity & Society* 21 (1): 67–83.

Sacksteder, William. 1989. "Mutually Acceptable Glory as a Cause of Conflict." In *The Causes of Quarrel—Essays on Peace, War and Thomas Hobbes*, edited by Peter Caws, 97–113. Boston: Beacon Press.

Santi, Victor A. 1979. *La Gloria nel Pensiero di Machiavelli*. Ravenna: Longo.

Sartre, Jean-Paul. [1943]. 1989. *Being and Nothingness*. Translated and with an introduction by Hazel E. Barnes. New York: Washington Square Press.

Schaar, John H. 1981. "The Case for Patriotism." In *Legitimacy in the Modern State*, edited by John H. Schaar, 285–312. New Brunswick: Transaction Books.

Schaefer, David Lewis. 1990. *The Political Philosophy of Montaigne*. Ithaca: Cornell University Press.

Schedlitzki, Doris, and Gareth Edwards. 2014. *Studying Leadership: Traditional and Critical Approaches*. London: Sage.

Schelling, Thomas. 1960. *The Strategy of Conflict*. Cambridge: Harvard University Press.

Schumpeter, Joseph. 1942. *Capitalism, Socialism, and Democracy*. New York: HarperCollins.

Seligman, Edwin R. A. 1902. "The Economic Interpretation of History." *Political Science Quarterly*, March, 17 (1): 71–98.

Shaw, Richard, and Chris Eichbaum. 2015. "Following the Yellow Brick Road: Theorizing the Third Element in Executive Government." *International Journal of Public Administration* 38 (1): 66–74.

Shaw, Richard, and Chris Eichbaum. 2017. "Politicians, Political Advisors and the Vocabulary of Public Service Bargains." *Public Administration* 95 (2): 312–26.

Shaw, Tamsin. 2014. "The 'Last Man' Problem: Nietzsche and Weber on Political Attitudes to Suffering." In *Nietzsche as Political Philosopher*, edited by Manuel Knoll and Barry Stocker, 345–80. Berlin: De Gruyter.

Shergold, Peter. 2007. "What Really Happens in the Australian Public Service: An Alternative View." *Australian Journal of Public Administration* 66 (3): 367–70.

Siedentop, Larry. 2014. *Inventing the Individual: The Origins of Western Liberalism.* Harvard: Harvard University Press.

Sigelman, Lee, and Robert S. Goldfarb. 2012. "The Influence of Economics on Political Science: By What Pathway?" *Journal of Economic Methodology* 19 (1): 1–19.

Slagle, R. 1995. "Anthony In Defense of Queer Nation: From Identity Politics to a Politics of Difference." *Western Journal of Communication* 59 (2): 85–102.

Slomp, Gabriella. 2000. *Thomas Hobbes and the Political Philosophy of Glory.* Houndmills: Macmillan Press.

Smith, Adam. [1901]. 2007. *Wealth of Nations.* Edited by Charles J. Bullock. New York: Cosimo.

Smith, Anthony D. 1998. *Nationalism and Modernism: A Critical Survey of Recent Theories of Nations and Nationalism.* New York: Routledge.

Smith, John E. 1973. "Hegel's Critique of Kant." *The Review of Metaphysics* 26 (3): 438–60.

Smither, Edward L. 2016. "Rise of Monasticism." In *Missionary Monks: An Introduction to the History and Theology of Missionary Monasticism*, edited by Edward L. Smither, chapter 2, 14–26. Eugene: Cascade Books.

Spencer, Herbert. 1873. "Is There a Social Science?" In *The Study of Sociology*, by Herbert Spencer. London: Henry S. King.

Spencer, Philip, and Howard Wollman, eds. 2005. *Nations and Nationalism: A Reader.* New Brunswick: Rutgers University Press.

Stalley, R. F. 1975. "Plato's Argument for the Division of the Reasoning and Appetitive Elements within the Soul." *Phronesis* 20 (2): 110–28.

Stauth, Georg. 1992. "Nietzsche, Weber, and the Affirmative Sociology of Culture." *European Journal of Sociology/Archives Européennes de Sociologie* 33 (2): 219–47.

Steinberger, Peter J. 1989. "Ruling: Guardians and Philosopher-Kings." *American Political Science Review* 83 (4): 1207–25.

Stewart, Frank Henderson. 1994. *Honor.* Chicago: University of Chicago Press.

Strauss, Leo. 1953. *The Political Philosophy of Hobbes, Its Basis and Its Genesis.* Chicago: University of Chicago Press.

Strauss, Leo. 1958. *Thoughts on Machiavelli.* Chicago: University of Chicago Press.

Strauss, Leo. 1959. *What Is Political Philosophy? And Other Studies.* New York: The Free Press.

Strauss, Leo. 2001. *On Plato's Symposium.* Edited with foreword by Seth Benardete. Chicago: University of Chicago Press.

Street, John. 2004. "Celebrity Politicians: Popular Culture and Political Representation." *British Journal of Politics and International Relations* 6 (4): 435–52.

Sullivan, Vickie. 1996. *Machiavelli's Three Romes: Religion, Human Liberty, and Politics Reformed*. DeKalb: Northern Illinois University Press.

't Hart, Paul, and Karen Tindall. 2009. "Leadership by the Famous: Celebrity as Political Capital." In *Dispersed Democratic Leadership: Origins, Dynamics, & Implications*, edited by John Kane, Haig Patapan, and Paul 't Hart, 255–78. Oxford: Oxford University Press.

Tamir, Yael. 1993. *Liberal Nationalism*. Princeton: Princeton University Press.

Tan, Kenneth Paul. 2009. "Who's Afraid of Catherine Lim? The State in Patriarchal Singapore." *Asian Studies Review* 33 (1): 43–62.

Tan, Kenneth Paul. 2012. "The Ideology of Pragmatism: Neo-Liberal Globalisation and Political Authoritarianism in Singapore." *Journal of Contemporary Asia* 42 (1): 67–92.

Tan Kok-Chor. 2004. "The Limits of Patriotism." In *Justice Without Borders: Cosmopolitanism, Nationalism, and Patriotism*, edited by Tan Kok-Chor, 135–62. Cambridge: Cambridge University Press.

Tarling, Nicholas, ed. 1999. *Cambridge History of Southeast Asia*. Cambridge: Cambridge University Press.

Tarnopolsky, Christina H. 2010. *Prudes, Perverts and Tyrants: Plato's Gorgias and the Politics of Shame*. Princeton: Princeton University Press.

Taylor, Charles. 1994. *Multiculturalism and the "Politics of Recognition."* Princeton: Princeton University Press.

Tendi, Blessing-Miles. 2010. *Making History in Mugabe's Zimbabwe: Politics, Intellectuals and the Media*. Oxford: Peter Lang.

Tessitore, Aristide. 1996. *Reading Aristotle's Ethics: Virtue, Rhetoric, and Political Philosophy*. Albany: State University of New York Press.

Tetlock, Philip E. 2005. *Expert Political Judgment*. Princeton: Princeton University Press.

Thompson, Dennis. 1983. "Ascribing Responsibility to Advisers in Government." *Ethics* 93 (3): 546–60.

Tiernan, Anne. 2007. *Power Without Responsibility*. Sydney: UNSW Press.

Tocqueville, Alexis. [1835; 1840]. 2000. *Democracy in America*. Translated and edited by Harvey C. Mansfield and Delba Winthrop. Chicago: University of Chicago Press.

Trilling, Lionel. 1972. *Sincerity and Authenticity*. Oxford: Oxford University Press.

Trottier, Tracey, Montgomery Van Wart, and XiaoHu Wang. 2008. "Examining the Nature and Significance of Leadership in Government Organizations." *Public Administration Review* 68 (2): 319–33.

Tully, James. 1995. *Strange Multiplicity: Constitutionalism in the Age of Diversity*. Cambridge: Cambridge University Press.

Turner, F. M. 1981. *The Greek Heritage in Victorian Britain*. New Haven: Yale University Press.

Turner, Nick, Julian Barling, Olga Epitropaki, Vicky Butcher, and Caroline Milner. 2002. "Transformational Leadership and Moral Reasoning." *Journal of Applied Psychology* 87 (2): 304–11.

Turner, Stephen. 2003. "Charisma Reconsidered." *Journal of Classical Sociology* 3 (1): 5–26.

Uhr, John. 2015. *Prudential Public Leadership: Promoting Ethics in Public Policy and Administration*. New York: Palgrave Macmillan.

Vanden Houten, Art. 2002. "Prudence in Hobbes's Political Philosophy." *History of Political Thought* 23 (2): 266–87.

Varotti, Carlo. 1998. *Gloria e Ambizione Politica nel Rinascimento. Da Petrarca a Machiavelli*. Milan: Bruno Mondadori.

Viroli, Maurizio. 1995. *For Love of Country: An Essay on Patriotism and Nationalism*. Oxford: Oxford University Press.

Viroli, Maurizio. 1998. "The Power of Words." In *Machiavelli*, by Maurizio Viroli, 73–113. Oxford: Oxford University Press.

von Vacano, Diego A. 2007. *The Art of Power: Machiavelli, Nietzsche, and the Making of Aesthetic Political Theory*. Lanham: Lexington Books.

Wagner, Ross J. 2016. "The Prophets in the New Testament." In *The Oxford Handbook of the Prophets*, edited by Carolyn Sharp, chapter 21, 373–87. Oxford: Oxford University Press.

Waltz, Kenneth. 1979. *Theory of International Politics*. Boston: Addison-Wesley.

Walzer, Michael. 1974. "Civility and Civic Virtue in Contemporary America." *Social Research*, winter, 41 (4): 593–611.

Wang, Zheng. 2008. "National Humiliation, History Education, and the Politics of Historical Memory: Patriotic Education Campaign in China." *International Studies Quarterly* 52 (4): 783–806.

Warren, Mark E. 1992. "Max Weber's Nietzschean Conception of Power." *History of the Human Sciences* 5 (3): 19–37.

Weber, Max. 1978a. *Economy and Society*. Edited by Guenther Roth and Claus Wittich. Berkeley: University of California Press.

Weber, Max. 1978b. "Politics as a Vocation." In *From Max Weber*, edited by H. H. Gerth and C. Wright Mills. New York: Oxford University Press.

Weir, Allison. 2008. "Global Feminism and Transformative Identity Politics." *Hypatia* 23 (4): 110–33.

Weiss, Linda. 2000. "Developmental States in Transition: Adapting, Dismantling, Innovating, Not 'Normalizing.'" *The Pacific Review* 13 (1): 21–55.

Welsh, Alexander. 2008. *What Is Honor? A Question of Moral Imperatives*. New Haven: Yale University Press.

Westphal, Kenneth R. 1991. "Hegel's Critique of Kant's Moral World View." *Philosophical Topics* 19 (2): 133–76.

Wheelan, Frederick G. 2004. *Hume and Machiavelli: Political Realism and Liberal Thought*. Lanham: Lexington Books.

Wiethoff, William E. 1974. "Machiavelli's The Prince: Rhetorical Influence in Civil Philosophy." *Western Speech* 38 (2): 98–107.

Wiethoff, William E. 1991. "A Machiavellian Perspective on the Rhetorical Criticism of Political Discourse." *Quarterly Journal of Speech* 77 (3): 309–26.

Williams, Melissa, Rosemary Nagy, and Jon Elster. 2012. *Transitional Justice: NOMOS LI*. New York: New York University Press.

Williams, Robert R. 1997. *Hegel's Ethics of Recognition*. Los Angeles: University of California Press.

Wilson, J. R. S. 1995. "Thrasymachus and the *Thumos*: A Further Case of Prolepsis in *Republic* I." *Classical Quarterly* 45 (1): 58–67.

Wilson, Suze. 2013. "Situated Knowledge: A Foucauldian Reading of Ancient and Modern Classics of Leadership Thought." *Leadership* 9 (9): 43–61.

Winkler, Ingo. 2010. *Contemporary Leadership Theories: Enhancing the Understanding of the Complexity, Subjectivity and Dynamic of Leadership*. Heidelberg: Springer-Verlag.

Wong, Ben, and Xunming Huang. 2010. "Political Legitimacy in Singapore." *Politics and Policy* 38 (3): 523–43.

Woods, Michael. 1987. "Plato's Division of the Soul." *Proceedings of the British Academy* 73, 23–47.

Wyatt-Brown, Bertram. 1982. *Southern Honor: Ethics and Behaviour in the Old South*. New York: Oxford University Press.

Yap, Sonny, Richard Lim, and Leong Weng Kam. 2009. *Men in White: The Untold Story of Singapore's Ruling Political Party*. Singapore: Singapore Press.

Yong, Ben, and Robert Hazell. 2014. *Special Advisors*. Oxford: Hart Publishing.

Young, Shaun P., ed. 2009. *Reflections on Rawls: An Assessment of His Legacy*. Abingdon: Ashgate.

Yukl, Gary A. 2010. *Leadership in Organizations*. Boston: Pearson Learning Solution.

Zakaria, Fareed. 1994. "Culture Is Destiny—A Conversation with Lee Kuan Yew." *Foreign Affairs* 73 (2): 109–26.

Zaleznik, Abraham. 1992. "Managers and Leaders: Are They Different?" *Harvard Business Review* 70 (2): 126–35.

Zmora, Hillay. 2007. "World Without a Saving Grace: Glory and Immortality in Machiavelli." *History of Political Thought* 28 (3): 449–68.

Zuckert, Catherine. 2009. *Plato's Philosophers: The Coherence of the Dialogues*. Chicago: University of Chicago Press.

INDEX

www.ingramcontent.com/pod-product-compliance
Lightning Source LLC
Chambersburg PA
CBHW030358270326
41926CB00009B/1166